AF553890

UNIVERSAL HISTORY OF MUSIC,

UNIVERSAL HISTORY OF MUSIC,

COMPILED FROM DIVERS SOURCES

TOGETHER WITH

VARIOUS ORIGINAL NOTES ON HINDU MUSIC

BY

RAJA SIR SOURINDRO MOHUN TAGORE, Mus. Doc.;
KNIGHT OF THE UNITED KINGDOM OF GREAT BRITAIN AND IRELAND;
COMPANION OF THE MOST EMINENT ORDER OF THE INDIAN EMPIRE;
FOUNDER AND PRESIDENT OF THE BENGAL MUSIC SCHOOL AND
OF THE BENGAL ROYAL ACADEMY OF MUSIC; GRAND CROSS,
COMMANDER, OR CHEVALIER, OF DIVERS IMPERIAL,
ROYAL, ECCLESIASTICAL, OR REPUBLICAN ORDERS, AND
HONORARY PATRON, PRESIDENT, OR MEMBER, OF
VARIOUS LITERARY OR SCIENTIFIC SOCIETIES,
OF ASIA, EUROPE, AFRICA, AMERICA,
AND OCEANIA; "NAWAB SHAHZADA"
OF THE PERSIAN EMPIRE; MASTER
OF MUSIC; SANGITA-NAYAKA;
&C. &C. &C.

Low Price Publications

2011

First Published 1896

Reprinted in **LPP**
1990, 1999, 2011

ISBN 10: 81-7536-156-5
ISBN 13: 978-81-7536-156-0

Published by
Low Price Publications
A-6, Second Floor, Nimri Commercial Centre,
Ashok Vihar Phase-IV, Delhi 110 052 (INDIA)
Tel.: +91 11 27302453 Fax.: +91 11 47061936
E-mail: info@Lppindia.com
Website: www.Lppindia.com

Printed at
IIP Printers
Delhi

PRINTED IN INDIA

To

The Hon'ble Sir Alexander Mackenzie,

K. C. S. I.

&c. &c. &c.

Lieutenant-Governor of Bengal,

This Book is, with permission,

Most Respectfully Dedicated

by

His Honor's most obedient servant,

S. M. TAGORE.

PREFACE.

THE following pages furnish an account of the music of various nations, civilized or uncivilized, on the face of the habitable globe. It must be acknowledged, however, that this treatise does not pretend to be exhaustive, nor are the descriptions characterised by a uniformity of system in the manipulation of the subject. Specimens of the songs of different nations have been given in this book, not only because Music and Poetry are, according to Sanskrit lore, presided over by one and the same deity, Sarasvatí, and are, therefore, intimately connected with each other, but also because an acquaintance with the spirit of a nation's songs facilitates the understanding of the spirit of its music and poetry which are but the outward expression of the inner workings of a nation's heart.

A few facts concerning Hindu music are given a place in the Appendix. To enter into details of the kind in the body of the work would be going beyond its general scope.

My acknowledgments are pre-eminently due to the authors of the several valuable works from which I have gleaned the materials for this compilation. They have been alluded to in some portion or other of the book. To those whom I may have omitted to mention by name and to others, including editors of Encyclopædias, Musical Dictionaries and Gazetteers, and publishers of general history and geography, I take this opportunity of tendering my grateful thanks.

S. M. TAGORE.

HARA KUMAR BHAVAN;
PATHURIAGHATA RAJBATI,
Calcutta, 31st August, 1896.

CONTENTS.

AFRICA.

EUROPE.

AMERICA.

OCEANIA.

APPENDIX.

A Few Facts Concerning Hindu Music.

UNIVERSAL HISTORY OF MUSIC.

INTRODUCTION.

MUSIC pervades all nature. It is co-eval with the creation. There is nothing in nature that arouses our attention or affects our feelings so quickly as a sound. The murmuring of water, the sighs of the zephyrs, the whispers of the evening breeze, the roar of the storms, the chirpings of the birds, the cries of the animals, the hum of distant multitudes, and the concussion of sonorous bodies, excite in our minds feelings of pleasure, pain, or fear, and contain in them the germs of music. A musical sound is a noise, no doubt, but every noise is not a musical sound. There is a marked difference between the two. Noise is a confused combination of sounds resulting from the concussion of non-elastic bodies ; musical sound is a pure harmonious effect, produced from a simple elastic body, such as the tone of a bell. It flies further and is heard at a greater distance than a noise. The musical instruments played at a gathering may be heard at a distance of a mile, but the noise made by the people at the gathering, however overpowering it may be on the spot, is scarcely audible at a similar distance. Sound

(Sanskrit, *Náda*) has been described as either inarticulate (Dhanyátmaka), or articulate (Varnátmaka). Instrumental music is considered inarticulate, and vocal music articulate. By the curious structure of the vocal organs, man is capable of making a greater variety of tones than any other animal, and has at his disposal the power of giving expression to every emotion. The human voice, in its tone and accent, is undoubtedly the purest and most sonorous of any which distinguishes the vocal animals. In those countries where man may be said, like a plant, to grow and flourish, the voice expands, ripens, and attains to perfection; but in the Northern and colder regions, where the mouth is more constantly kept closed, the voice is restricted and escapes with difficulty. Hence it is that the Afghan, Dutch and similar other languages are so guttural that in the delivery of some of their words, the speakers seem as if they are choked; and hence it is that in India, Greece, Italy and other Southern countries, the climate of which is noted so much for its beauty and mildness, the vocal art has risen to so much fame.

Time plays an important part in music, and like music itself is born in nature.* The vibrations of the pulse or the manner of our walking furnishes correct notions of time. If we listen to the sound of our own step, we find it equal and regular; corresponding with what is called ordinary time in music. Probably the time in which we walk is regulated by the action of the heart, and those who step alike have pulses beating in

* The crowing of the cock covers all the time-measures of music, *i. e.*, half a unit, a unit (short), two units (long), and three or more units in succession, thus:—

kuk	*ku*	*ku*	*ku*
½	1	2	3

corresponding, respectively, with the *Ardha*, *Hrasva*, *Dirgha*, and *Pluta* measures of Hindu music.

the same time. Soldiers are compelled to preserve an exact pace, when marching in a body. Armies are moved with the greatest regularity in the time of a march which is always in common time. Artisans, such as smiths, tailors, and paviors, who work in unison with the pulse, acquire accurate habits of keeping time. Stage-coachmen have the faculty of ascertaining the lapse of time, almost with the regularity of a watch, by an attention to the pace of their horses. Sir Gore Ousley says that the Persians vary the rhythm in so masterly a manner that their music not only pleases the ignorant, but even the learned. The most effectual and ready way to acquire a knowledge of musical time is that of playing in concert; and the larger the band, the greater is the chance of its being correctly kept.

The mere recurrence of sounds at regular intervals does not represent all the properties of musical sound. Accent is necessary to add beauty and grace to the time, such as rhythm and ear will approve. The ear takes no pleasure in listening to a series of monotonous sounds: it tires and grows weary with the uniformity. Owing to the peculiar structure of the ear, it is unfitted to receive two sounds of equal force in succession. The different degrees of loud and soft constitute one of its greatest pleasures. An accented sound invariably deprives the following one of its energy, and this is only natural, for after the weight of voice has been thrown upon the accented note, the next one is uttered under some degree of exhaustion and is rendered weaker in consequence. If we listen to the trotting of a horse or the tread of our own feet, we cannot fail to notice that each alternate step is louder than the other, and here nature furnishes us with the idea of accent. The musical measures of a nation are mostly founded on the

time which they generally adopt in the ordinary pursuits of life. It has already been remarked that the walking pace of a man is in common time, and that armies are always moved in this measure. In Venice where the people are constantly moving upon the water, the oars are thrown in the movement of triple time, which is speedily communicated to the wave ; and hence it is that all their celebrated airs and barcarolles are written in triple time. Rousseau says that these airs are composed and sung by the gondoliers and have so much melody and an accent so pleasing that there is scarcely a musician in Italy who does not insist upon knowing or singing them.

Rhythm may be said to be the map or ground-plan upon which a musical composition proceeds. It is to the ear what order and regularity are to the eye. And herein, too, nature furnishes the idea. When we observe the symmetry of the human form, we find the arms, the hands, the eyes, the fingers, equidistant from a line drawn down the nose, through the centre of the body A similar regularity is observed in the vegetable tribes, and the very principles of architecture are dependant on these due proportions. Though the ear can receive only one impression at a time and has to wait for the coming sounds to form a musical idea, yet in this succession it demands the same order which to the eye is presented at once. Music and Poetry have been combined from time immemorial. There is a Sanskrit stanza to the effect that Music and Poetry are the two teats of Sarasvatí, the Goddess of the two arts. Plutarch says that in the early times such was the fondness for rhythm and numbers that all instruction was given in musical verse. Voltaire remarks that before Herodotus the Greeks wrote all history in verse, which custom they

borrowed from the Egyptians. The Egyptians, in their turn, might have most probably derived their idea from the Hindus whose sacred and classical writings were all clothed in verse, such as the Mahábhárata, the Rámáyana, the Tantras, the Puránas, &c. The object of history being to preserve to posterity the memory of great men, the verse was laid hold of to assist the memory. A boy who beats a drum may be innocent of all knowledge of melody and harmony and yet have an ear for rhythm; and such is exactly the case with those who play the cymbals or musical cups in the melo-dramatic performances in Hindusthan which popularly go by the name of *Játtrás.* The jugglers of India, who exhibit such extraordinary feats with swords, cups and bells, depend upon the rhythm of the movement for the success of their performance. The bells are of different gravities, and are thrown with a certain velocity, so that they shall fall into the hand in the time of quavers and semi-quavers, and from their being hollow and made like a coral bell they give a jingling sound, by which they are more easily caught. Rhythm is as much necessary to please the ear as to relieve man in the common pursuits of labour. The regularity with which the smith throws his hammer on the anvil, the woodman his axe on the timber, and the *palki* bearer of India hums out his jargon, serves to charm away the *ennni* which these men feel in the discharge of their laborious duties. Without rhythm no music can be considered beautiful. Ideas that may in themselves be good and pleasing lose their charm, if bereft of the symmetry which rhythm gives them. A confused heap of colored stones affords no pleasure to the eye, but viewed in a kaleidoscope, they delight us by the beauty of their arrangement and the infinity of their combinations. Rhythm is at the root of every form in which man desires to manifest his

feelings, whether it is by throwing the voice into song, the speech into verse, or the gestures into dance. Dancing has been described as an art in which the "sentiments of the mind and passions are expressed by measured steps or bounds, that are made in cadence, by regulated motions of the body, and graceful gestures; all of which can only be successfully produced by that law of nature called rhythm". To mark out the rhythm as a governing principle in these motions, music has been found to be the most efficient method. In the dances of the savage *Santálas** and other nations this is simply done by the clapping of hands, or the beating of a drum or sticks together, but since melody and the phrases of music can make the finest gradations in rhythm perceptible to the ear, not only grace, but passion and sentiment have followed as natural expressions in the motion and carriage of the human form.

Rhythm connects the musician and the poet into a brotherhood. The painter, however, is in larger sympathy with the musician; so much so that he describes his picture in a language made up of musical terms. The musician returns the compliment and attributes to his favorite art another quality which he denominates *color*:—and here nature supplies another idea. If, as Newton supposed, the impulse upon the nerves of the eye produced by color is similar in kind or degree to that produced upon the ear by sounds, the impression upon the sensorium or seat of sensation in the brain will probably be the same, or so nearly so, that the ideas of the respective external objects will be associated in the mind. On the basis of this theory, the different musical

---

**Santálas* i. e., *Samatálas*, from *sama*, equal, and *tála*, measure: alluding to the regularity of their movements in dancing.

instruments have been characterised by corresponding colours and fancifully classed as under:—

WIND INSTRUMENTS.

Trombone	... Deep red.	Flute	...Sky blue.
Trumpet	... Scarlet.	Diapason	.Deeper blue.
Clarionet	... Orange.	Double Diapason.	.Purple.
Oboe	... Yellow.	Horn	...Violet.
Bassoon (Alto)	... Deep yellow.		

STRINGED INSTRUMENTS.

Violin	... Pink.	Violoncello	... Red.
Viola	... Rose.	Double Bass	... Deep crimson red.

In connection with the above, it should be understood that the lowest notes of each instrument partake of the darkest shades of its color, and as they ascend they become of a lighter hue. As regards the human voice, the lowest tones, *i.e.*, those formed in the chest, partake of the most sombre hues and forcibly express our inmost feelings; as they ascend, they become more bright and cheerful, expressing the more lively sensations of mirth and joy. There is thus independently of words, a language of nature, in which the passions find a universal and an instinctive utterance, and if these are attended to, it will be found that they may all be referred to the gradations of the musical scale. According to Sanskrit authorities the seven notes are respectively represented by the following colours:—Black, tawny, golden, white, yellow, purple, and green,

resembling very nearly those mentioned in Field's Chromatics*

---

* The seven principal notes of Hindu Music, *sa, ri, ga, ma, pa, dha, ni.* corresponding to the notes of European Music, *C, D, E, F, G, A, B*, are based on phonological principles, these notes being related to the seven principal vowel sounds in the Sanskrit language, thus :—

Sa, ri, ga, ma, pa, dha, ni.

अ आ इ उ ए ओ

Hindu Music is divided into three *Grámas*, namely, the *Sa* gráma, the *Ga* gráma, and the *Ma* gráma. The idea of these *Grámas* seems to be connected with that of the three primitive vowels, *a* (अ), *i* (इ), and *u* (उ), from which, according to philologists, all the various vowel sounds in the Aryan languages have been developed. The three *Grámas* are thus indicated :--

Sa, o ga, ma, o, o, o.

अ इ उ

The twenty-one *Múrchhanás* spoken of in Hindu music are thus traced :—

(Vowels)

1	2	3	4	5	6	7	8	9	10	11	12	13	14
अ	आ	इ	ई	उ	ऊ	ऋ	ॠ	ऌ	ॡ	ए	ऐ	ओ	औ

(Consonants)

15	16	17	18	19	20	21
क group	च group	ट group	त group	प group	य group	श group.

The forty-nine *Kuta-tánas* are derived from the 16 vowels and 33 consonants that form the alphabet of the Sanskrit language. The vowels enumerated above are 14 in number, and to these the two and : are to be added, thus making up the total number 16. The consonants are

5 of the क group—*viz.*, क, ख, ग, घ, ङ,
5 ,, च ,, *viz.*, च, छ, ज, झ, ञ,
5 ,, ट ,, *viz.*, ट, ठ, ड, ढ, ण,
5 ,, त ,, *viz.*, त, थ, द, ध, न,
5 ,, प ,, *viz.*, प, फ, ब, भ, म,
4 ,, य ,, *viz.*, य, र, ल, व,
4 ,, श ,, *viz.*, श, ष, स, ह,
—
33

In the Sanskrit Grammar *Kalápa* occurs the following aphorism :—

सिद्धो वर्ण समाम्नाय:

Harmony is an effect inherent in nature. Every sound is a mixture of three tones, or, the first, third and fifth, in the same way as a ray of light is composed of three prismatic colors, namely, blue, red and yellow, which are the colors attributed, respectively, to C, E, and G of the major diatonic scale. This union is called the common chord. The musical scale*, which has been formed from an observation of the effects of every sound in nature,

which means that the *varnas* (letters of the alphabet, are *Siddha*, *i. e.*, eternal or self-manifested. So are the musical notes.

The principal notes are seven just as, according to the *Ayurveda* (Medical science of the Hindus), the constituent parts of the body are seven, namely,

मेद (Marrow), मांस (Flesh), मज्जा (Pith), अस्थि (Bone), शुक्र (Semen), वसा (Fat), and शोणित (Blood).

The days of the week are seven ; the oceans of the world, according to *Paurânic* geography, are also seven.

* The musical scale is derived, according to Sanskrit authors, from the cries of birds and beasts in the following order :—

C	... Peacock.	C to G	...	Kokil (a sweet-voiced Indian bird).
C to D	... Bull.			
C to E	... Goat.	C to A	...	Horse.
C to F	... Jackal.	C to B	..	Elephant.

The cries of birds have furnished hints for several musical compositions in Europe.

The vocal organs of both man and beast present a general resemblance to each other. Some of the quadrumana have large sacs between the thyroid cartilage and the *os hyoideum*, which have much to do with modifying and increasing the resonance of the voice. The bray of the ass has been traced to two large sacs existing between the vocal chords and the inner surface of the thyroid cartilage. A few of the Mammalia, as for instance, the giraffe, the porcupine, and the armadillo, have no vocal chords, and are therefore mute. Birds possess a superior larynx which differs considerably from that of the Mammâlia, and has nothing to do with the production of sound. Below this is the inferior larynx at the lower end of the trachea; just before it bifurcates into the two bronchi. This is the organ of voice, and differs a great deal, both in form and structure, in the several species of birds. In some birds the inferior larynx has as many as five muscles, in others, none, as in the case of vultures. The two membranes, *membrana semilunaris*, and *membrana tympaniformis* (the latter being highly developed in singing birds), which are attached to the thin rod of bone (*os transversale*), correspond to the vocal chords in the Mammalia, sounds being produced by the vibration of their margins. The various notes are caused by changes in the degree of tension of the membranes, by differences in the force of the air-current, and by changes in the length and degree of tension of the trachea and other parts. The range of the voice in birds is usually within an octave, but may be much greater. The sounds produced by most insects are pro-

B

may be called the *prism* of the art whereby all combinations of sound are divisible into their component parts. The Sanskrit authorities divide the notes into castes, C, F, and G (each of which contains 4 *srutis*) being *Bráhmanas*; D and A (each having 3 *srutis*) being Kshatriyas; E and B (having 2 *srutis* each) being Vaisyas; and the sharps and flats being Sudras (or *pariahs*, these having lost caste, so to speak, by the relative values of the notes they represented being affected). This grouping furnishes the key to the combination that should be resorted to in setting a musical piece to harmony. The arrangement of the colors, too, furnishes an important guide in the arrangement of chords.

duced externally and not internally. The stridulation of the cricket or grass-hopper is made by rubbing certain file-like organs against the edges of membranous drums on the wings. The pitch of the sounds produced by the cricket is high, consisting of 4,096 vibrations per second. The buzzing of flies and gnats is produced by the rapid vibration of two rudimentary posterior wings called *halteres*. The humming of humble-bees, beetles, and the like, is due to the passage of the air through the spiracles. Fish, with few exceptions, have no special sonorous apparatus. It is possible that the air-bladder opening into the pharynx which is possessed by some fish may enable them to emit sounds; and the fact that they can emit sounds, and sweet ones too, is testified to by Lieutenant White, Sir James Emerson Tennant, and other European travellers who had personal opportunities of listening to the music produced by the finny denizens of the deep.

NATIONAL MUSIC.

IT has been generally accepted that most countries have a music of their own, the character of which may be called national. The primitive tones of the human voice are much the same in all countries and prior to the progress of the art and to the period when the music of one country came to exercise some influence over that of another, the songs of a nation could express only the sensations of the heart, and have been little better than the mere tones of the voice. The Moors have exercised a perceptible influence upon the music of Spain. The well-known German "Dessauer Marsch" is of Italian origin. Certain authorities doubt if the English National Anthem is not an importation from abroad. The adoption occurs oftenest in a nation whose music has a less marked national character, and between nations whose music does not differ widely in its prominent features. In the case of civilized nations where music is cultivated on scientific principles in the upper strata of society, and where it has reached a high degree of development, one must look to the less educated classes for obtaining a strictly correct idea of their national music. National music means a faithful expression of national feelings, and these feelings are best manifested under circumstances that are not controlled by extraneous influences. The shepherd tending his flock, the fisherman mending his nets, the labourer in the paddy field, the cartman driving his cart,

has no inducement to sing his favorite tune, unless he is prompted to it by the emotions of his heart. The professional musician, on the other hand, has several inducements to compose or perform music which he does not really feel. The peculiar character of the popular music of a nation depends to a large extent upon the climate of the country, upon the occupation and habits of the people, and, as some go to the length of asserting, upon the food upon which they chiefly subsist. National airs are mostly without instrumental accompaniment, and this could hardly be otherwise, for the people generally sing at their daily occupations and on similar occasions where an instrument could scarcely be used, not to mention the practice that is required to enable one to play upon an instrument. The only instrument used on such occasions may be the drum, or some such thing that can mark out the rhythm; and it is only in countries where music has made some progress that stringed instruments are used.

The study of the music of various nations is advan tageous to the musician for a number of reasons. The variety of rhythm and modulation and the deep and beautiful expression that prevail in some of the melodies may present to the student excellent models in composition. The study is important from an ethnological point of view, as it affords him an insight into the inward man, and displays the character and temperament of different races, and the relation they bear to one another. It is also important from a historical standpoint, for it shows the different stages of progress which music has made in different countries. Having dwelt on some of the aspects of music in as succinct a manner as the scope of the present book will allow, and having for our object the presentation to the student of a birds'-eye view

of music as it prevails in the civilized world, we shall now proceed to our task, after making a few observations on the music of the savage nations of both the new and old hemispheres

---

THE SAVAGE NATIONS.

THE collection of tunes made by G. W. Steller shows that the people of Kamtschatka possess music far more expressive and beautiful than their ignorance and their wretched life would lead one to suppose.* The natives of the Fuegian Archipelago are said to possess a fine ear and great fondness for music. In his "Narrative of the United States Exploring Expedition," Captain Wilkes states that one of them sang with promptness and precision the diatonic and chromatic scales which had been played to him upon the violin. The Esquimaux, when visited by Captain Parry, had no instruments except a species of drum and tambourine, though they were found to be very fond of music. They had songs but these were characterised by neither variety, compass, nor melody: When conquered by the Spaniards the Mexicans were found to possess two drums as their chief instruments. The one was called the *Huehuetl* and the other, the *Teponaztli*. They had, besides, horns, sea-shells,

* The Kamtschadales have a kind of dance called the *Bachia*, or Bear dance in which two persons imitate the attitudes, tricks, and uncouth postures of two bears while the spectators singing incessantly repeat the words *Bachia da hog*! Tilesius, who witnessed one of these performances and wrote down one of the tunes employed, remarks that the dancers emitted at intervals a grunting sound, *hog*, or *ugh*, which is supposed to be an imitation of the noise made by the animals which they represented. The people of Kamtschatka evince an extraordinary talent for extempore songs. It is related that when two Russian officers and a naturalist visited them the natives soon commemorated in a song what they had observed regarding the doings of the visitors and of their servants. The *Aangitsch songs* form a particular class of national songs of the Kamtschadales, their name and origin being derived from a wild duck (*Anas Glacialis*) which appears in Kamtschatka at a certain season in large flocks. The notes of this bird are C, E, G, C, F, A, of the major diatonic scale.

and little pipes, as also an instrument used by their dancers, and designated the *Ajacaxtli.* From the description given of it, this instrument appears to have been little better than a child's rattle. The music of the Indians of North-West America, as described by Mr. Weld in his "Travels in North America", was very rude and indifferent, and equally devoid of melody and variety. Their celebrated war-song was little better than a dull recitative. Singing and dancing went hand in hand. The only instrument they used in addition to the drum was a flute formed of a thick cane or reed. The tones of this instrument admitted of a pleasing modulation; but Mr. Weld never came across an Indian, including those who were in the habit of singing, who could play a regular air upon it. Captain Hall who visited the Creek Indians in 1828, was present at one of their grand ball plays which, he was informed, was "a perfectly genuine unsophisticated display of the Indians, who had resided on the spot from time immemorial." At this festival were present "two musicians, one of whom was hammering away with his fingers on a drum, formed of a piece of deer skin, stretched over the hollowed trunk of a tree, while the other kept tune with a large gourd containing a handful of gravel." Soon after the arrival of Captain Cook at Otaheite, he was treated to a specimen of native music by one of the chiefs. Four persons played upon flutes, which sounded like German flutes; the performer, instead of applying the instrument to his mouth, blew into it with one nostril, while he stopped the other with his thumb. To these instruments four other persons sung. The Captain and his fellow-voyagers found, to their surprise, that generally they were the subjects of the songs, which were unpremeditated. The Otaheiteans possessed drums which, however, were beat with the hands. At Amsterdam, one of

the Friendly Isles, the Captain and his officers were entertained by the women with songs, and they accompanied the music by snapping their fingers. Here only three instruments were found, *viz.*, a flute, another wind instrument (like the Syrinx or Pan's pipe), and a drum. In his description of the Tonga Islands (which represent a part of the Friendly group), Mr. Mariner remarks that the inhabitants are fond of singing, and that on festive occasions they go singing about all night. Some of their songs have neither rhyme nor regular measure; but there are others that have both. They also sing a kind of lament over the corpses of the dead. The Indians of Chili used flutes made of the bones of the enemies whom they had slain in war; they likewise made them of the bones of animals; but the Indians of war danced only to the former. In his work entitled the "Historical Relation of the Kingdom of Chili," Alonso de Ovalle mentions that their way of singing was to raise their voices altogether upon the same note; and that at the conclusion of each song, they played upon the flutes and a kind of trumpet. The Indians of Brazil also used pipes made of human bones. The Bachapins, a tribe of the Caffres, have only one instrument called the *Lichákå* which is simply a reed pipe, and which is capable of producing only one note. When several players meet, some of these pipes are tuned in unison, while others take different notes in the scale, the interval between the lowest and the highest pipe comprising about twelve notes. Burchell in his *Travels* says that there is no particular air in their music, though a certain cadence is perceptible now and then. He supposes that prior to 1812 when he visited the tribe they had not heard European airs; and that when he, for the first time, played some on the violin, several boys who

had heard them attentively, soon picked them up and sung them to him with surprising readiness and precision. It would appear that love-songs and serenades are not the monopoly of civilized lovers; for we find that the North-American Indian blows his little courting whistle; that the Bushman in South Africa twangs the solitary string of his bow-shaped *gorah*; and that the Corsican youth sings his melancholy *vocero* referring to death in the prime of life. In his work entitled "Voyage of His Majesty's ship *Alceste*," John M'Leod mentions that in the island of Formosa, "when a young man fixes his affections, he hovers about the house where the object of his regard resides, and plays upon some musical instrument, which signal the lady answers by coming out to meet him, and to settle the matter, provided he is to her taste; should it be otherwise, she takes no notice, the gentleman 'whistles in vain' and must try his fortune elsewhere." Captain Cook observed that the Sandwich Islanders while engaged in preparing their favorite drink, called *ava* (which is expressed from the root of a kind of pepper plant) invariably sang hymns. When the liquor was prepared, the chief among them, after chanting by himself for some time and being responded to by the people in chorus, would pour some of the *ava* on the ground, evidently as a libation to the gods. Marco Polo, who travelled in Asia during the latter half of the thirteenth century, relates of the Grand Khan of Tartary thus;—"when drink is called for by him, and the page in waiting has presented it, he retires three paces and kneels down, upon which the courtiers and all who are present, in like manner make their prostration. At the same moment all the musical instruments, of which there is a numerous band, begin to play, and continue to do so until he has ceased drinking, when all

the company recover their posture; and this reverential salutation is made so often as His Majesty drinks." Francisco Travassos Valdez, in his work called "Six Years of a Traveller's Life in Western Africa," relates of the Kafirs in Loanda, Lower Guinea, that if a death occurs among them, the friends of the deceased performed songs and dances not only at the funeral, but resume this manifestation of grief at the expiration of eight days, and then again at the close of a month. In her "Ten Months in the Fiji Islands," Mrs. Smythe remarks that the natives possess some songs which are said to be so ancient that many of the words are no longer intelligible. Bowdich, when he enquired about the antiquity of a popular air which he frequently heard sung by the Negroes in Ashanti, was told that "the song was made when the country was made." The music of the aboriginal tribes of Western, Southern, and Eastern Africa presents surprising points of similarity. The Negroes are proverbially fond of music. "The general excellence of the Negro ear for music," observes Dr. Charles Pickering in his work on "The Races of Man," "is a subject of common remark in the United States." He goes further and states that much of the popular music in the United States can be traced to a Negro source. Remarking on the musical talent evinced by the Negro slaves in Georgia, Mrs. Fanny Kemble says in her "Journal,"—"with a very little skilful adaptation and instrumentation, I think one or two barbaric chants and choruses might be evoked from them that would make the fortune of an opera." The music of the American Indians has very little in common with that of the Negroes. The instruments which were in use among the Indians when America was discovered, and those subsequently found in old tombs and other places, where they had lain

undisturbed for several centuries, point more to Asia than Africa as the country whence they were imported. These genuine evidences of the progress made in music by the American Indians before they came in contact with the European and African races, go to support the theory that America was in the very remote past colonised by the Hindus. The use of the rattle in incantations and of songs for the cure of diseases is common to the aborigines of America and Africa. The *maraca* of the Brazilian Indians is a rattle made of a gourd containing grains of maize and having a wooden handle attached to it. Precisely similar is the *pehi* of the Indians of Guinea which is used by the sorcerers in their incantations. (called *obiah*) for the purpose of expelling a malady or inflicting one. The same kind of rattle is to be found with most Negro tribes in Africa and with the Kafirs in Eastern Africa. Again, the Indians on the Rio Haupes (a tributary of the Rio Negro, South America) possess a musical instrument called *Juruparis* or "devil," which is said to be an object of very great veneration. Women are never allowed to see these instruments, nor young men either, until they have been subjected to a series of fastings and other preparations. Captain R. F. Burton mentions an equally mysterious instrument which the Negroes in Abeokuta, Western Africa, are in the habit of sounding on certain peculiar occasions to terrify their women. The Rev. Dr. J. Lewis Krapf relates that the Wanika, a Kafir tribe near Zanzibar, make use of an instrument called *muansa-wa-kurri* which is held in great veneration and awe. It is always brought into play when the Wanika people sacrifice or pray for rain, or are going to strangle a misshapen child in the wood, or promulgate any new laws. It is only those who are initiated into the mystery of

the *muansa* that are allowed to hear the bellow of this terrible instrument.

The development of music is found to be much slower than that of other arts, and this is specially the case with the music of uncivilized countries. But curious as the fact may appear, it has been observed that some of the savage nations possess a kind of notation, rude though it well may be, but calculated to help the memory of the singer in a very suggestive method. In his work entitled "Information respecting the History, Condition, and Prospects of the Indian Tribes of the United States," Dr. H. R. Schoolcraft tells us that the North American Indians paint pictures upon birch-bark or some other suitable material to which the singer refers as to a book. Dr. Schoolcraft has published several of these mysterious representations. In one of the war-songs, there are only four symbolic figures, *viz.*—

1. The sun.
2. A warrior pointing with one hand to the sky, and with the other to the earth.
3. A warrior appearing under the symbol of the moon.
4. Venus, the evening star, called "The Eastern woman."

These figures recall to the mind of the singer a whole verse, each symbol representing a particular sentiment as the following translation will explain :—

1. I am rising to seek the war-path;
2. The earth and the sky are before me.
3. I walk by day and by night,
4. And the evening star is my guide.

In another war-song are depicted :—

1. The hero with his war-club and magic rattle.
2. Birds of prey flying in the sky.
3. The hero lying slain in the battle-field.
4. The hero appearing as a spirit in the sky.

The interpretation of the above is as follows :—

1. I devote my body to battle.
2. I take courage from the flight of eagles.
3. I am willing to be numbered with the slain;
4. For even then my name shall be repeated with praise.

Mr. G. Catlin, in his " Letters and Notes on the manners, customs, and condition of the North American Indians," gives a fac-simile of a song of the Chippeway Indians in North America. From this chart it would appear that besides the suggestive figures such as those described above, there are certain symbols which are no doubt musical signs. The traveller Kohl relates, in his " Wanderings round Lake Superior," that an Indian, named Kitagiguan (or The Spotted Feather), gave him a music lesson, in which the master took one of the birch-bark books in his lap, and, pointing with his finger to certain of the depicted figures, proceeded to instruct his pupil by remarking that those signs meant nothing further than that they showed him how he should go on singing. Pointing to some others he observed :—"This sign signifies that the same voice and the same tune continue; and this sign indicates that the voice shall go up."

The music of other savage or semi-savage nations will be noticed further on under the headings of the countries to which they respectively belong.

ASIA

CHINA.

CHINA is one of the oldest countries in the world, and it is no wonder, therefore, that the invention of the music of that country should be attributed to Fo Hi, its first prince, who was, according to some authorities, contemporary to, and according to some others, identical with Noah. Chao-Hao, and after him Confucius, greatly improved the art. The latter is said to have compiled a work on the science, but according to M. Klaproth it was burnt by command of Emperor Shihuang-ti, who flourished about 246 B. C. Music was held in high estimation among the early Chinese. It was called "the Science of Sciences; the rich source from which all the others spring." Father Amiot speaks enthusiastically of the skill of the Chinese in the musical art. He goes to the extent of saying that Linghen Kouie (who is said to have lived 1000 years before Orpheus and to have remarked,—"when I strike harmonious chords, the beasts of the field encompass me, leaping for joy",) was superior to Hermes Trismegistus and that the *Kin* of Pin-mou-kai far excelled the lyre of Amphion. Father Alvarez Semedo, in his work entitled "The History of the Great and Renowned Monarchy of China," gives an account of the music and musical instruments of this nation. He mentions therein that Confucius took great pains in having the people instructed in music. There were wandering minstrels, and blind minstrels who went about the country, singing or playing at feasts and

festivals, and marriages and birth-days. The priests also used music in their offices and funeral ceremonies; and this sacred music was somewhat like the *canto-fermo* of the Romish Church. The Chinese sang in unison and not in harmony. Their singing was with one voice, accompanied by a single instrument. Their first instrument was of metal and contained "bells of all sorts, cymbals, sistra," &c. The second was made of jasper, "like the Italian squadra." They had the ordinary drum, the kettle-drum, the violin, the viol (with silk strings), the flute, a kind of wooden castanets, as also an instrument like the syrinx or Pan's pipe. In addition to these there is one instrument—the most ancient on record—called the *Hiuen*, which Father Amiot attempted to trace 3000 years before the Christian era. It is in the form of an egg pierced with five holes, two being at the top and three at the bottom. Dr. Burney makes mention of one instrument which he saw in Paris with the Abbé Arnaud of the French Academy. It was a kind of harmonicon, consisting of bars of wood of different lengths, as sonorous as if they had been of metal. A specimen of this was observed by Carl Engel in the Museum of the United Service Institution, London. Two of the most important of Chinese instruments are the *King* and the *Cheng*. The *King* consists of stones cut into the shape of a carpenter's square, each stone being suspended by the corner in a wooden frame. It is played by being beat with a round mallet like a gong, which latter is also a Chinese instrument. The *King* had, according to Father Amiot, 25 bridges, of which 5 were blue, 5 red, 5 yellow, 5 white and 5 black. The *Cheng* has a gourd or bamboo for its basis, and represents, in the arrangement of its reed or bamboo pipes, the column of an organ. It has from 13 to 19 pipes which emit sound either by blowing or inhaling, so that a

tone may be continued to any length. It does not sound till a hole is stopped, and as many openings as are covered by the fingers, so many sounds are produced. Duets may, therefore, be played on a single instrument or even chords. The tone of the *Cheng* is not loud enough for a theatre or concert hall, but in a small room it is known to discourse exquisite music.

According to the Chinese, there are eight different kinds of musical sound in nature, named as below, and their instruments are classified accordingly:—(1) sound of skin; (2) sound of stone; (3) sound of metal; (4) sound of silk; (5) sound of wood; (6) sound of bamboo; (7) sound of gourd; and (8) sound of baked earth. Under heading (1) come the varieties of the *Kou* (drum) *viz.*, *Ying Kou*, *Kin Kou*, *Tsu Kou*, *Tao Kou*, *Pang-Kou*, *Thai-pang-kou* and the *Chi-sian* (tambourine). Under heading (2) are comprised the *King* and its modern variety the *Pien-King*, *Tse King*, *Yu-ty* and *Yu-hsiao* (flutes), and *Hai-lo* (conch-trumpet). No. (3) includes the varieties of the *Chung* (bell), the *Lo* (gong), the *Po* (cymbals), the *La-pa* or long trumpet and *Hao tung*, a long. cylindrical instrument. No. (4) is represented by *Kin* or "the scholar's lute," the favourite instrument of Confucius, the *Se*, the *Pepa* (balloon guitar), *San-Heen*, *Yue-Kin*, *Hu-Kin*, *Ur-Heen* (two-stringed violin), and *Yang-Kin* also called the foreign harpsichord, because it is also found in Syria, Turkey and Egypt. No. (5) is now represented by the *Chu* (a rectangular box), the *Yu* in the form of a crouching tiger resting on a rectangular box, the *Mu-Yu* or "wooden fish," shaped like a skull, the *Pai-pan*, and *Shon-pan*, the last two being varieties of castanets. The wind-instruments come under class (6) and consist of varieties of the *Pai-hao* or pipes, the *Ty* or flute, and the *Sona* or clarionet. Under head-

ing (7) comes the *Cheng* or the "mouth-organ" already described. Class (8) is represented by the *Hsuan*, a kind of ocarina said to have been invented 2700 years before the Christian era. It is described as "a reddish yellow cone of baked clay or porcelain, ornamented with designs of dragons, clouds, &c., and pierced with six holes,—one at the apex to blow through, three in front, and two behind."

In his work, entitled "The Chinese as they are" (London, 1841), Mr. Tradescant Lay mentions the Chinese *Pepa*, a kind of guitar with four strings. "It is often used at festal rites of a religious character, and accompanied by the three-stringed guitar (*San-Heen*); so that we see something like music in parts, though of a very humble kind." Of the latter instrument he remarks:—"The sounds of the *San-Heen* are low and dull, which adapt it for the purpose of subduing the shrill sounds of the *Pepa* by something like a bass. Performers do not appear to have anything like a score,—one plays from memory or in learning from notes, while the other accompanies him according to the best ideas of harmony he is master of." Of another instrument, the *Yue-Kin* or "full-moon guitar", he remarks: "I once saw a musician at one of the strolling theatres who displayed a great deal of execution upon it, with very pleasing effect. On another occasion it was used as an accompaniment to the *Ur-Heen* (a species of fiddle), and, as the musician understood his business, the result had something peculiarly merry and exhilarating about it." The Chinese dulcimer, *Yang-Kin*, is furnished with brass strings which are struck with two small hammers; "when touched by a skilful hand, it yields a very gay and lively combination of harmonious and melodious sounds."

Music enters largely into the composition of the Chinese drama; and in remarking on the songs with which their plays are interspersed, Bishop Hurd, in his "Discourse on Poetical imitation", states that they evince a remarkable likeness to the ancient chorus of the Greek pieces. But the Chinese do not make use of music in their dramatic representations merely with the object of affording amusement. The aid of music is invoked when the author has reached the climax of passion, and only when words alone are found inadequate to convey the desired expression. Sir George Staunton says that at Turon in Cochin China, the embassy were treated to a performance of a kind of historical opera, in which the recitative, the air, and the chorus were as regular as upon the Italian stage. Some of the female performers were "by no means despicable singers." "At Zhe-hol", adds Sir George, "the singers had such a command over their voices as to resemble the musical glasses at a distance." The English officers who accompanied Lord Macartney on his embassy shewed a great contempt for Chinese music, and compared their military and theatrical bands to the "confused jingle and jargon of Bartholomew Fair." Mr. Ellis remarks—"Myriads of cracked penny trumpets give the best idea of Chinese military music." About 18 years ago a troupe of Chinese artistes gave some performances at the Opera House, Calcutta, and the newspapers of the time were full of bitter complaints made by the neighbouring Europeans against the company for disturbing the peace of night. The Chinese, in return, show their utmost indifference for English music, for when Lord Macartney's band was heard by them, they declared that it was not made for Chinese ears; and yet they seemed perfectly well aware of what should be the effect of music; as, on a previous occasion, when two of Rameau's best pieces

were played to them, one of the Chinese people remarked after the performance was over:—"Our melodies go from the ear to the heart, and from the heart to the mind; we feel them; we understand them; but the music which you have just played we neither feel nor understand—it does not move us." He further observed—"Music is the language of feeling; all our passions have their corresponding tones and proper language; and therefore music,to be good, must be in accord with the passion it pretends to express."

From the result of the investigations which Father Amiot made, during his residence in Pekin, regarding the science and history of Chinese music, it would appear that the ancient Chinese divided the octave into the twelve equal parts. The scale, as commonly used, consisted, however, of only five notes, which were called *koung, chang, kio, tché, yu,* corresponding with the European F, G, A, C, D. The intervals corresponding with the European B and E were called *Pien-tché* and *Pien-koung,* respectively. F was considered the principal or normal key, just as C is regarded in European music. Converted into the "C" scale, the Chinese scale would stand C, D, E, G, A, *i. e.,* the notes F and B would be avoided. These two intervals were used only in exceptional cases; and almost all the musical instruments were constructed with a view to the pentatonic scale. The *Hiuen,* as already stated, had only five holes through which this scale would be emitted. The *Kin* was similarly constructed. Another very old instrument called the *ou,* which was in the shape of a crouching tiger, had six notes, corresponding to F, G, A, C, D, F. The modern instruments are constructed to suit the pentatonic scale. It is said that when Prince Tsai-yu, towards the close of the sixteenth century of the Christian era, attempted

to introduce a diatonic scale by the inclusion of *Pien-tché* and *Pim-koung,* the innovation met with strong opposition at the hands of the musicians. Apparently the diatonic scale never became popular, as almost all the tunes collected by Europeans in China are strictly based on the pentatonic series. This scale seems to be the earliest in existence,* and the simplest of all. Children in their first attempts to intone the diatonic scale after it has been sung to them are apt to omit the *fourth* and *seventh.* From this fact it would appear that the pentatonic series comes most naturally to those whose ear has not been accustomed to any particular scale. On account of the similarity of scales, Chinese music bears a strong resemblance to the Scottish. But as Dr. Burney thinks there is no reason to conclude that the one borrowed it from the other, especially having regard to the fact that the Chinese are extremely tenacious of old customs, it may safely be asserted in the language of the learned Doctor that the pentatonic scale is " natural to a people of simple manners during the infancy of civilization and the arts among them." The uses of this scale among other nations will be noticed when they come to be dealt with.

The earliest information of the existence of a system of musical notation among the Chinese is to be found in a manuscript of Father Amiot transcribed by Laborde in Paris in 1780. They seem to have a certain system for vocal music and another kind for certain of their instruments. Fétis mentions a Chinese treatise on the art of playing the *Kin,* or " Scholars' Lute," which contains a notation peculiar to that instrument. Carl Engel

* This is borne out by the fact that the six principal *Rágas* (melody types of the Hindus) which, with reference to their mythological genesis, sprang from the five mouths of Mahádeva and the mouth of Párvatí include one, the (*Megha*), which is practically of the pentatonic scale.

reproduces the words and music of a Chinese song "Siau Chok," and attempts an explanation of the various symbols used to denote duration of time and to indicate the higher octaves. In the "Journal of the North China Branch of the Royal Asiatic Society, Shanghai, 1859," The Rev. E. W. Syle thus describes the mode in which the Chinese add the musical notation to the words of a song:—"The words are written down in a severe and stately column, and the music is left to find room for itself in the best way it can. All the vocalization that is to be done upon any particular word is made, as it were, to flow off from it sideways and downwards; the performer must look sharp after his notes and rests and beats among the odds and ends of writing that appear to the uninstructed like the after-thoughts of hasty composition."

In China great attention is paid by the State to the cultivation of music. The connection of the State with music is shown by the names of the notes of the oldest musical scale, *F* being called Emperor; *G*, Prime Minister; A, loyal subjects; *C*, state of affairs; and *D*, mirror the world. One of nine tribunals who have charge of the general affairs of the State superintends the musical rites and ceremonies. The professors of music have a higher status than those of Mathematics and have their college in the enclosure of the Imperial Palace. It is said that the Library at Pekin includes 482 works on music.

China is no exception to the custom of singing by beggars with a view to solicit alms. The Chinese beggars use castanets made of bamboo. In his "Personal narrative of three years' service in China" published in London in 1863, Lt.-Col. Fisher mentions that in Canton, there exists a poor-law which provides that no beggar who enters a shop or a similar place and sounds

his bamboo-sticks shall be turned out without having first received some alms; but when only the smallest coin—the twentieth part of a penny in value,—has been given him, he is bound to go away at once. Regarding the quality of voice of the Chinese, Col. Fisher remarks:—"On no single part of the coast [of China] from North to South, did I ever hear a man sing from his lungs; it was invariably the head voice or falsetto, and very absurd it was to see a great big man emit such sounds out of his body." Sir John Barrow, who published his "Travels in China" in 1804, makes mention of a song of Chinese boatmen, who sing in chorus at time of sowing, the object being to combine "cheerfulness with regularity." At the time of his visit to China he found the *Moo-lee-wha* or the song in praise of the flower *moo-lee* to be "one of the most popular songs in the whole country." The following is a translation of that interesting composition, the music of which has been reproduced in the *Victoria Sámrájyam*; *

How delightful this branch of fresh flowers!
One morning, one day, it was dropped in my house.
I, the owner, will wear it not out of doors,
But I will hold the fresh flower and be happy.
How delightful this branch of the Moo-lee flower!
In the full plot of flowers blooming none excels it,
I, the owner, will wear this gathered branch,
Wear it, yet fear, the flower seen, men will envy.

* By the author.

SIAM.

THE people of Siam seem to have made as great an advance in music as any of the oriental nations. They say that their instruments and much of their music have been derived from Burmah, Pegu, or China, while these nations, in their turn, consider the Siamese as their superiors in musical proficiency and attribute to them the invention of their principal instruments.

The *Ranat* or the Harmonicon is the characteristic instrument of Siam. There are four varieties of this instrument of which *Ranat Thong* and *Ranat Lek* are made of metal, and *Ranat Ek* and *Ranat Thoom* are made of wood. Gongs are very popular among the Siamese. The *Khong yai* consists of a circular frame-work in which are suspended by strings sixteen gongs. The player squats in the middle of the circle. The *Khong Lek* is a smaller instrument of a similar kind and consists of twenty-one gongs. The varieties of the drum go by the names of *Talot Pote* (a small hand-drum chiefly used in the Laos states); *Taphone* (a larger hand-drum); *Song-nah* (of a narrow cylindrical shape); and the *Thone* (a small vase-shaped hand-drum). The *Klong-Khek* (Malay drum) and the *Klong-Yai* (Kettle drums) are among the chief varieties that are beaten with sticks. The *Tuk-kay*, or "alligator", is the most characteristic stringed instrument the country. This instrument is placed on the ground at time of playing and the performer presses the strings

(of which one is brass, and the others are of silk) on the frets, and strikes them with an ivory plectrum. Of the instruments of the violin species are the *Saw Tai* and the *Saw Samsai,* both being mounted with three strings. The *Saw Duang* and *Saw Oo,* which are two-stringed violins differing only in size, bear a close resemblance to the ordinary Chinese fiddle. The *Pee,* which is the most important wind instrument of Siam, may be made either of marble, ivory, or ebony. Another instrument of this class is known as *Peechawar,* or Java flute, which has seven holes and is generally made of ivory. Bamboo flutes are also in use. The *Klui* is a variety in which the pitch may be altered by covering one of the holes with a membrane. In Laos and Siam there is a species of organ constructed on a principle similar to the Chinese *Cheng,* though entirely dissimilar in outward look. The name for cymbals is *Charp* and that for castanets, *Ching.* The latter is used by the conductor of an orchestra to keep time during the performance. The orchestra, like the instruments, is divided into two classes,—*Mahoree* or "light-sounding," and *Bhimbhat* or "heavy-sounding," the former being intended for in-door performances and the latter, like the brass bands of Europe, for out-door purposes.

In his account of *Siam and Cochin China,* Mr. Crawfurd remarks that a Siamese band "ought not to consist of less than ten instruments. The first of these in rank is a kind of staccato, in the form of a semi-circle, within which the player sits, striking with two small hammers the notes, or keys, which consist of inverted vessels of brass. The second is another staccato, of the same materials, but less compass, in the form of a boat; the third, a violin with three strings; the fourth, a guitar with four strings, played with a bit of wood fastened to the finger; the fifth, a flute; and the sixth, a flageolet.

To these are occasionally added an instrument with four strings, in the form of a boat; and the band is completed by the addition of a drum, cymbals, and castanets." At the International Inventions Exhibition held at South Kensington, London, 1885, the King of Siam caused to be exhibited specimens of the principle instruments used in that country, and a Siamese orchestra gave performances of their national music.

The music of the Siamese is characterised by a great deal of softness, playful sweetness, and simplicity. It differs from that of othe similar people in being played in a minor key; and many of their melodies are, according to Crawfurd, analogous to the Scotch and Irish tunes.. There is no harsh or jarring sound, no sudden or unexpected transition, no disagreeable sharpness in their music. "Its principal character", observes Mr. George Finlayson, in his work entitled *Mission to Siam and Huè*, "is that of being soft, lively, sweet, and cheerful, to a degree which seemed to us quite surprising. They have arrived beyond the point of being pleased with mere sound; the musician aimed at far higher views, that of interesting the feelings, awakening thought, or exciting the passions. Accordingly, they have their different kinds of music, to which they have recourse, according as they wish to produce one or the other of these effects. Their pieces of music are very numerous. A performer of some notoriety who exhibited before us stated that he knew 150 tunes." A number of Siamese tunes collected by Captain James Low, of the Madras Army; were published in the "Journal of the Royal Asiatic Society," Volume IV, London, 1837. Among these is "Phriyadun", or the King of Siam's March, which consists of only four different intervals, but it is evidently founded upon the pentatonic scale, like all

the other Siamese melodies in Captain Low's collection. "Cha lok loang" and "Cha Hong" are among the popular airs of Siam. The following two translations of songs give some idea of the spirit of Siamese poetry :—

I.

A mother's merits, who can say
How inappreciable they ?
A mother's merits, earth can bring
Nought 'gainst them in the scale to weigh.
The fire-fly's light's a lovely thing;
But those are bright as noon-tide ray.
Wide is the air, vast heaven's arched hall ;
Yet they are narrow, they are small,
With mother's merits when compared :
The sea, the stream, the water-fall,
Mount Meru * to its summit bared,
Are trifling and unworthy all.
Yes ! mother's merits, high and true,
They can eclipse, outweigh, outvie
The earth, with towering Mount Meru,
And the huge ocean and the sky.

II.

Hateful, repulsive to the eye,
The ugly vulture floats on high ;
Yet harmless, faultless in his ways
Upon the dead alone he preys ;
And all his acts in every place
Are useful to the human race.
The snowy Ibis, beautiful
And white as softest cotton-wool,
Preys on the living, and its joys
Spring from the life that it destroys.
So wicked men look sleek and fair
Even when most mischievous they are.

* The holy mountain of the Buddhists.

JAPAN

CONSIDERING the circumstance of the Chinese and the Japanese possessing much in common in religion and usages, and having regard to the fact that the musical instruments of these two nations bear a strong resemblance to each other, it will require no stretch of imagination to conclude that the spirit of the music of both should be substantially the same. As might be expected, the pentatonic scale is mostly in use in Japan. The specimen of a Japanese song published with music in "All the Year Round," London, May 11th, 1861, shows that the melody is constructed upon the pentatonic scale. It is, however, not in *Major*, like similar melodies, but in *Minor*,—*F sharp* being the tonick. This specimen was obtained from the Japanese envoys, who, with a suite of seventy officers and attendants, visited the United States of America, shortly before the publication of the article on "Music among the Japanese" in the journal alluded to. Siebold's work, published in Leyden in 1832, contains some beautiful drawings of the musical instruments of Japan.* According to the traditions of the Japanese,

* The author of the present work has in his collection the following instruments of Japan presented to him in 1878 by His Majesty the Mikado of Japan:—

A pair of time-beaters.
A kagura flute.
A mouth-organ.
A flageolet and reed.
A flute.
A koma flute.
A Japanese harp with bridges.
A lute with plectrum and strings.
A harp with bridges and finger-tips.
A gong and sticks.
A large drum and sticks.
A small drum and sticks.

Amaterasu, the goddess of the sun, hid herself in a cave, being offended by the other divinities, and refused to come out until she was charmed out of it by the music which the gods had invented with a view to bring her out. This is the mythological account of the origin of Japanese music. Historically, however, it has been asserted that Japan derived its music from India through China and Corea. It is said that in 453 of the Christian era, the King of Shiragi (in Corea) being deeply grieved at the news of the death of the Emperor of Japan sent eighty ships full of presents with eighty musicians of different kinds. This is the first authentic record of the musical connection between the two countries. A great impetus was given to the cultivation of music with the introduction of Buddhism in 552 of the Christian era. Prince Shotoku commanded the people to learn music, and it is related of him that when he overthrew Moriganodaijin, he led on his army to the tune of *Bairo*, a piece of classical music. From the beginning of the seventh century, when communication was first opened between Japan and China, the classical music and musical instruments of the latter came to be introduced into the former country. Since the tenth century, however, when the relations between the two countries became strained, the cultivation of the classical music of China has been given up, and popular music has come into greater prominence in the country. Japanese musicians are divided into four classes—the first being called Gakkunine (who devote themselves exclusively to sacred music and from whom the orchestra of the Mikado is recruited); the second, Guenin (who are practical players and perform secular music alone); the third, the corporation of what are called *Feki-blind* musicians, who perform both sacred and secular music; and the fourth being designated Ghekos or singing-girls who

sing the popular songs of the day and are forbidden to take part in sacred music. The Buddhist chants in Japan are accompanied by the free use of the gong and drums. Music is extensively cultivated in Japan; there is scarcely a house in which a musical instrument of some kind does not find a place, and there is scarcely a class of women who is not proficient in the art. The Japanese are a highly imitative people and are gifted with a very accurate ear; and it is no wonder, therefore, that European melodies are heard whistled with precision in most of the streets of the capital cities. In the year 1878, the Japanese Government appointed a Commission to enquire into the character of European music with a view to ascertain its fitness for introduction into the school system of the country. In 1880, a national institute of music was opened in connection with the normal school of Tokio and the services of Mr. Luther Whiting secured as instructor of music.

The Japanese instruments are divided into two classes—perfect and imperfect; the former being represented by those used for sacred music, the latter embracing all others. This distinction has reference to details of construction and ornamentation, to the character of strings, to the manner of tuning, and so forth. The most important of the stringed instruments are the *Koto*, the *Samisen*, the *Kokiu*, and the *Biwa*. The *Koto* has several varieties (from the *Summa-koto* with its single string to the *Lono-koto* with its 13 strings), and one of these, called *Schikenkin* or *Kinno-koto*, corresponds to the *Kin* of China. The *Samisen* (*Siamisen*) is a three-stringed guitar frequently used to accompany songs, and is the favorite instrument of the Gheko. The *Kokiu* is a four-stringed instrument of the violin class, while the *Biwa*, the favourite of the *Feki-blind* musicians, is some-

what like the Chinese *Pepa*. It is called after the Biwa lake, from the fact of the outlines of its shores resembling the body of this instrument. It is used both for classical and popular music. Among the wind instruments of Japan, may be mentioned the *Fuye* or *Teki* (the flute), and its varieties the *Riyuteki*, *Shakuhachi*, *Seouno-fuye* (Pan pipes), and *Shichiriki*. The *Sona* and *Cheng* of China appear in Japan under the names of *Heang-ti* and *Sho*. The *Rappakai* or conch trumpet is used as a war horn and also at religious festivals. *Taiko* is the Japanese name for drum, so called after a celebrated warrior. The varieties of the drums are *O-Tzudzumi* and *Ko-Tzudzumi* (hand-drums), *Jamagairou-guine-taico* (great war-drum), and *Kagura-Taiko* (a large drum used in the Buddhist temples). The *Doo*, or gong, appears in several varieties, and so do the *Nihoihagi* or cymbals. The *Mokkine* is a kind of Xylophone consisting of 16 wooden keys of unequal length, played with two wooden-tipped drum-sticks. The *Mokugyo* is a hollow wooden drum with which the Buddhist Priests accompany their prayers. The *Soezoew* consists of a cluster of bells attached to a handle. The orchestra plays an important part in the theatres of Japan which, though of a comparatively recent origin, have become very popular in the country. In martial scenes the *Taiko*, or bass drum, is very freely used. The plan of arranging the representations may be noticed *en passant*. Supposing five plays are to be acted in a day, the performers go through the first act of the first play, then the first act of the second play, and so on, until they have successively taken the first act of every play. They then take the second act of each play, and so on until the whole is concluded. The object of this rather singular custom is to enable spectators wishing to follow a

particular play to see one act, go away, and come again in time for the next act.

As regards the question whether the Japanese had any system of musical notation, it is stated by Saris, whose account dates as far back as the year 1611, that "their tunes were pricked." Referring to the present times it has been asserted that the Japanese possess for their sacred music alone a relatively complete system of notation. They have no signs to indicate the time. Like the Chinese, they write their music in verticle lines from right to left. In vocal music the words are written to the left of the lines.

The following translation of a Japanese song appeared in the "Manners and Customs of the Japanese in the Nineteenth Century," which was published in New York in 1845 :—

> Upright in heart be thou, and pure,
> So shall the blessing of God,
> Through eternity be upon thee;
> Clamorous prayers shall not avail,
> But truly a clear conscience,
> That worships and fears in silence.

The following is a song of a Japanese girl :—

> Yes! eager is my longing
> To look upon thy face,
> With thee some words to speak'
> But this I must renounce ;
> For should it in my dwelling
> Once chance to be divulged,
> That I with thee had spoken.
> Then grievous were the trouble
> Would surely light on me :
> For certain my good name
> Were lost for evermore.

———

COREA.

THE people of Corea are passionately fond of music, though, like the Chinese, the upper classes consider it undignified to take part in instrumental music and prefer listening to the performances of paid musicians. The women, too, seldom take part in instrumental performances. Singing is popular with both sexes and among all classes of people. Dancing is held in great favour, but men and women never dance together, and generally only one person at a time takes part in the performance. The dance consists of a slow movement of the feet, with a backward and forward motion of the body, similar to the dancing of the Spanish Gypsies. The Coreans, who gave their music to the Japanese, received theirs from the Chinese. But they are a highly conservative people, and the pentatonic scale is still in use among them. It is rather peculiar that music plays little part in the Buddhist rites practised in Corea, and that it seldom finds a place in the theatrical performances which are conducted by the Buddhists and patronised by the lower classes.

Of the wind instruments of Corea, the *Nallari,* or clarionet is the most popular. The *Toungsyo,* or flute, is one of the commonest instruments of the country, and is depended upon by many a musician as the means of earning his livelihood. The Rev. G. W. Gilmore, who was resident in Corea for som time, attempted to buy a specimen from a blind musician, and was told that he

would part with it if the Reverend gentleman undertook to support him during the rest of his natural life. The *Saihwang* corresponds with the *Cheng* of China and *Sho* of Japan. During the last few years, some brass bugles have been imported from America, and these are played before the King in his progress from one palace to another. The *Komounko* is the most characteristic instrument of Corea. It is said to be the direct ancestor of the Japanese instruments of the *Koto* kind, though it differs from the ordinary variety of the *Koto* in several essential particulars. The *Yang-Kum* is a smaller variety of the *Yang-Kin* of China. The *Haggum,* or violin, is, in principle, the same as the *Ur-Heen* of China. The most important variety of the Corean drum is known as the *Chan-Gou,* which consists of a frame of hollow wood, in the shape of an hour-glass. It is beaten on one head with a stick, and on the other with the fingers. A variety of sounds is produced by the player beating on the top, or on the edge, or between the two, by using alternately the fingers and the entire fists. Orchestral performances are held in private houses, specially at dances, and dinner-parties, the musicians playing in a room adjoining that in which the party is held. On such occasions, the *Komounko,* the *Haggum,* flutes, and the *Chang Gou* are commonly used. The *Yang-Kum* is sometimes added.

THIBET.

THIBET may appropriately be called the head-quarters of Buddhism, which, of all religions in the world, has the largest number of adherents. There is scarcely any religious denomination on the face of the earth in whose sacred ceremonies music holds a more prominent place than Buddhism, though its tenets contain strict injunctions against the encouragement of secular music. The temple music in Thibet is specially remarkable for the large and powerful brass instruments used in it, combined with various other instruments of equal power. The trumpets of the Buddhist priests in Thibet are noted for their enormous size. The *Drilbu* is the little hand-bell which they use in connection with the religious ceremonials, which are said to resemble those of the Roman Catholic Church in some respects. In his "Account of the Embassy to the Court of Teshoo-Lama, in Thibet," London, 1800, Captain Samuel Turner says that in Thibet "there is no religious edifice but what is adorned with the head of the lion at every angle, having bells pendant from his lower jaw, and the same figure is equally common at every projection of the palace walls." Captain Turner was informed by the Buddhist priests in Thibet that "their music was written down in characters which they learnt." The Captain

describes an annual ceremony in honor of the dead, performed by the Buddhists, which he witnessed in Teshoo-Loomboo, the residence of the famous Teshoo-Lama. On that occasion all the inhabitants of the town illuminated their house-tops. The summits of the buildings belonging to the Buddhist monastery, and the dwellings of the villagers in the distance, were similarly lighted up. Sounds of the bell and various musical instruments broke the tranquillity of the night, and when the noise subsided, the people chanted their prayers in memory of their ancestors. These observances, adds Captain Turner, "were all so calculated, by their solemnity, to produce serious reflection, that I believe no human ceremony could possibly have been contrived more effectually to impress the mind with sentiments of awe."

BURMAH.

THE Burmese are very fond of music and poetry, and, like the Chinese, have an extreme aversion for European music. Captain Henry Yule, who went to Burmah in 1855 in connection with the mission sent to the Court of Ava by the Governor-General of India, has translated into English one of the Burmese dramas. In this the hero is represented as having had presented to him by a *nát* (a sprite) a golden harp, and when he sings and plays "the wild elephants of the forest come around him, and are obedient to his voice and harp." The same drama shows that the Burmese are acquainted with the power of music for the expression of various emotions. A sprite addresses the band—"So now, as I am about to fly, strike up a victorious melody, O leader of the orchestra!" Afterwards, it says, "Now, that I may easily reach the large tree in my own mountain from this country of Kauthambi, play a soft and simple air, O leader of the orchestra." And a hunter in the forest concludes his monologue by addressing the orchestra—"Now, as I go on a grand expedition, burst forth like thunder!"

The principal stringed instrument of Burmah is the *Soung*, or *Soum*, a harp, which in shape "somewhat resembles a canoe with a deck." The *Thro* is an important instrument of the violin class. The Indian

Sárindá is als found in the country. The *Tuk-kay* of Siam appears in Burmah under the name of *Megyoung*. The flute is called the *Puloay*, and, along with the oboe, forms an important adjunct to the orchestra. The *Ranat* of Siam is known in Burmah as *Pattala*. Gongs of various kinds are in use, and are sometimes combined into an instrument called *Kyee-wain*, which corresponds to the *Klong-yai*, or gong-organ of Siam. This instrument is considered an essential part of the orchestra. The cymbals used are chiefly divided into *Ya-gwin* (big cymbals) and *Than-hin* (small cymbals). The *Kyee-zee* is a plate of sonorous brass of a triangular shape, used by Buddhists to attract attention to their offerings. The *Khew* is a small bell hung from the roofs of Buddhist temples. The gigantic bamboo castanets, called *Wahle Khoht*, play an important part in the orchestra. The *Seing-weing* consists of a carved circular frame round which a number of drums are hung.

Several of the Burmese instruments were captured in war and taken to England by Colonel Miles with whose consent they were exhibited in the Egyptian Hall, Piccadilly, London. They consisted of—

1. The *Patola**—a kind of guitar, fantastically shaped like an alligator.

2. The *Soum*—A kind of harp. This instrument has 13 silken strings, to the ends of which are attached tasselled cords, which are bound round the curved upper part of the frame in a way which admits of their being pushed up or down. By this means the instrument is tuned, as the tension of the strings can thus be increased

* Modern writers remark that the *Puttala* or *Patola* is a percussive instrument resembling the *Ranat* of Siam, and that the alligator-shaped guitar is called the *Megyoung*, which has been mentioned above.

or diminished at pleasure. These cords are made to serve also as ornamental appendages, as in the Assyrian harp.

3. The *Turr,* otherwise called the *Thro,* or violin, very nearly resembling the European instrument, and most elaborately carved and ornamented.

4. An instrument of the oboe species, but with the bell-end of the common trumpet.

5. The *Tom-Tom,* or Indian drum.

6. The *Harmoncia,* a boat-shaped instrument, hollow, and with bars of metal crossing it transversely. It was tuned to the natural minor scale of Europe.

7. A set ot *Gongs,* 16 in number, of different sizes, suspended to two sticks of bamboo, tuned nearly according to the diatonic scale, played upon with a small hammer.

8. A *Gong,* made of very thin metal and producing a somewhat soft sound.

9. *Cymbals.*

10. *Flutes,* or *Fifes.*

11. The following is a description of this item, taken from the catalogue which was sold to the visitors :—

"It is a triangular piece of compound metal, seven inches and a half in width, and four in depth, an analysis of which shews it to be composed of silver, copper, and bell-metal. It is of sacred origin and use, and is perfectly unique in this country. Its history is, that at the capture of Tavoy, the high-priest,

an active and leading officer, became a prisoner with the viceroy and second commander; the two last were immediately confined, but to the former, Colonel Miles gave instant liberty. In token of his gratitude for this unexpected mark of clemency, he took from his person this talisman, and gave it to the Colonel, as the most valuable gift it was in his power to bestow. When struck, the hearers, be they whom they might, were compelled immediately to fall down on their faces, in token of submission. The sound it emits is powerful and beautiful."

Besides the above, the Burmese have another instrument which the writer who describes it in the *Quarterly Musical Review, Vol. VII,* calls a *Cat,* as it is in the form of that animal sitting, with its legs folded under. it, and its tail brought in a semicircle over its back, and to these the strings are attached. It has usually 12 or 13 strings, and, supposing the lowest to be D, the scale does not rise by tones and half tones, D, E, F, G, but thus,—1st string D; 2nd, F; 3rd, A. The 4th then begins with G, and the two following are B and D. The 7th string, again, begins with C. The 8th and 9th are E and G; and so on with the remainder. The other stringed instruments play in concert with this one; and a bass is formed by means of a circular instrument called a *Boandah* which consists of a number of different sized drums, which the musician strikes with violence. *

In the description of the "Golden Pagoda" at Rangoon, in his work "Six Months in British Burmah," (London, 1858), Mr. Christopher Winter mentions

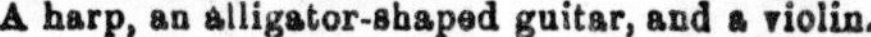

* The writer of the present work received a present of the following musical instruments, from His Majesty the King Theebaw of Burmah in the year 1878—

A harp, an alligator-shaped guitar, and a violin.

a large Burmese bell, under which, he says, he was able to stand upright with ease. He further states :—" There is, in a pagoda in Maulmain, a great bell suspended in the usual way between two posts; it has an inscription in the Burmese character. The bell is suspended in front of the temple; and when an offering has been made, or some religious duty performed, it is generally struck by the devotee once or twice with a deer's horn, several of which are usually placed near the bell."

The sacrificial ceremonies in the Buddhist temples in Burmah are accompanied by solemn chanting by the priests, and by dancing by chosen maidens, to the tune of the oboe and drum. The Burmese plays (or operas, strictly speaking), consist of a combination of acting, singing, dancing, and orchestral accompaniment. The subject of the representations is usually mythological, the adventures of the Hindu deity Ráma being a special favorite. It is said that the royal library at the capital contained a large number of works on the theory of music. It is considered treasonable to sing a new song before the king, and it has been asserted that the great singer Moung Thah Byaw was several times condemned to death for transgressing this injunction.

An interesting collection of Burmese melodies was presented to the Royal Asiatic Society, London, by Mr. Fowle, who resided for many years at Rangoon. It contains thirty different pieces, which, according to Mr. Fowle, include all the principal popular tunes of the Burmese: most of them are of considerable length. From the letter of Mr. Fowle to the Secretary of the Asiatic Society, it would appear that these melodies have been arranged for the instrument *Thro*. Traces of the pentatonic scale are to be found in these tunes.

The following translation of a Burmese Morning Hymn is taken from "Four Years in Burmah" by W. H. Marshall; London, 1860, Vol. II:—

Hail the sun's bright rays
    Chasing the night!
Our voices applaud
    The great Giver of Light!
Hail to the flowers,
    Fresh from their beds,
Rich with the fragrance
    The night-dew sheds!
Hail to the bird who
    With musical voice
Bids the sleeper awake
    And come forth and rejoice!
Lo! the broad river,
    The source of our food!
Hail to the Giver—
    Munificent Buddh.

INDIA.

HINDU PERIOD.

WITH the Hindus, music is of divine origin. In fact, it is considered as divinity itself. Before the creation of the world, an all-pervading sound rang through space. Brahmá, the Creator, Vishnu, the Preserver, and Mahádeva, the Destroyer, who comprise the Hindu Triad, were not only fond of music but were practical musicians themselves. Vishnu holds the *Sankha* (the conch-trumpet) in one of his hands, and this *Sankha*, according to some of the Puránas, was one of the valuable articles or gems, recovered from the deep, at the churning of the ocean. On one occasion Vishnu is said to have been so charmed with the vocal performance Mahádeva that he began to melt, and thus gave birth to the sacred Ganges. Mahádeva invented the *Pináka*, the father of stringed instruments. It was out of his five mouths that five of the original *Rágas* (melody-types) of Hindu music were produced; the sixth springing from the mouth of his consort Párvatí, these being respectively named Srí, Vasanta, Bhairava, Panchama, Megha, and Nata-Náráyana. After slaying the demon Tripura, Mahádeva was so much elated with joy, that he began to dance, and Brahmá prepared the drum (with which he asked Ganesa, the son of Mahádeva, to keep time to the performance) out of the earth, saturated with the demon's

blood, his skin serving as the skin with which the instrument was covered at its two heads. It is further stated that Mahádeva composed the *Rága Sankara-Vijaya*, in commemoration of this victory. Brahmá added six *Ráginís* to each of the principal *Rágas* and began to impart a knowledge of music to five of his disciples. Of these, Huhu and Tumburu (the inventor of the stringed instrument called after him, *Tumburá*) cultivated and spread the knowledge of vocal music; Rambhá, the celestial female dancer, learnt and taught dancing; and Nárada (the inventor of the *Mahatí Víná*, the principal stringed instrument) and Bharata (the father of the drama) practised the theory of music. Each of these musicians composed a musical treatise, but the one produced by Bharata had currency on earth. It was he who, out of the combination of the six *Rágas* and thirty six *Ráginís*, composed 48 *Ráginís* and designated them as their children. Innumerable combinations followed and it is said that each of the sixteen thousand milk-maids, with whom Vishnu in his incarnation of Krishna in the *Dwápara Yuga* held dalliance in Brindavan, composed a *Rágini* for his delectation. The court of Indra teemed with celestial musicians who entertained him with songs and dance and dramatic exhibitions. Brahmá created the four *Vedas* (or revealed scriptures of the Hindus) and, out of them, four *Upa-Vedas* of which *Gandharva Veda* (musical science) was one. This was evolved out of the *Sáma Veda*. The hymns in the *Sáma Veda* used to be chanted according to rules laid down which are still followed in most parts of India. Sarasvatí, the consort of Brahmá, presides over the letters and music.

Coming down to the heroic ages described in the Rámáyana and Mahábhárata, it will be found that music

was cultivated and encouraged by the princes and the people. It is related that Bhagiratha escorted the river Ganges from her heavenly residence to the terrestrial earth, blowing a conch all along the journey. Lava and Kusa chanted the Rámáyana in the presence of their father, to the accompaniment of the *Viná* which was taught them by the sage Válmiki, the father of metrical composition in Sanskrit. Several instruments used in the field of battle are mentioned in the Rámáyana. Rávana, the ten-headed giant-king of Lanká (Ceylon), is credited with the invention of the *Rávanastram*, the prototype of stringed instruments of the violin kind. The Mahábhárata also abounds in descriptions of the musical instruments of war. The conch-trumpet was much in use at this time. Krishna used the conch called *Pánchajanya*. The five Pandava brothers, Yudhisthira, Bhíma, Arjjuna, Nakula, and Sahadeva, respectively, used the conches named Ananta-vijaya, Paundra, Devadatta, Sughosha, and Manipushpa. Krishna is credited with the invention of the *Muralí* (flute). He was such a dexterous player on this instrument that the milk-maids of Vrindavan neglected their domestic duties and ran to listen to its strains while the river Jumuna in bewildered ecstacy forgot its onward course.

Coming further down to the period of tangible history, one might observe that music held a high place in polite society. In *Mrichchhakatik Nátaka,* which is the oldest drama extant and is said to have been written at, or shortly before, the beginning of the Christian era, Rebhila is mentioned as a distinguished musician of Oujjein in Malwa, and Chárudatta is described as returning home late at night from a concert given by Rebhila. This concert is also

described as including a performance on the "tuneful Vina" which "cheers the lonely heart and lends new lustre to the social meeting." Kalidasa who flourished in the reign of Vikramaditya (B. C. 56), King of Oujjein, who was a great patron of learning, mentions in his drama, called *Málavikágnimitra*, that the principal queen Dháriní sent her attendant maid to the *Sangíta-sálá* or music saloon, to enquire of Ganadása about the progress made by his pupil, Málaviká, in dancing and singing. In a subsequent portion of the play, Málaviká is described as singing an *Upa-gána* or prelude, and a *Chatuspada Vastu* in *Madhya-laya* (andante time). The play mentions the name of Haradatta, another professor of music. The classical dramas speak of the *Vaitálikas* being in attendance on the kings. They are, as Professor Wilson puts it, "a sort of poetical warder or bard who announce the fixed periods of the day, dawn, noon, or evening, in measured lines and occasionally pour forth strains arising from any incidental occurrence." It may be observed here *en passant* that the original name of the bard of Hindustan, (which has now been corrupted into *Bhát*) was Bárdai, which Abul Fazil has translated as "musician." It is perhaps more than a mere coincidence that the name and functions of the Bárdái and the Celtic Bards should be found almost identical.

The following are some of the principal treatises of music belonging to the Hindu period —*Sangita Ratnákara* by Sárangadeva; *Sangíta Darpana* by Dámodara Misra; *Sangita Párijáta* by Ahavala Sastri; *Nárada Samhitá* and *Náradí Sikshá* by Rishi Nárada; *Bharata Samhitá* by Rishi Bharata; *Narttaka Nirnaya* by Pundarika Vichchila; *Sangíta Náráyana* by Gajapati Narayanadeva; *Sangíta-Sára* by Harináyaka; *Rága Bibodha* by Somesvara; *Dhvani Manjarí* by Visvavasu;

Rága Sarvasva-Sára by Silhana; *Sangíta Bháskara* by Bháskarácharya; *Sangítárnava* by Kallinátha; *Sangíta Bháshya* by Rishi Matangaja; *Tándava-tarangesvara* by Andhúka Bhatta; *Tumburu Samhitá*; *Kohalíya*; *Gíta Siddhánta Bháskara* by Rámánanda Tírthasvámí; and *Rangodaya* by Sámbhavácharya.

MAHOMEDAN PERIOD.

THE Mahomedans as a ruling nation came in contact with the people of India for the first time in the 11th century, and since then a change has been worked into the musical system of the country. The Mahomedans did not much encourage the theory of the art, but they patronized practical musicians and were themselves instrumental in composing or introducing several styles of songs or devising new forms of musical instruments. It is related by Mahomedan historians of the period that when Dacca was invaded by Alla-uddin in 1294 (after Christ) and the conquest of the South of India was completed some years later (about 1310), by his Mogul general Malik Kafur, the profession of music was found to be in such a flourishing condition that all the musicians and their Hindu preceptors were taken with the royal armies and settled in the North. It is said that the celebrated Persian poet and musician Amir Khusru came to India during the rule of Alla-uddin and defeated in a contest the musician of the South, Náyaka Gopal, who had come to Delhi with a view to challenge the musicians of the court. Amir Khusru is reported to have given the name of *Setár* to the *Tritantrí Víná* of the classic days and to have divided the *Rágas* into twelve *Mokams* which were subsequently subdivided by other

Mahomedan musicians into 24 *Sobhas* and 48 *Gusvas*. Rajah Mán who ruled in Gwalior (1486—1516) was a great lover of music. It is said that he brought the *Dhrupada* style of song to its present state and that he composed several songs in this style. Sultan Hossein Shirki (of the Shirki family which flourished in Jounpur in the 15th century) introduced the style of song which has come to be known as the *Kheyal*. During the reign of the Mogul Emperor Akbar (1550—1605), music made considerable progress and received substantial encouragement. It was in his court that the famous musician Tansen (pupil of the venerable Haridas Swami) flourished. Tansen, who was formerly in the service of Rajah Ram, is said to have received from him one crore of *Tankas* as a present. The Emperor Akbar is mentioned in the *Ain-i-Akbari* as being excessively fond of music and having a perfect knowledge of its principles. In another portion of the *Ain* it is stated that he was an excellent hand at performing, especially on the *Naqqarah*. His court teemed with musicians of various nationalities, Hindus, Iranis, Turanis, Kashmiris, both men and women. The musicians were divided into three classes, *Gayandahs*, singers; *Khwánandahs*, chanters; and *Sazandahs*, players. The principal singers and musicians came from Gwalior, Mashad, Tabriz, and Kashmir. The schools in Kashmir had been founded by Irani and Turani musicians under the patronage of Zain-ul-Abidin, King of Kashmir. The Gwalior school dated from the time of Rajah Mán Tunwar, in whose court as well as in that of his son Vikramjit, the famous Náyaka Baksu lived. When Vikramjit lost his throne, Baksu went to Rajah Kirat of Kalinjar. Shortly after, he accepted a situation in the court of Sultan Bahadur (1526—1536) at Guzrat. Ramdas and Mahapatar, both of whom had been with Islem Shah at Lucknow, were among the court musicians of

Akbar. The number of the principal musicians named in the *Ain* is 36, and included Tansen, Tantaranga (his son), Baz Bahadur (ruler of Malwa, and inventor of the style of singing known as *Baz-khai*), Birmandal Khan (player on the *Sarmandal*), and Qasim, surnamed Koh-bar, who invented an instrument intermediate between the *Qubuz* and the *Rabab*. The following were the instruments used in the *Naqqarah-khanah* :—(1) the *Kuwargah*, commonly called *Damamah* (18 pairs more or less); (2) the *Naqqarah* (20 pairs more or less); (3) the *Duhul* (of which four were used); (4) the *Karana* or *Karrana* (made of metal :—never blown fewer than four); (5) the *Surna* (Persian and Indian kinds—nine blown together); (6) the *Nafir* (Persian, European, and Indian kinds—some of each kind being blown); (7) the *Sing* (made of brass in the shape of a cow's horn; blown two together); and (8) *Sanj* (cymbals, of which three pairs were used). The *Ain* gives details of how and when the band played and other music was performed for the amusement of the Emperor. The following stringed instruments are described in the *Ain* as being in use at the time:—The *Junter* (which is mounted with 16 frets and six wires, and has half of a gourd attached at each end of the neck); the *Bheen* (something like the *Junter*, but having only 3 strings); the *Kinner* (having a longer neck than the *Bheen*, and the gourd with two strings); the *Sirbheen* (like the *Bheen* but without the frets); the *Ambriti* (having one iron wire, and only one gourds placed under the middle of the neck which is smaller than that of the *Sirbheen*); the *Rebab* (having strings of gut, numbering in some 6, in others 12, and in some others, 18); the *Sirmandal*, (resembling the *Quanun* and having 21 strings, some of which are of iron, some of brass, and some of gut); the *Saringee* (also called Soorbotan—of the shape of a bow, with two hollow cups inverted at

each end; mounted with one string of gut resembling a bow string, and played with a plectrun); the *Adhowtee* (having a gourd with two wires); and the *Kingerah* (resembling the *Bheen* but having only two strings of gut, and smaller gourds). Seven varieties of the drum are mentioned—*viz.*, the *Pukuwej*, *Awej*, *Dehl*, *Dheddeh*, *Irdahwej*, *Duff* and *Kenjir*. Only two percussive instruments are described, these being the *Tal*, (a pair of brass cups with broad mouths); and the *Kut-h Tal*, (resembling small fish and made of wood or stone a set consisting of four). The wind instruments were the *Shehna*, (the same as the Persian *Sirna* or *trumpet*); the *Mushk* (called in Persian *Nai Amban* or the bagpipe); the *Moorle* (a kind of flute); and the *Owpunk* (a hollow tube, an ell long, with a hole in the centre, in which is placed a small reed). The songs of Vidyápati (who adorned the court of Siva Sinha of Tirhut, Behar, in the 14th century) were in vogue in the time of Akbar. It was also in this reign that Mira Bai, the wife of a Rana of Udaipur and a celebrated songstress and composer of hymns, flourished. The Emperor had opportunities of listening to her excellent vocal performances. The blind poet and musician Suradas, who is said to have composed 125,000 *Vishnupadas* (hymns to *Vishnu*) lived also in this reign. Suradas was the son of Ramdas, who has been already described as one of the musicians of Akbar's court. The following singers are named as belonging to the reign of Akbar's son Jehangir (1605—1627):—Jehangirdad; Chatr Khan; Parwizdad; Khurramdad; Makhu; Hamzan. It was in the reign of this Emperor that Tulsidas died. Tulsidas was a popular composer of hymns regarding Ráma and Sítá. During Shahjehan's reign (1628—1658), the following musicians lived:—Jaganath (who received from Shahjehan the title of *Kabrái*); Dirang Khan; and Lal Khan upon whom was conferred the title of *Gan-*

samundar (ocean of singing excellence). Lal Khan was son-in-law to Bilas, who was a son of Tansen. Jaganath and Dirang Khan were both weighed in silver and received each 4,500 rupees. Aurangzebe, who succeded Shahjehan to the throne of Delhi and occupied it from 1658 to 1707, abolished the court singers and musicians. A curious incident is related as having taken place after the order was promulgated. The court musicians brought a bier in front of the *Jharokah* (the window where the Emperors used to show themselves daily to the people), and attracted the attention of the Emperor by their loud lamentations. On Aurangzebe appearing at the window and asking whom they had on the bier, the musicians replied "Melody is dead, and we are going to the grave yard." "Very well," said the Emperor, "make the grave deep, so that neither voice nor echo may issue from it." During the years the ten successors of Aurangzebe ruled in Delhi (1707—1857), music continued to be cultivated but not with the vigour it had attained in the preceding reigns. Mahomed Shah was the last of the Emperors who had renowed musicians flourishing in his time. There are several vocal compositions extant which are associated with his name. The famous songstress Shori brought the *Tappá* song to its present degree of perfection in this reign. It is said that her husband Golam Nubi. composed the songs and coupled them with her name. The chief feature of music of the Mahomedan period was the combination of the Hindu style with the Persian one. Some types of classical music were brought out under Persian names, while some entirely new ones were introduced such as the *Trivat*, the *Terana*, the *Gazal*, the *Rekhta*, the *Quol*, the *Qulbana*, the *Gúl Nuksh*, the *Maulud*, &c. The Mahomedan musicians did not write any original works on music; what they composed were merely the *rechauffe* of Sanskrit treatises

on the subject, and among those might be particularized the *Toftel Hind* by Mirza Khan. The style of music they cultivated is now the standard high class music of India, leaving out of course, the provincial airs which are noticed later on. Some of the eminent religious reformers of India were born during the Mahomedan period and contributed to the making of a literature of hymns in this country. Among these were Kabir who flourished (1380—1420) in the reign of Sikandar Lodi. Kabir is credited with having created the sacred literature of Hindi, composed a number of songs himself, and caused a good many more to be composed by his followers and successors. Jayadeva, who was a native of Birbhum in Bengal, composed his melodious stanzas in Sanskrit in the 12th century. Nának, who flourished in 1469, and Chaitanya, who was born at Nuddea in Bengal in 1486, gave a strong impetus to the vocal literature of the religion they respectively represented and preached. Dádu, a religious reformer, was born at Ahmedabad in 1544. The *Abhángas* or spiritual poems of Tukárám or Tukobá, who flourished about 1609, represented the highest flight which Marathi poetry reached. Chandidás, who was contemporary to Vidyápati, was a native Brahmin of Birbhum, and was the first Bengali whose sweet stanzas were set to music and sung as the original *Kirtan* songs of Bengal. The performances of *Kirtan* songs used to take place so early as Akbar's time as mention of them is made in the *Ain*.

BRITISH PERIOD.

UNDER this heading will be noticed not only what has taken place in different parts of the country during British rule, but also what has continued since the preceding periods.

THE NORTH-WESTERN PROVINCES.

Lucknow is celebrated for the musicians, vocal and instrumental, as well as dancers, male and female, that have been supplied to various Indian courts from time to time. The court of Rampur has always maintained a high standard of efficiency in the department of music. Benares is noted for its temple music. The chants that are sung in the temple of *Visvesvara* are characterised by great solemnity. The *Nowbut,* which is an out-door band, said to have been invented by Alexander the Great, and held in favour in all Mahomedan courts, is engaged in Hindu temples as well. The *Nowbut* which plays in the temple of *Visvesvara* and at the *Dasásvamedha* Ghat at Benares is of a very high order of merit. Bajpai and Babu Mahesh Chunder Sirkar (a native of Bengal) were two of the best *Setár*-players of Benares of the modern day. The latter was an amateur. Vrindavan and Muttra are the cradle of much of the festive and periodical songs that are sung in connection with Krishna's career. The *Hori* is sung in celebration of the *Dol Játtrá* festival; the *Jhulan* or *Hindola,* at the swinging festival which takes place about the full moon of August; and the *Bádhái,* on the occasion of the birth of Krishna. The *Chaubes* of Muttra and Vrindavan are great vocalists. To the principal shrines of Vrindavan are attached a number of musicians who sing and play at regular intervals. The *Thumri* song, which is sung by the Nautch-girls, is composed in an impure dialect of the Vraja Bháshá. The beggars at Muttra and Vrindavan sing stanzas from Jayadeva or other songs celebrating the loves of Rádhá and Krishna. The *Rásadhári Játtrá* which is much in vogue in these provinces is a characteristic representation of the early career of Rádhá and Krishna, in melodious song, graceful dance, and captivating con-

versation. Lucknow and Benares were once noted for their dancing girls. The *Taza-ba-Taza* and *Hili-mili-pania* are two of the light songs sung by these girls which find much favour in European ears. Jivan Shah and his brother Piyar Khan were two distinguished players on the *Víná* who flourished at Benares in the latter part of the 13th century.

CENTRAL INDIA AND RAJPUTANA.

According to Sir John Malcolm, most of the villages in Central India have attached to them men and women of the Nutt or Bamallee tribes (a kind of wandering gipsies), who have among them rude musicians and minstrels whose music and songs form the principal entertainment of the peasantry. These musicians are divided into two classes, *Chárims* and *Bháts*. They boast of a celestial origin and exercise a great deal of influence over the people. The bards attached to the courts of the Feudatory Princes (who, by the way, as a rule, keep a number of good musicians in their establishment), used to compose and sing the chivalrous events of ancient and mediæval times, relating to the glories of the Rajput race in general and to those of the progenitors of their employers in particular. The Rajputs are all fond of music. The chief of Kotah is mentioned by Col. James Tod as having kept the largest band of his time in Central India. The *Meshek* or the Indian bagpipe is known to the Rajputs. The *Chohán* is described by the celebrated poet Chand as master of the art of music, both vocal and instrumental. The *Tooraye* is mentioned by Col. Tod as a trumpet much in favour in the mountainous regions of Central India. He also speaks in high terms of the performances of the hermits singing the praises of Pataliswara from their

pinnacled abode of Abu. Colonel Meadows Taylor says that the *sing* (horn) is indispensable in all processions, temple services, and specially at marriages and other festivities in Central or Southern India, and that this instrument is also blown by the village watchman at sunset and again at certain hours during the night. In the large cities every *mahulla* or ward is stated to have a horn-blower attached to its night watchmen or police. The horn is used to play wailing blasts for the dead at the funerals of the lower classes of the Hindus, and sometimes at the cremations of Hindu Princes. The *Karkhás* are the war-songs of the Rajputs or hymns in praise of their kings. These are generally sung by a class of singers called *Dháris.* The *Dádrá* and *Nuktá* are sung in the dialect spoken in the Districts of Bundelkhund and Bughelkhund and are confined to the lower classes. Col. Tod describes the *Rás-mandal,* or the mystic dance, which he compares with the Pyhrric dance, or the fire-dance of the Egyptians, and which he frequently witnessed at the Gwalior court. In this dance Krishna is represented with a radiant crown in a dancing attitude, playing on the flute to the nymphs encircling him, each holding a musical instrument. These nymphs are also called the *no-Rágini,* from the *Rágini* or mode of song over which each presides, and *no-rasa,* or nine passions excited by the power of music. Col. Tod observes: "the movements of those who personate the deity and his fair companions are full of grace, and the dialogue is replete with harmony." He asks if the *Rás-mandal* is not typical of the zodiacal phenomena and whether in this a trace cannot be found of the origin of Apollo and the sacred nine. He adds that "in each sign a musical nymph is sculptured in *alto-relievo* in the vaulted temples dedicated to the god, or in secular edifices by way of ornament, as in the triumphal column of Chitor.'

Gwalior has been the seat of much musical learning and the nursery of many eminent musicians of India. The Library of the Bikanir State, a catalogue of which was prepared by Rajah (then Doctor) Rajendra Lala Mitra, C. I. E., contains some of the old Sanskrit treatises on music. The Rana of Udaipur of the time when Col. Tod was there is mentioned by him as a great patron of the art of music. Maharajah Ram Sing, the predecessor of the present ruler of Jaipur, was also a great lover of music. He had some eminent musicians in his establishment. In the temple of *Govindji* situated within the compound of the Jaipur palace, sacred music is regularly performed. The Bhils or aborigines inhabiting the hilly regions of Rajputana and Central India have a music of their own which they vigorously practice in company.

CENTRAL PROVINCES.

At the instance of Mr. Colin Browning, Inspector-General of Education of the Central Provinces, music was introduced in 1877 into Government Vernacular Schools in the District of Raipur and taught according to the vocal manual *Gitávali* which was published in Hindi at his request by the author of the present work.

HYDERABAD.

His Highness the present Nizam of Hyderabad maintains in his establishment a number of musicians, chiefly Mahomedan, who perform the Mahomedan style of music.

MYSORE AND COORG.

The rulers of Mysore have ever been known to encourage music and musicians. The music of this

country partakes largely of the character of the music of Southern India which will be noticed further on His Highness Chama Rajendra Woodayar Bahadur, G.C.S.I., the late Maharajah of Mysore, was a great lover and a practical performer of music. Under his auspices, a music school was started in the capital for the purpose of promoting the study of Hindu music. Savaya Sachi, Shamana, and Sheshana are three of the distinguished musicians of Mysore of the present century.

The people of Coorg celebrate the *Huttari* or harvest festival with great *eclat*. The ceremonies proper last for seven days and are accompanied by much singing and dancing. The time for these performances is from sunset till after 10 o'clock. When the assembly is full,—the attendance of all males from six to sixty being religiously enforced,—a space is marked out for the performances. At a little distance, a band of musicians, two Holeyas or slave horn-blowers, and two Meda-drummers, sit near a fire. The horns are large and made of brass. The drums are a *pare* (large drum) and a *kudike-pare* (kettle-drum of a smaller size). The *Huttari*-chants resound in every house during the night. Four after-*Huttari* days are added to the festive week. On the eighth day, the *Wrukolu*, or village stick-dance, takes place. Four women—a pair leading and a second pair following—come forward, all beating cymbals and chanting ancient songs or impromptu verses. When they have arrived at the place of meeting, they sit down in groups with the children, and look at the dances which are performed only by the males who go through the evolutions peculiar to the country, beating small sticks, of which they carry one in each hand, while they move to the time of the music played at a little distance by a group of Holeyas. Theatrical exhibitions are added to

these performances. After dinner, on the ninth day, the *Nádukolu* commences--this being an assembly of the whole district. The programme of the *Urukolu* is repeated, only on a larger scale. While the music and the dances continue, a couple of men from different villages and armed with a small shield and a long rattan, come forward from opposite sides and step into the ring with a defiant shout. Keeping time with the music, they approach and evade each other, swinging their rattans and dealing blows at the legs of the opponent and warding them off with their shield. The mock-fight thus introduced sometimes takes a serious turn and has often to be stopped by the spectators. In the afternoon of the tenth day, the *Devarakolu* (stick-dance in honor of Bhagavati) takes place in every village. The proceedings are the same as on the two preceding days. On the 11th day the festivities are closed with a large public dinner to which *eclat* is given by the united exertions of the musicians, bards, and drummers. The guests who assemble at the house of the bridegroom before he sets out for the house of the bride are treated to a dinner and music. If the house be wealthy an improvisatore is engaged to sing the praise of each guest before his face. The guests at the house of the bride receive similar compliments. The bridal procession includes singing and music. The Coorgis have some very pleasing wedding songs, cremation songs, and nursery rhymes; these last are sung only by the women, and as they would not repeat them for the information of foreigners, difficulty has been felt by Europeans in procuring samples.

BOMBAY.

In the Mahratta country ballads and love-songs are numerous, whether of the Mahomedan period, the Mahratta risings against them, and the more recent

English and Mahratta wars, and are full of local adventure and spirited description. The *Sárangí* is as much used in the Bombay Presidency as elsewhere, and it is related that Captain Giberne, of the Bombay Army, was so fond of it that he preferred one of these instruments to his own violin for concerted pieces in which the violin took a soprano part. The *Holar-cha-soonai*, specimens of which along with various other Indian instruments were presented by Colonel P. T. French to the Irish Academy of Music, are described as being somewhat like the flageolets in appearance and the bagpipes in sound. These are occasionally used in the *Nobut* in the Mahratta countries where the players of these pipes are called *Gursee*. The office of piper is hereditary in every village or town, and accompanied by portions of land, and certain proportions of the crops at harvest time. The office of *Gursee* involves sweeping the temples, lighting the lamps, and officiating at certain ceremonies; and the *Gursee* is entitled to certain perquisites on all occasions of marriages, festivals, funerals, and the like. The *Zicree* species of song which is full of spiritual and moral sentiments originated in Guzrat, it being sung in the dialect of that country. It was introduced into the other parts of the country by Quazi Mahmood. The court of Baroda is noted for the number of efficient musicians it included in its establishment. One of the distinguished musicians of this court, Mowla Buksh, made a tour of India, and won the admiration of all who could appreciate music, by his performances on the *Víná* and *Jaltaranga*. He visited Calcutta in 1874 and was awarded a gold medal by the President of the Bengal Music School at a public meeting held at the school on the 28th November of that year. He is equally conversant with the music of Northern and Southern India, and sings Sanskrit hymns with a re-

markably correct pronunciation of the language. The theatres of the Parsis of Bombay have generally songs of the Mahomedan style sung in them. The *Gáyan Samáj* which has been recently started at Poona has for its object the cultivation and encouragement of Hindu music and has done much to propagate a knowledge of the art among the people.

MADRAS.

The influence which a contact with foreign nations exercised over the habits, doings, and arts of the Hindus having been less strong in the south of India, Hindu music in its original purity appears to have been maintained and cultivated there as a science long after it had ceased as such in the north. There are still to be found in the south musical works in the Telegu, Canarese, and Tamil languages. The practical music of the south (or Karnatic music, as distinguished from Hindustani music which prevails there to a certain extent) being more in accordance with the rules laid down in the classical works, it differs in essential particulars from what is performed in the north. There are some *Rágins* current there that are entirely unknown to the musicians of the Mahomedan school of the north; again there are some others sung in the south that are known under different names in the north. The elaborate system of solmization, and the rhythmic arrangements chiefly differentiate the music of the south from that of the north. Certain musical instruments are found in the Presidency which have no counterparts in other portions of India, while there are others in use which are modifications of those used elsewhere, or bear different names. A bagpipe called *Ttty* was taken from Coimbatoor and deposited some years ago in the East India Museum,

London. A drawing of a similar instrument is given in Sonnerat's "Voyage aux Indes Orientales", where it is called *Tourti.* The *Viná* is extensively practised in the Presidency. Colonel Meadows Taylor mentions that on one occasion he heard a *Viná*-player of the south execute on his instrument a great portion of Beethoven's Sonata in A. The musician explained that "having once taught an English lady a good deal of his own music, which she played upon the piano, she had in turn taught him this Sonata, which he preferred, he said, above all other English music." Col. Taylor remarks that his version of it was "really very beautiful." The Madrasi hymn is a characteristic music of the country. One Bisvanath Sastri, a native of the south, visited Calcutta in 1872, and was awarded a silver medal by the President of the Bengal Music School where he gave a performance on the 19th August of that year and charmed the audience by his vocal performances, and specially by his elaborate solmization. His Highness the present ruler of Travancore has introduced the study of Hindu music into the girls' schools in the State where vocal music and performance on the *Viná* are regularly taught. The Musical Association which has lately been established in Madras has made considerable progress in propagating a correct knowledge of the science and art among the native people. The Svarajotas and Vernams (ballads), Kruthis and Kirthanas (sacred songs), Javadis and Pathams (love songs), are among the styles of vocal composition peculiar to Madras. Tanjore is now-a-days the chief seat of music in Southern India as it has been so since early times. The Maharajahs of Tanjore have liberally encouraged musicians and the cultivation of music. Among the renowned musicians of the present century in Southern India might be named Tigya Raj, who was a native of Trivadi in the Tanjore District and

a pupil of Venkatraman Iyer; Siama Sastri; Sabharayya Sastri, a native of Pudukota; Kshetrya, (who was also a poet and composer of a large number of love songs); Nathiva Vadivelu (who is said to have introduced the use of the European violin into Southern India); Kalyana Krishna Iyer, a *Víná*-player in the service of the Maharajah of Travancore; Suryanarayan Rao Pantulu, a *Víná*-player in the service of the Maharajah of Vizianagram; and Mahadeva Iyer, a violinist in the service of the Maharajah of Travancore. The late Maharajah Kola Shékhara of Travancore was a composer of no ordinary repute.

The folk-songs of Southern India in the several dialects that prevail there contain in many of them deep spiritual and moral sentiments, some of these being the productions of eminent poets of the times when they were composed. They embrace a variety of topics; in fact the Southern people have songs for every event in life. "They cut the first sheaves of harvest to a song," observes Mr. Charles E. Glover, "they come into life, are married, and die to the music of some chant, song, or requiem." The "Dasarapada" of the Canarese is a song of the *Dasaras* (or Dasas), or slaves, who, from being attached originally to some of the pagodas as menial servants, have become, in course of time, a singing caste. Those who are not attached to a temple obtain a livelihood by begging. The Bagada and Kota tribes who live about the Neilgherry hills have some very beautiful chants in their *repèrtoire.* The Bagadas specially are a musical race. They play on the pipe and also sing. The village people will sometimes join the singer of an evening and dance to the song. Prior to a corpse being taken for cremation, the male relations circle round it and dancing and singing go on, in which sometimes the

females will take a part. The Malayalam songs are mostly of an amourous type and relate to the love-quarrels of some of the *Pauránic* deities. Mr. Glover has collected a specimen of "riddle" songs, which class of composition, he says, holds a high place in the lower literature of some of the Dravidian tongues. The Telegu language, which is called the Italian of the East, and which has been compared with Greek for flexibility and fullness, contains a large number of serious songs. The thousands of quatrans of purely popular love which go by his name are said to have been either composed or arranged by Vemana who lived about the end of the twelfth century. The Telegus were once a very great nation. "All over the Indian Seas," remarks Mr. Glover, "we find the tokens of a great Telugu dominion. What are the Klings of the Malay Peninsula, but Kalingas, a branch of the great Kalinga or Telinga nation? Who built the monster temples of Sumatra, Java and the Archipelago, whose towering summits still point to the heaven of Swerga? No other people than the Telegus, the Phœnicians of the Indian ocean. In Burmah and Siam are the foot-prints of the same people." Telegu beggars are frequently found in Calcutta singing hymns in their national style. The Tamil language is spoken by 20 millions of people, who form the foremost of the Dravidian nations. The better classes are fond of the *Adwaita* songs, *i. e.*, songs relating to the *non-dual* system of Hindu theology. At the other extreme are the "labor" songs. Midway between the two and common to all classes, except the very lowest, are the songs of the *Cural* which is the most venerated and popular book south of the Godavery. The *Cural* is considered as "essentially the literary treasure, the poetic mouth-piece, the highest type of verbal and moral excellence among the Tamil people." The

author of the *Cural* is Tiruvalluva, "the holy pariah," who flourished about the third century of the Christian era. The legends about his birth and early career, and the story of his work successfully standing the test to which it was put, have served to give a mythical interest to the *Cural.* Pattanattu and Patirakiriyar, both of whom lived in the 10th century, composed several moral songs which are also very popular in the Tamil countries. Such is the tenacity of the natives for their national institutions, that even the Christian converts recruited from the lower classes would not take kindly to the European music and songs, and steps had to be taken to compose songs and poems. in imitation of those so popular among the worshippers of Vishnu and Siva, and to have them set to popular indigenous music. The "labor" songs have attached to each stanza a refrain such as "Yo Ho! Yo Ho!", or "Heave O! Heave O!" or "Ho! Ho! work hard!", or similar expressions serving as stimulants to physical ex[illegible]ns. The *Bayaderes* are dancing-girls attached to the pagodas, and they are not despised to the same extent as Nautch-girls are in other parts of India. The *Bayadere's* song has found a place in the "labor" songs of the Tamil people, and its presence there is accounted for by the "re-active feeling which makes the worker dream of the idle, and the hungry delight in visions of luxurious meals." The "labor" songs represent the utterance of an illiterate class. Some of them are possessed of much humour, such as the song of the "Wife," which, in view of its general application, is reproduced below:—

> To every man is tied a wife,
> She clings to him as long as life.
> Yo Ho! Heave O!
>
> Of all our wealth she takes two-thirds,
> Yet thinks we pick up more like birds.
> Yo Ho! Heave O!

If any day we give her none,
You'd think her wrath would ne'er be done.
Yo Ho! Heave O!

While still 'tis dark she turns us out,
But sleeps for two hours more, no doubt!
Yo Ho! Heave O!

We toil all day, with spade or bar;
To bring our dinner 'tis too far.
Yo Ho! Heave O!

Oh! How we strain and heave and sweat;
While she buys cloths and runs in debt!
Yo Ho! Heave O!

No moment may we stay to rest;
She works an hour a day at best.
Yo Ho! Heave O!

We are too busy e'en to eat;
She scarcely ever leaves her seat.
Yo Ho! Heave O!

What comes of all the wages we earn?
Ah! That from her no man can learn.
Yo Ho! Heave O!

Our breasts are bruised by rope and pole;
That ne'er prevents her daily stroll.
Yo Ho! Heave O!

Our pain is more than we can bear;
She combs and oils her jet-black hair.
Yo Ho! Heave O!

Sometimes we faint through heat and toil;
To sweep the house her cloth would soil!
Yo Ho! Heave O!

'Tis well if we may earn some pice;
At home her mouth is filled with rice.
Yo Ho! Heave O!

We rest,—the master stops our pay,—
She scolds and bawls till morn is grey.
Yo Ho! Heave O!

How strange and odd a world is this,
To us the work, to them the bliss!
Yo Ho! Heave O!

THE PUNJAB.

Delhi was at one time the emporium of music. Even in the present day, some eminent musicians are found there. At Lahore music is cultivated to a great extent. In the Golden Temple at Amritsar, where the sacred *Grunth* is deposited, singing and chanting take place all through the day. Mahamahopadhyaya Sirdar Sir Atar Sing, K. C. I. E., Chief of Bhadour in Ludhiana, is a great patron of music and successfully cultivates the theory and practice of the art. He has some old treatises on music in his possession. In a leader which appeared in the *Times* of November 23rd, 1864, the writer, in describing a certain diplomatic demonstration held in India in the presence of Feudatory Chiefs, remarks that the Indian ear loves of all European music that of the Scottish bagpipe alone. "When the pipers of the 93rd were ordered out to play, the gratification of Her Majesty's princely vassals was complete. Three times were the pipes brought up and played round the great tent to the delight of the company ; and the Maharajah of Kashmir, we are informed, has sent an embassy to Sealkote for the express purpose of getting instruction on the instrument from the Highland corps quartered there, while another hill chieftain has bespoken the genuine article direct from Edinburgh." At one time Kashmir was noted for the dancing girls sent out to different parts of the country. The *Tuppá* song which has been re-modelled by Shoree originated among the camel-drivers of the Punjab.

NEPAL.

The Nepalese are broadly divided into two races, *viz.*, the *Newars* and the *Parbuttiahs*. There are certain musical instruments which are peculiar to either race,

and there are certain others common to both. The *Newars* are extremely fond of music, and many of the higher and middle castes practice it professionally, or indulge in it as amateurs. Among the instruments in use among them are the (1) *Phúnga*, or the "musical instrument of the gods," a trumpet made of copper and played at every religious ceremony; (2) the *Mohalli*, or flageolet, to which the laborers dance and which is employed at feasts and weddings; (3) the *Beaugh*, or clarionet; (4) the *Dishi*, or drum; (5) The *Beh*, or *Krishna-beh*, the pastoral flute of Krishna. Among the *Parbuttiahs*, the lowest castes of whom generally furnish professional musicians, the following instruments are in use; (1) the *Sinhga*, or *Nara Singha*, or horn made entirely of copper and composed of 4 pieces put together in the shape of a cow's horn; (2) the *Nag-pheni* or *Turi*, almost similarly constructed as the *Singha*, but of a smaller size; (3) the *Muralli*, a small clarionet made of a single piece of bamboo, and looking the same as the *Beaugh*; and (4) the *Dholuck* which has only one end covered with leather. Among the instruments common to both the races are the *Bansuli*, or "rural flute", and cymbals of various sizes which are employed at all social and religious ceremonies. Several instruments belonging to other parts of India are also used in Nepal, such as the *Sárangí* and *Setár*. European instruments, such as horns, bugles, trumpets &c, have been imitated or bodily introduced into the country. There are some old Sanskrit treatises on music to be found in Nepal. Latterly, much attention has been paid by the Maharajah's Darbar to the subject of music, and an institution has been opened in the chief city where Hindu music is taught to students by competent professors. Some years ago a collection of Nepalese musical instruments was presented by Dr. A. Campbell to the Asiatic Society of Bengal

and deposited in the Calcutta Museum. The music of Nepal is essentially the same as that which prevails in other parts of the country. The Gurkhas creditably play European airs in the military bands which have been organized and are conducted under the supervision of European band-masters.

BENGAL, BEHAR, AND ORISSA.

It is on record that Mahapatar, one of the musicians in the Court of Akbar, was once sent as ambassador to Mukund Deo of Orissa. The lower classes of the people of Orissa use a trumpet called *Benu*, which is made of a long piece of bamboo. The *Játtrás*, which they hold in honor of the deity Satyanáráyana, consist of the playing of the *Khol* and cymbals and the singing of chants or recitatives, the combined effect of which is by no means soporofic in its tendency. Sometimes, companies are observed performing *Játtrás* in the Bengali style. The *palki*-bearers of Orissa are well known for the extempore poetry they make while carrying the *palki* with its contents on their shoulders. In his "Popular Account of the Manners and Customs of India", London, 1847, the Revd. Charles Acland has translated a song which the bearers sang on an occasion when they carried Mrs. Acland. The words run as follow :—

Sh's not heavy, cubbadar !
Little baba, cubbudar !
Carry her swiftly, cubbadar !
Pretty baba, cubbadar ! cubbadar ! cubbadar !
Trim the torches, cubbadar !
For the road's rough, cubbadar !
Here the bridge is, cubbadar !
Pass it swiftly, cubbadar, cubbadar !
Carry her gently, cubbadar !
Little baba, cubbadar !
Sing so cheerily, cubbadar !
Pretty baba, cubbadar, cubbadar, cubbadar.

The verses which the bearers improvised on the occasion when they carried the Revd. gentleman himself were by no means complimentary to his person, as the following translation will show :—

O, what a heavy bag !
No, it's an elephant ;
He is an awful weight !
Let's throw his palkee down—
Let's set him in the mud—
Let's leave him to his fate.
No, for he'll be angry then ;
Ay, and he will beat us then
With a thick stick.
Then let's make haste and get along,
Jump along quick !

"And then," says Mr. Acland, "suiting the action to the word, off they set in a nasty jog-trot, which rattled every bone in my body, keeping chorus all the time of 'jump along quick, jump along quick', until they were obliged to stop for laughing."

Golam Rezza, and his son Ali Rezza, noblemen of Patna, a district of Behar, were noted players on the *Setár*, and the style of their execution has been followed in some parts of the country. The principal aristocratic houses in Behar have continued to patronise music. The Maharajah Sir Lachmiswar Sing, K. C. I. E., the present chief of Durbhanga, is a great admirer of the art. He plays on the *Setár* excellently well, and has in his service a performer on the *Sarod*, who is considered one of the best players on the instrument of the present day. Maharajah Newal Kissore Bahadoor, the grand-father of the late Maharajah Harendra Kissore of Bettia, composed a large number of songs on Durgá or Kálí, which are associated with his name and are reverently sung by Hindu musicians hailing from the province. Behar claims to

have given birth to Vidyápati, whose mellifluous stanzas on the loves of Rádhá and Krishna are considered the ideal of lyric songs and are extensively utilized in the *Kirtanas* and *Játtrá* performances of Bengal which are noticed further on. The following is a translation of one of Vidyápati's lyrics made by Mr. O. C. Dutt, a prominent member of the Rambagan Dutt family of Calcutta, very appropriately called by Captain D. L. Richardson "a nest of singing birds" :—

O vain the attempt to describe the sweet pleasures,
The exquisite bliss which from Love doth proceed,
For they change every moment, and lo ! at his bidding,
New pleasures and sweeter each other succeed.

From my birth, I may say, I have looked on Love's features,
But my eyes are insatiate,—would see them more clear,
Tho' oft have I heard his low tones of endearment,
Their accents seem new, O so new to the ear !

With him have I pass'd long nights of deep rapture,
But no trace of those transports,—tho' long have I griev'd ;
For cycles I've kept him enshrined in my bosom,
Still my heart's bitter anguish remains unrelieved.

O Love has been worshipped by poets unnumber'd,
But none has the spirit of Love e'er divined,
Says sage Vidyapati,—to give balm for the heart-ache,
In hundreds of thousands not one shall we find.

In Bengal the strains were simultaneously taken up by Chandidás, a native of Birbhum, and a contemporary of Vidyápati. Chandidás is considered the earliest writer of lyrical literature in Bengal, and his melodious effusions are also recited or sung in *Kirtanas* and in *Játtrás* of the ancient style. The following is a translation of one of Chandidás's songs representing Rádhá's appeal to

Krishna which, even in the foreign garb in which it has been clothed by Mr. R. C. Dutt, C. I. E., (of the Bengal Civil Service, and another "singing bird" of the Rambagan "nest"), so characteristically depicts the loving heart of the Hindu heroine :—

Love ! what more shall I say ?
In life, in death, in after-life,
I'll be thy duteous wife.
Yes ! to thy feet my heart is tied
By silken ties of love,
I offer all,—my heart and soul ;
I'll be your doating slave !
I've thought if in this wide, wide world
Another friend I own,
In loving tones to name my name,
Alas ! Alas ! there's none !
On earth, in heaven, in after-world,
Alas ! who loveth me ?
Oh ! to thy feet, I turn for help,
To thee alone ! to thee !
Oh ! do not spurn me—I am weak,
Oh do not turn away.
I've thought and felt, without thy help,
I have no other way.
If for a moment thee I miss,
A death-like trance I own ;
I'll keep and nurse thee on my heart,
E'en as a precious stone.

Another native of Birbhum was Jayadeva, who flourished in the 12th century and whose Sanskrit lyric called the *Gíta Govinda* has also furnished songs for *Kirtana* and *Játtrá* performances. His language was highly poetic and eminently suited for music. The first stanza of one of his songs, beginning with the words "Viharati hariríha sarasa vasante," has thus been rendered into English by Sir Edwin Arnold, K. C. S. I.—

I know where Krishna tarries in these early days of spring,
When every wind from warm Malay brings fragrance on its wing;
Brings fragrance stolen far away from thickets of the clove,
In jungles where the bees hum and the Koil flutes her love;
He dances with the dancers, of a merry morrice one,
All in the budding spring-time, for 'tis sad to be alone.

Bengal has been prolific in reformers and devotees whose feeling compositions have contributed so much to enrich the religious literature and national songs of the country. The *Kirtana* is one of the earliest national songs of Bengal. As has already been mentioned, Vidyápati and Chandidás were the pioneers in the field of this kind of religious song. Chaitanya, the promulgator of the doctrine of *Bhakti* or faith, who flourished in Nuddea in the fifteenth century, introduced the *Nagara-Sankirtana* for the street processions in which *Kirtana* songs were sung in chorus in a somewhat different style, to the accompaniment of the *Khol* and *Karatála* (cymbals). His contemporaries, disciples, and followers, among whom were Brindávan Dás, Murári Dás, and Govinda Dás, composed a large number of *Kirtanas* which now form the standard songs in this line. The District of Burdwan produced several *Kirtana*-singers of note. The *Kirtanas* have for their subject the praises of Krishna, his early career, and the loves of Rádhá and Krishna. As the people expressed a desire to see the adventures of Krishna represented not only in words but also in action, the *Játtrá* came to be introduced. The original *Játtrá* was a melo-dramatic performance in which the classical stanzas of Vidyápati, Chandidás, and other

early composers preponderated, and these compositions were sung either *solo* or in chorus. Prem Chánd and Paramánanda were among the earliest leaders of the *Játtrá*. Govinda, a disciple of the latter, and Badan followed in their wake and were prominent singers in the middle of the present century. The *Játtrás* being the direct outcome of the *Kirtanas** had also for their subjects the career of Krishna and in this sense were somewhat like the *Mysteries* of mediæval Europe. Latterly, however, other subjects from the Puránas as also incidents from the Mahábhárata, or from popular legends, have been chosen for representation, and the *Dhol*, *Tablá*, *Mandirá*, violin and other instruments have been introduced. The *Khol* and *Karatála* are essentially the instruments employed in musical performances of a religious nature. The *Chandí* songs, which are based on the incidents described in his work by Mukundaráma Chuckerbutty, who lived in the 16th century, are also sung to these instruments. Jagannáth Swarnakár was a well known singer of *Chandí* songs: his grandson Rájanaráyana made a name in this direction in the third quarter of the present century. The *Rámáyana* songs, which are based on the popular version of that great epic made by Kírtibás Ojhá of the Nuddea District, who flourished in the 16th century, are sung to the rhythmic accompaniment of the *Mandirá* alone. Ramprasad Sen contributed a great deal to enrich the literature of devotional songs by his compositions on the Goddess *Káli*. He was

* The *Dhap* song is a compromise between the *Játtrá* and *Kirtana*. It is sung in the manner of the *Kirtana*, the music having more of the character of the *Játtrá* than of the *Kirtana*. About 60 years ago this kind of singing was introduced by Mohun Dass Baul. His disciple, Madhu Sudan Kaora, popularly known as Madhu Kán, composed a large number of pieces of this kind, which are still popular in the country.

born in 1720 and received much encouragement at the hands of Maharajah Krishna Chunder of Nuddea, who was a great patron of literature and the art of music. The songs of Ramprasad are full of devotional fervour and up to this day furnish the means of livelihood to many a Hindu mendicant. Maharajah Srish Chunder, the grand-son of Maharajah Krishna Chunder, composed a number of religious songs which are held in much regard by the followers of Kálí.

The *Kabi* song had its rise at the time of Maharajah Nava Kissen of Sobhabazar, Calcutta, who flourished during the rule of Lord Clive. The creators of this kind of song were Rasu Nrising, Nalu Nanda Lal, and Raghunath Das. Haru Thakur used to entertain the Maharajah with these compositions and eventually received help from him to form a company. At first the company was formed of amateurs, but latterly it became a professional one. Haru Thakur, who could compose the songs, is considered the first professional *Kabi-wala*. His contemporaries were Nityananda Bairagi, Bhabani Churn Banik, Bhimdas Malakar, and others, who started an antagonistic company, whose object was to sing replies to the questions mooted by Haru's party; the replies being at that time framed previous to the performance taking place and after the subject-matter had been ascertained from the opening party. After the death of Maharajah Nava Kissen, Haru Thakur gave up the profession, and Nilu Chuckerbutty and his brother Ramprasad on one side, and Bhola Nath Moira on the other, all disciples of Haru Thakur, formed two companies. At this time several other companies were started, led by Mohan Sirkar, Nilmani Patuni, Anthony (a Eurasian), and others. Prominent among those who composed the songs for these companies was Ram Bose of Sulkea (in

the District of Howrah, situated opposite to Calcutta, on the banks of the Hugli). It was he who introduced the system of composing replies and rejoinders on the spot. At one time *Kabi*-singing was the rage in Calcutta and other places in Bengal. After the death of the master-composers (whose effusions may still he heard repeated by the old men of this country), the *Kabi* system began to decline. Later on, Mohan Chand Bose of Bagbazar (in Calcutta) introduced the *Dándá Kabi* and, shortly after, the *Half Akrai* *, which were cultivated, and are to some extent even now practised, by amateur parties. The difference between the two classes of singing was this :—The former was sung standing and to the accompaniment of the *Dhol* and *Kansi*, exactly on the lines of the original *Kabi* ; the latter was sung sitting, and to the accompaniment of the *Dholak*, *Tumburá*, violin, *Mandirá*, and other instruments employed in the drawing-room. The subjects of these performances were the same as those of the original *Kabi*, *viz.*, hymns to *Kálí*, the adventures of Krishna, love and the pangs of separation, and sallies of an erotic nature. Umpires were selected to decide on the merits of the musical performance of the two parties and on the propriety of the questions and the correctness of their answers. A rival party to that of Mohan Chand at Bagbazar was started at Jorasanko (also in Calcutta), for which Ram Chand Mukherjee used to compose the songs.

* Kului Chunder Sen was a musician with Maharajah Nava Kissen. He was the originator of a system of singing, then called *Akrai*, which was improved upon by his sister's son, Ramnidhi Gupta, who started two amateur companies, about 1806. The chief feature of the *Akrai* lay in the preponderance of instrumental music. At that time the system of singing reply-songs was not in vogue : the musical compositions were rather difficult of rendering, and hence, perhaps, the *Akrai* style of singing was discontinued after a few performances. It was when Mohan Chand (who was a disciple of Ramnidhi) devised the *Half Akrai*, on the system now in use, that the *Akrai* came to be called *Full Akrai*, in contradistinction to the term *Half Akrai*.

Both Mohan Chand and Ram Chand composed tunes for the songs for the companies they led, and these have been followed as standard airs up to the present date. The well-known poet Iswar Chunder Gupta (born 1809), and his contemporary Gopal Chunder Bannerji of Bhowanipore, used to compose songs for some of the companies of the latter days. Mano Mohan Bose, a dramatist and poet (born about 1833), is considered one of the best living composers of this kind of song. The *Dándó Kabi* and *Half Akrai* performances have always been confined to gentlemen amateurs. The music and composition represented by the *Half Akrai* and *Dándá Kabi* being beyond the reach and comprehension of the masses, the *Pánchálí* was introduced in about the first quarter of the present century. It consists of alternate recitation and singing, the subjects being chosen from the Rámáyana, Mahábhárata and Bhágavata. Dasarathi Ray was the first great leader of a professional company of this kind. He was born in 1804 and died in 1857, and was the composer of several pieces which he and his brother Tinkari performed. The *Pánchálí* is an *ex-parte* affair so far as composition is concerned, but two companies are sometimes employed to perform and their respective excellence has to be decided by umpires. Sanyasi Chuckerbutty was the last singer of the *Pánchálí* who excelled in the professional line. This kind of performance is, like the professional *Kabi*, going out of fashion. Sometimes gentlemen amateurs organize *Pánchálí* companies for special performances, and among those started in the recent times might be mentioned the parties of Agarpara (a village about 8 miles north of Calcutta), Jorasanko, Bag Bazar, and Bow Bazar, in Calcutta, and Bhowanipore and Kalighat in the suburbs of Calcutta. Respectable Bengali gentlemen from time to time start amateur *Játtrás* which are a

combination of the professional *Játtrá* and dramatic acting. They also sing in chorus in street processions such as issue on the occasions of the *Rath Játtrá* and *Dol Játtrá* festivals. The songs sung on such occasions are composed and set to music on the lines of the *Half Akrai*. Amateur theatricals are started now and then in Calcutta and other parts of Bengal. The first Bengali amateur theatre was started in 1858 at the Belgatchia Villa of Rajah Pratap Narain Singh of Paikpara in the suburbs of Calcutta, under the supervision of some of the prominent members of the educated Hindu society of Calcutta. Maharajah Bahadur Sir Joteendro Mohun Tagore, K. C. S. I., took an active part in its get-up, and composed for the orchestra organised for it a few airs which are the first of their kind. This orchestra consisted mostly of European instruments. Later on, when theatricals began annually to be given at the Maharajah's family residence in Pathuriaghatta Street, Calcutta, the orchestra was made up entirely of Indian instruments, and most of the airs played in it were composed by the author of this publication. Some professional theatres have, within the last 25 years, been set up in Calcutta in most of whose orchestras Hindu music is played on European instruments. Amateur parties are sometimes formed in imitation of the *Báuls*, a sect of religious mendicants who dance and sing to the music of *Ektárá*, *Gopíjantra* and *Ananda Laharí*.

The old Rajahs of Bissenpur in the District of Bankura were famous for the impetus they gave to the cause of music by encouraging musicians and fostering its practice in the country. At one time the progress made here was so great, and the number of musicians it produced so large, that the country came to be designated the "Delhi of Bengal." Ram Sankar Bhattacharya

was one of the most distinguished musicians of the place. The tradition for its love of music has in the modern days been kept up in the country by the establishment of a Musical Society at Bankura in connection with which two Music Schools were opened in 1883, one at Bankura and the other at Bissenpur, chiefly with the object of training teachers for the benefit of the surrounding *Patsalas* (primary schools). Mr. J. Anderson, at that time the Magistrate of the District, helped a great deal in the establishment of the schools, where elementary music began to be taught by means of a manual of vocal music, called *Gíta-pravesa,* which the writer of the present publication prepared for the purpose.

Music plays an important part in the service of the Brahmo Somajes or Theistic Churches of the country Rajah Ram Mohan Roy (1776—1833), who established what is called the *Adi* (or first) Brahmo Somaj in Calcutta in 1830, composed a number of hymns which were sung here as well as elsewhere. At the present time hymns set to high class music are sung here under the supervision of the talented members of the familyof *Maharshi* Debendro Nath Tagore, the present head of the *Somaj.* In the *Brahmo Somaj of India* which was opened by Babu Keshub Chunder Sen in 1869 in another part of the town, hymns composed in the *Kirtan* and other popular styles are sung to the accompaniment of the church organ and the *Khol.* The songs sung by the members and followers of this Somaj in their street processions are quite in keeping with the national style.

In some of the Native Christian Churches, hymns are sung to the music of the country. A few years ago a *Játtrá* was started in the District of Nuddea where

some of the incidents related in the Bible were rendered in the melo-dramatic style. Sometime ago the Christian Missionaries adopted the style of the *Kathaks* for the propagation of their religion. The *Kathaks* are learned Bráhmanas who elucidate the texts of the Hindu *Sástra* or relate the Puránas by means of recitations and songs. Among the most noted of them in the modern days were Krishna Mohan, Dharanidhar, and Sridhar.

The aristocratic families of Bengal and specially of Calcutta have always encouraged musicians who visited them from time to time. Some of them were practical musicians. The late Maharajah Mahatab Chand of Burdwan composed a large number of songs and patronised Ramapati Banerji who also composed some excellent songs in praise of the Goddess Kálí. Babu Ashutosh Deb of Calcutta, popularly known as Shatu Babu, kept a number of distinguished musicians on his establishment. He was a skilful player on the *Setár*, and the composer of many songs. Rajah Sir Radha Kant Deb Bahadur, K. C. S. I., Babu Gopi Mohan Tagore, and Babu Prosunno Cumar Tagore, C. S. I., were great lovers of music and supported several musicians, among whom might be mentioned the songstress Hira, the *Mridanga*-player Golam Abbas, the vocalist Haddu Khan, the *Sur-Sringár* player Kashim Ali Khan, and the *Rabáb* player Basud Khan. His Majesty Wajed Ali Shah, the ex-King of Oudh, who, since the annexation of Oudh in 1856, resided at Matiabruj in the suburbs of Calcutta, kept some very good musicians on his staff, among whom Taz Khan is still living. His Majesty was a practical musician himself and is said to have been the originator of the kind of song known as "Lucknow Thumri." His Highness the Nawab Nazim of Bengal, father of the present Nawab,

had some distinguished musicians in his court. One of them, Ata Hossain, had accompanied His Highness to England where he gave some specimens of his skill before H. R. H. the Prince of Wales. Ata Hossain received a silver medal from the President of the Bengal Music School in May 1883 when he visited Calcutta. The first Bengali treatise on music was written about 50 years ago by Babu Radha Mohan Sen of Calcutta. The first treatise in the same language, written on a systematic plan, embodying the theory and practice of music, was brought out by Professor Khetra Mohan Goswami in the year 1868. He composed several airs for the *Setár* and the orchestra, as also a number of songs which he published later on in his work called *Kantha Kaumudí*, or a treatise on vocal music. Among the distinguished vocalists of the third quarter of the present century were Ahmud Khan and Gopal Prasad. The latter's brothers, Luchmi Prasad and Sarada Sahay, were first-class players on the *Víná* and the *Setár*. The present Maharajah of Hill Tipperah is well-known for the encouragement he gives to the art. He is himself a practical musician of no ordinary ability. Madan Mohan is a good *Mridanga* player of the day. Lala Kebul Kissen, Kadau Sing, and Badau Sing also distinguished themselves in this line two decades ago. The *Tuppá* songs composed by Babu Ramnidhi Gupta, who flourished in about the first quarter of the present century, are still popular among those Bengalis who sing or listen to erotic compositions.

The year 1881 is full of importance to the history of Indian music. It was on the 3rd of August of this year that a school of music named the Bengal Music School—the first of its kind in India—was established in Calcutta, where vocal music and some of the drawing-room instru-

ments began to be taught with the aid of books and according to a system of notation. It was founded by and has ever since been under the presidency of the writer of the present work. In the year 1881, the Bengal Academy of Music was founded by him. The object of this institution is mainly to encourage the study and practice of Hindu music by the establishment of schools and by the awarding of complimentary titles and insignias thereof to distinguished musicians. These two institutions have always received the encouragement of the highest officials of the land. The Marquess of Dufferin and Ava, while he was Viceroy and Governor-General of India, was the High Protector of the Academy. Since 1880, the Bengal Music School has been receiving a grant-in-aid from the Government of Bengal. Some years ago, a class for teaching theoretical music, as also one for the teaching of *Vedic* chants, were opened at the Sanskrit College of Calcutta,—both with the support of the present writer and the sanction of the Government obtained by him. He has with him a distinguished musician Babu Kally Prosonno Banerji who plays skilfully on the *Víná, Sur-báhár* and *Setár*. His performances on the *Nyástaranga*, an instrument peculiar to India, have always challenged the admiration of his listeners, among whom might be named Their Royal Highnesses the Prince of Wales, and the Duke and the Duchess of Connaught, the Earl of Northbrook, the Marquess of Dufferin and Ava, the Marquess and Marchioness of Ripon, besides distinguished Government officials and visitors from Europe and America. Since the foundation of the Bengal Music School, the science and art of music have received considerable attention at the hands of the Indian people, and several books have been published tending to a clear understanding of the subject. In view of the help of the Government

of the land, the exertions of friends, and the interest shown in it by the Indian people at large, the revival of Hindu music and its restoration to its pristine glory and purity may fairly be considered as an accomplished fact.

CEYLON.

IT appears that music was formerly cultivated in Ceylon, and reduced to principles. Pieces of music in regular notes might be seen in some of the old books in the Pali language. The gamut was termed *Septa Souere* (Sanskrit, *Sapta Swara,* or the seven notes.) There were no particular signs for these notes, each of them being formed of as many letters as were necessary for their pronunciation. The Singalese have several instruments in use. They are very fond of the trumpet, called *Hoveneve,* or *Horanawa,* which they consecrate to the temples. Their horn, named *Kombone,* is said to produce as annoying a sound as their trumpet. They have a kind of hautboy, which, however, is not so unpleasant as the others. It is very narrow, considering its length. The two extremities are tied by cat-gut strings to the belt on which the instrument hangs; this belt goes over the shoulder. They have several kinds of drums. The *Daoul,* a long and narrow instrument, is struck with a curved stick called *Daoul kadipone,* the left hand only being used. The Tammetam (Tom-tom ?) is a kind of kettle, covered with a skin on the top, and beat with an instrument called *Kaddipow.* The *Ravani,* (perhaps so called in honor of Rávana, the monster-king of Ceylon of the mythological days), is a sort of timbrel, *minus* the bells. It is held with the left hand, and the fingers of the right are made to slide on it. It is placed on the

ground and three or four people together (sometimes women) beat it continuously for hours without reference to musical time. The *Odikie* or *Udakea* is the best of all their drums, and capable of producing a good effect in a piece of music. It is the instrument of the man of taste, and the performer, therefore, is paid more liberally than those on the other varieties of the drum. The *Berrigodea* is a kind of long drum made of jack-wood, covered with deer-skin, and beat with the hands. The *Tallea,* made of brass, is beat with a stick. M. Sonnerat, in his *Voyage aux Indes Orientales,* (Paris, 1806), says that the Hindus maintain that the *Ravanastron,* one of their old instruments played with the bow, was invented about 5,000 years ago by Rávana, a mighty king of Ceylon. The *Venah* or *Venavah* is a stringed instrument sometimes seen in the hands of strolling beggars. It is mounted with wo strings of different kinds (one made of a species of flax and the other of horse-hair), and is played with a bow which is also made of horse-hair and has bells attached to it. The hollow of the instrument is half a cocoa-nut shell, polished, covered with the dried skin of a lizard, and perforated below. The people of Ceylon are very fond of hearing songs. When on his travels, a great man has often one vocalist before and another behind his *palki.* These two men, each in their turn, sing stanzas of an intermediate length, for it so happens sometimes that the singer, quite taken up with the subject, gives some *extempore* verses. The songs are either religious, in which case the virtues of Buddha and other gods are extolled ; or they are historical, and then the virtuous actions of some of their kings are recited. Sometimes the songs relate a love adventure. But in all cases the air is a mournful one, gay music among the Singalese being an uncommon thing. The measure is constantly changing, the movement remaining the

same—always slow. The most admired tune of the Singalese is what is called the "Horse-trot," from the resemblance which it bears to the sound of the trotting of a horse.

PERSIA.

THERE is every reason to think that music was more generally cultivated and brought to a much higher pitch of perfection before the conquest of this country by the Mahomedans in the seventh century of the Christian Era than it has been since. Music was performed at the courts of Susa and Persepolis. Athenæus mentions that Darius had in his harem no less than 329 female musicians. Xenophon substantially supports the remarks of Athenæus. In the time of the Sassanides, music was employed in all the festivities of the Persian court. Fétis holds that the music of ancient Persia bore a resemblance to that of India. One of the results of the Mahomedan conquest was the destruction of the arts and literature of the Persians. From the letter of William Erskine to Sir John Malcolm, which was published in the Transactions of the Literary Society of Bombay, Vol II, it would appear that, when the Mussulmans conquered Persia, Saad, the son of Abu-wakhas, wrote to Omar, (who was the second Caliph after Mahomed), to be allowed to send a number of books to him. Omar's answer was, to throw them into the water, as useless to the faith. This order was so completely carried out, by the burning of all books, that the only musical work now known to exist in the Persian language is one entitled *Heela Imaeli*, mentioned in a catalogue of MSS. appended to Mr. Fraser's History of Nadir Shah. The third part of this book treats of

musical instruments. It is said that music was introduced into Persia by Gjemshid, or Giamschid, the fifth sovereign of the first, or Pischdalian dynasty. Nizami, a Persian writer, describes in enthusiastic terms the musical entertainments of Parviz, a Persian monarch, who flourished about 590 of the Christian Era, as being in a style of great magnificence. Anim, a musician of Hindusthan, states that the seven primary modes were in use among the Persians before the reign of this monarch. Sir William Jones speaks of their having 84 modes, "which they distribute, according to an idea of locality, into twelve rooms, twenty-four recesses, and forty-eight angles or corners." The principal modes, like those of the Greeks, are called after the different countries or cities; as the mode of Ispahan, the mode of Irak, the mode of Hijaz, and so on. Considering the softness of the Persian language, the strong accentuation of the words, and the tenderness of the songs that are written in it, Sir William concludes that "the Persians must have a natural and affecting melody, which is, certainly, true music; but they seem to be very little acquainted with the theory of that sublime art." In his "History of Persia," Sir John Malcolm says: "The Persians deem music a science, but it is one in which they do not appear to have made much progress. They have a gamut and notes, and a different description of melody, that is adapted to various strains, such as the pathetic, voluptuous, joyous, and war-like. The voice is accompanied by instruments of which they have a number; but they cannot be said to be further advanced in this science than the Indians, from whom they are supposed to have borrowed it."

The first writers in Persia who treated music as a science were Arabs, who adopted the musical instru-

ments of the Persians. From their works it would appear that the compass of the octave was divided into 17 intervals, there being consequently two intervals between each whole tone; in other words, the octave was divided into 17 one-third tones. Towards the end of the thirteenth century, however, some theorists adopted a system in which the octave was divided into twelve intervals, like the semi-tones of the chromatic scale of Europe.

M. Taugoin, in his "Journey in Persia", describes the "funeral games" of the Persians, in which music plays an important part. These games are called the *Tazias*, or Desolations; and they were instituted in memory of the martyrdom of the Imams Hassan and Hossain, who perished at Kerbela in a great battle against the false Caliph Yezid. During this solemn festival, the Mollahs, stationed in pulpits, chant in a mournful tone, sacred hymns and lamentations, and the whole auditory respond to them with tears and deep-drawn sighs. Music forms also a part of the nuptial ceremonies of the Persians. M. Von Hussard, an amateur of music, who held an official situation in Persia, took to Europe some of the choruses of the Persian dervishes, which appeared to be possessed of considerable musical merit. These dervishes hold meetings on certain days, at which their superior presides, and they dance to the music of the flute and the drum, whisking themselves round with great swiftness. Of the various sects into which the dervishes are divided, the *Mewliach*, or *Mewlewi*, are the most devoted to music. These choruses are described in the *Harmonicon* as having "considerable originality and force of expression," and as being "throughout, faithful to the meaning and spirit of the poetry." Further on: "The change of time that sometimes occurs exactly resembles the French dramatic

music: it does not offend the ear, and never appears to be out of its proper place. The compass amounts to no more than an octave and a half, from C to F; consequently these songs transposed according to circumstances, are within the compass of every voice." Kotzebue, in his *Narrative of the Russian Embassy to Persia in 1817*, says that when the ambassador arrived at Erivan, "the troops presented arms, the drums beat, and the fifes played the English national air of 'God Save the King.'" The programme of the musical entertainments given to the ambassador and his suite included "a guitar, a sort of violin of three strings, two tambarines, and a singer. . . . Three handsome boys had small metal castanets, which they struck in time with the dance." In the year 1834, a troop of Persian soldiers went to Warsaw. A certain Russian Prince who was there at the time gave them an entertainment a part of which consisted of a grand concert of their own music. The leader of the band was ordered by his master the Prince to arrange the airs which the Persians were in the habit of singing, for the full orchestra. This was done, but it was a great disappointment to the Prince to be told by his Persian guests, after they had listened to the performance, that the arrangement with harmony entirely destroyed the beauty and charm of their melodies.

Though now rarely met with, the harp was formerly a well-known instrument in Persia. The celebrated Persian poet Amir Khusru (who flourished about the year 1315) makes the following mention of it in a poem entitled the *Mirah-i-Iskhandir*:—"The harp's soft notes to heaven ascended and from the flagon flowed the ruby wave; the lute's sweet tones angels from heaven attracted. The organ and the dulcimer, with gentle notes, a sooth-

ing charm diffused." Sir Robert Ker Porter gives some illustrations of the harp in his sketches from the old sculptures which exist on a stupendous rock, called Tackt-i-Bostan, situated near Kermanshah, ten days' journey north-east of Bagdad. These sculptures, which are said to have been executed during the reign of Khusru Parviz (towards the end of the sixth century of the Christian Era), include representations of boats filled with women playing upon harps resembling in construction those of the Assyrians. Major O'Neill remarks that "the figures are in perfect preservation, and the strings of the harp completely visible." Engravings of some Persian harps of a later date may be seen in Lane's edition of "The Arabian Nights' Entertainments." The harps are about 400 years old. The drawings from which the engravings are derived were received by Mr. Lane from Sir Gore Ouseley. The harp, called *Chang* in Persian and *Junk* in Arabic, is now almost entirely fallen into desuetude. The Persians have a dulcimer called *Santir*, which in point of construction and treatment is almost the same as the German *Hackbret*. Its antiquity in Persia is established to a certain extent by the representation of a Persian lady playing on it, of which Hommaire de Hell, in his "Voyage en Perse" has given a sketch taken from an illustration which is known to be very old. The other stringed instruments in present use in Persia are the *Oud* (or lute), the *Schtareh* (guitar,) the *Tar*, varieties of the *Tamboura*, the *Kemangeh* (literally, "bow-instrument"), and the *Rebab*. The *Schtareh* corresponds to the *Qitarah* of the Arabs and Moors. The *Tar*, which literally signifies "a string," is furnished with 24 frets of gut, mounted with five strings, and played with a plectrum of wax and brass. The *Tamboura* is with used in Persia, as elsewhere, to accompany

M

vocal music. The *Kemangeh* (otherwise called the *Kamancha*) is an instrument of the violin kind, and the parent of all the Arabic instruments of the same name. It is used to accompany both singing and dancing. The *Rebab* of Persia is an almost exact counterpart of the *Rebec,* which was formerly so popular in Western Europe. In his "Travels in various countries of the East, more particularly Persia," Vol I, London 1819, Sir William Ouseley states that he met with the bagpipe in Persia where it goes by the name of *Nei ambánah* (from *Nei,* a reed or pipe, and *ambanah,* a bag), and where also "it appears to have been more general in former ages than at present." That its construction is nearly identical with the Scottish instrument is evidenced by Sir William's remark that a Scotch gentleman "played on it several tunes of his own country, in a very pleasing manner, without any previous practice." Besides the bagpipe, the wind instruments of Persia consist of the *Nay* (or *Nei,* flute), the *Zourna* (or oboe), and the *Shaberba* (*Chabbabeh* or flageolet). The *Kouwal* is the largest specimen of the tambourine class. The hand drum *Dombeg* is very popular and is specially used to accompany social dances and singing. The *Dohl* is another variety of drum commonly used in the country. Castanets and cymbals are also in use. The Kurduis, a part of the military force of Persia, have bands whose instruments are, according to Kotzebue, "little drums fastened to the saddle of their horses, and a species of clarionet, of a harsh, squeaking tone." The voices of the Persian dervishes are described as specially good. Comparing Persian singers with the Arab musicians, Fétis remarks, with reference to the former, that "they sing with more taste, more expression; and the ornaments of their melodies are less numerous and better adapted to the character of the phrases." The Persians are especially

celebrated for their love-songs. The following two translations of Persian songs are taken from "Specimens of the Popular Poetry of Persia, &c.," by Alexander Chodzko, London, 1842:—

"The late Prince of Shiraz, the well-known Fermanfermah, having fallen in love with an Armenian girl, this song was composed and sung throughout all Persia."

A PERSIAN SONG.

Joy and bustle resound in Shiraz; a sugar-mouthed girl came there. Faith! Reyhana, come and embrace the Mussulman creed.

Truly! I will not turn to the Mussulman faith. I will not be a Mussulman. If I do so. I shall be killed. O, Shahzade! restore Reyhana to liberty.

I will give thee a turban and a calotte; I will give thee a Cashmere shawl and a satin petticoat; I will give thee a dagger richly set with diamonds. I will bestow on thee riches and plenty. Come, Reyhana, and embrace the Mussulman faith.

I do not want either a turban or a calotte. I entreat you in the name of Allah, Shahzade! restore me to liberty!

A PERSIAN LOVE SONG.

Ferruh walks proudly through the bazaar. I perceive her red dress. I am afraid she will come to me. Woe to me! Ferruh has kindled a fire in my soul! O do not be cruel—do not spill my blood!

Ferruh's dress is scarlet; her face shines, burns! Ferruh is a kid, born in the spring. O do not be cruel—do not spill my blood! Ferruh's eyes call me. My fancy dreams odd freaks. Her beauty makes a Mussulman of a Kafir. O do not be cruel—do not spill my blood!

I will write your name on a slip of paper; I will put it near my heart, and will keep it there. I will steal you from your father! Woe to me! O do not be cruel—do not spill my blood!

ARABIA

IN the olden days the Arabians seem to have had their musical instruments and names for the different notes. It has been asserted that an Arabian flute was not only known but also popular in Greece in the time of Menander. Their lutes and pipes were probably very simple, and Sir William Jones imagines their music "to have been little more than a natural and tuneful recitation of their elegiac verses, and love songs." According to Don Calmet, "the Arabs had rhyme, before the time of Mahomet, who died A. D. 632; and in the second century, they used a kind of poetry in measures similar to the Greeks, and set to music." After the wandering Bedouins had become conquerors of the world, they acquired a taste for the pleasures of life. Then the chanters and musicians of Greece and Persia went to Mecca and took service under the Arabs. Then flourished the celebrated chanters Meehit and Tawis Saib Hathir; and after them, Moid-ebn-Cherih who, along with others, improved the art of chanting until it reached the summit of perfection under the Abbassides. Bagdad was at that period the centre of musical excellence. Here, and at this period, were invented costumes for the dancers, castanets for their use, various kinds of dances, and a species of pantomime. The celebrated Haroun-al-

Rashid, who reigned from 786 to 809 of the Christian era, was a great lover and patron of music. In his reign flourished the famous flute-player Ishac. Wonderful effects are attributed to the music of the Caliph Abu-Nasir-Mahomed-al-Farabi who was called the Arabian Orpheus. From a collection of ancient Arabian MSS. in the British Museum, it would seem that the Arabians possessed a rude species of counterpoint prior to the year 1060.

The notes of the Arabic scale are designated by the numbers from 1 to 7, thus :—*Jek* (C), *Du* (D), *Si* (E), *Tschar* (F), *Peni* (G), *Schesch* (A), *Heft* (B flat.) The notes are sub-divided into 17 *one-third-tones,* in the following way :—

C D E F G A B flat (C)
. . . .

This scale came to be adopted by the Persians when they were subjugated by the Arabs, and as mentioned elsewhere, continued to be in use till it was modified into one of 12 intervals later on. The Arabs divide their music into two parts ; the *telif* (composition), or music, considered in its relation to melody ; and the *ikaa* (cadence of sounds), or the measured cessation of melody, regarding instrumental music only. They have four principal modes, from which are derived eight others ; and they have also six composite modes, formed out of the union of these. Their manner of noting music is by forming an oblong rectangle, which is divided by seven lines perpendicular to its sides, representing, together with the two extreme lines, eight intervals. The highest of these is called by a name signifying the interval of all the tones ; and the seven others, beginning with the lowest, contain the seven Persian names of numbers. Each of the lines is of

a different color, which must be remembered, as well as the name and the interval. The simplicity of character, attributed by Sir William Jones to the music of the ancient Arabs, seems now to have been lost, considering how complex is their system of notation.

The musical instruments of the Arabians are chiefly those of percussion, or thrummed with the fingers or nails. "They have indeed," says Dr. Burney, "a flute called *Nai* with ventages. The tube is a section of reed, with a mouth-piece of horn. It is to the sound of this flute that the Dervishes dance." The Arabs have also an instrument called the *Aoud*, or *El oud* (literally "wood"), which in name and shape, resembles a lute, and they ascribe as many marvellous effects to it as the Greeks did to the lyre of Amphion, or the Chinese to the *Kin* of Pin-mou-kai. "They tell you," says M. Ginguene, in an article on Arabian music in the *Encyclopedie Methodique*, "with the utmost gravity, that each of the strings of this instrument, four in number, has particular virtues; the first, for instance, acts as a specific against bile and phlegm; the second is a sovereign cure for the most inveterate melancholy and vapours; the third gives health and vigour to young people of both sexes; and lastly, the fourth string affords relief, the instant it is heard, to a sanguine temper and disposition." The power of these strings depends greatly on the manner they are manipulated. "They have," continnes the same writer, "a particular *pizzicato*, or pinch, for every action and passion; courage, liberality, and noble sentiments, are inspired by one mode of thrumming; love and pleasure by a second; the dance is inspired by a third; sleep and tranquility by a fourth." The Arabs have a kind of dulcimer called the *Kánun*; and a violin called *Kemangeh à goux.* With regard to the latter, M. Fétis observes:—"If we compare the *Omerti* with the Arab instrument *Kemangeh à goux,* we

at once perceived that the latter took its origin from the former", which is a Hindu instrument of the fiddle species. Further on, he says with reference to the *Rabab* of the Arabs, of which there are two varieties, *viz.*, *Rabab esh Moganny*, or "singer's Rabab", and *Rabab esh Sha'er*, or "poet's Rabab," that it is "only a modification of the *Ruana* of the Hindus, the only difference being in the body of the instrument." Some of the Arabic instruments are constructed so as to enable the performer to produce accurately the seventeen one-third tones of the scale. The frets on the *Tamboura*, (a species of mandoline with a long neck), for instance, are regulated with a view to this object. The *Kemangeh*, already mentioned, has its body commonly formed of a cocoa-nut shell, with a piece of skin extended over it, and is mounted with three strings of catgut or horse-hair. This instrument as well as the drum are commonly used by the itinerant musicians who accompany the dancing women. The *Marabba* is another instrument of the bow species. It is mounted with a string of horse-hair, and covered with a skin stretched upon the body. It accords well with the shrill voices of the singers in the coffee-houses. The Arab name for flute is *Nay*, of which the two most common varieties are the *Nay-chah* (large *Nay*) and *Nay-giref* (little *Nay*.) The *Shami* or *Chami*, and the *Sulami* belong to the flute species. Both are made of cane and pierced with several holes. The *Bouk* is a tube of metal, about forty-four inches long; contracted at the mouth, where a small reed is inserted, and enlarging towards the other end, where it is as wide as the hand. Most of the instruments in use in Turkey and Persia are met with in some parts of Arabia. The Sheriff of Mecca has a band of martial music, consisting of kettle-drums, trumpets, fifes, &c. Similar bands are kept by the Pashas at Aleppo and Smyrna.

In the course of his travels in Arabia, Mr. Buckingham observed that the church service at Assalt was very similar to that of the Greek churches in Asia Minor, the difference lying only in the language in which it was performed. At the church in Damascus, the sermon was followed up by fine peals of music on the organ, and the choristers, who were composed chiefly of children of both sexes, sang hymns, in responses to each other, in the Arabic tongue. In the ordinary amusements of the Arabs, music holds a prominent place. "In a coffee-house," continues Mr. Buckingham, "encounters at a sort of single-stick are animated by the sounds of a tambourine and fifes, which varied in their performance as the contest became closer." He came across a party who sang Arabic songs in thirds and fifths; and one sang an octave to the strain. The choral song, called *Djok*, is sometimes sung by the young men at night, in the coffee-houses, its measure being accompanied with the clapping of hands. The music of Arabia, as indeed of certain other Eastern nations, is remarkably florid in its style, the air (*cantus firmus*) being in some cases almost entirely hidden by the introduced passages and grace-notes. One of the famous Arabian songs is the "song of the Sakas, or water-carriers in Mecca," which is described by John Lewis Burckhardt, in his "Travels in Arabia", (London, 1829, Vol I), as "very affecting, from its simplicity and the purpose for which it is used." "The wealthier pilgrims," observes he, "frequently purchase the whole contents of a Saka's water-skin on quitting the mosque, especially at night, and order him to distribute it gratis among the poor. While pouring out the water into the wooden bowls with which every beggar is provided, they exclaim *Sebyl Allah ya atshan, Sebyl!* ("Hasten. O thirsty, to the ways of God!") and then break out

in this short song of three notes only, which I never heard without emotion." The words are : *Eddjenę wa el moy fezata ly Sahab es-Sabyl* ; that is, "Paradise and forgiveness be the lot of him who gave you this water !"

Singing is extremely popular with all classes of the Arabs. Many of their songs are soft and mournful in character, while others are cheerful and sprightly. Most of the melodies are simple, but they are so overlaid with trills and ornaments as to become almost unrecognizable. These variations are improvised by the singer, and form the chief beauty of the performance.

The following translation of an Arab extempore song is given in the "Narrative of Travels and Discoveries in Northern and Central Africa," by Denham and Clapperton ; London, 1826, Vol II :—

Oh ! She was beauty's self, and shone in matchless symmetry ! when shall I hear news of her ?—how support her absence and her loss ?

My hopes are but as the fantastic dreams of night ; yet with this hopelessness my love does but increase, even as a star shines the brightest in the blackest night.

O ! Mabrooka ! Thy head sinks too with sorrow at losing him whose thoughts are still of thee ; but as the desert-bird drops and smooths its wings, but to display the richness of its plumage, so will thy silent grief but cause thee to appear with increased charms !

Vain and cruel delusion ! At the moment of the possession of earthly happiness to doom us to melancholy despair, was as if the traveller should draw water to the brink of the well, and then see the wished-for draught snatched from his thirsty lips.

What she looks upon becomes graceful, enchanted by her loveliness ! Oh ! she is beauty's self, my polar star of life.

TURKESTAN.

The inhabitants of this country are of a hybrid stock—half Kirghiz half Persian, with an admixture of Kalmucks (Sans. *kála mukha* or black face). The Kalmucks use a kind of trumpet in their religious performances. This trumpet is usually far too long and too heavy to be held up by the performer himself; in processions there are attendants in front, who carry it before him, while in the temple it rests upon a frame, so that he has only to raise it slightly when blowing. M. Hommaire de Hell saw among the Kalmucks in the vicinity of the Caspian Sea an instrument of the guitar species similar to the *San-Heen* of the Chinese, or *Samisen* of the Japanese. This instrument is also considered almost identical with the Russian *Balalaika*, which is said to be of high antiquity and originally derived from the East. The following is a translation of a Kalmuk song:—

Having fettered my camel near the source of the river Manich, whose waters are bitter, I should like to sit with my Sogonda and play with her, snatching the smoking pipe from her.

The brand on my wild grey horse has the shape of a gun. If, after having him well bridled, I could run away from my Sogonda, should I be guilty?

The crows and the owlets sit in rows on the bushes. I should like to play with the sweet-tongued Sogonda, wresting a steel and a flint from her.

The grass is waving on the meadow ; the image of the beautiful Sogonda comes to my mind. What is she doing now ; she who shared her heart and thoughts with me ?

The following is the translation of a song representing an Astrakan Tartar's last farewell :—

My bay horse was fond of my singing a *tolgaw* * while I was riding. My bay horse will remain in the stables.

My Tarter girls, beautiful as the waves, remained in the tent. My beautiful Tartar girls will find a husband for themselves ; my bay horse will find a rider.

My old mother, after losing such a warrior as I, will stoop from grief, and will find a dark grave for herself.

* *Tolgaw*—The popular song of the Tartars.

TURKEY IN ASIA.

UNDER this heading will be briefly described, along with that of others, the music of some of the countries and cities that played prominent parts in ancient history. A succinct general account of such countries aud cities will not, perhaps, be found quite out of place here.

Assyria.—The first Great Empire of antiquity, celebrated in the Bible. Its limits are not ascertained, but it appears to correspond nearly to Kurdistan—the country of the Kurds, a rude and mountainous district, belonging partly to Asiatic Turkey and partly to Persia.

Babylon.—"The earliest post-deluvian city and the oldest in the world of which there are any traces remaining." Anciently the capital of the Babylonio-Chaldean Empire, in an extensive plain on the Euphrates River. The modern town Hillah occupies a portion of its site. The ruins of Birs Nimrod, on an elevated mound, are supposed to be the Tower of Babel of the Scripture, and the temple of Belus, described by Herodotus. Babylon is supposed to have been originally built 2230 B. C. It was at the height of its power in the time of Nebuchadnezzar. It was beseiged and taken by Cyrus, B. C. 538, and afterwards by Alexander the Great.

Chaldea.—Modern Irak-Arabi, a province comprehended in the modern pashalic of Bagdad. It is watered by the Tigris and the Euphrates.

Nineveh.—A famous city of antiquity, capital of the ancient kingdom of Assyria, the ruins of which occupy an extensive space around the village Nunia, on the East bank of the Tigris, opposite Mosul. The city was overthrown and its empire merged in that of Babylon in 625 B. C.

Palestine.—Called in Scripture also the *Land of Canaan;* the *Land of Promise;* the *Land of the Hebrews;* the *Land of Israel;* the *Land of Judah;* the *Land of Jehovah;* The *Holy Land.* The population comprises Syrians, Mahomedans, Druses, Maronites, Christians, Jews, and Turks. The Pasha resides at Beyrout, the chief commercial city, and under him is the Pasha of Jerusalem.

Phœnicia.—A tract of country in the north part of Palestine, in which Tyre and Sidon were chief cities. The people of Phœnicia were famous for their skill in navigation and their active encouragement of c ommerce.

Syria.—A province of Asiatic Turkey, famed in ancient history, lying along the east coast of the Mediterranean. It is now divided into the pashalics of Aleppo, Damascus, and Beyrout or Sidon. The trade of Syria is chiefly conducted by Christians, Jews, or Armenians. The Mahomedans are most numerous in the secondary towns and in the rural districts.

The musical instruments in present use in these countries are mostly those derived from Persian and Arabic sources.

ASSYRIA.

Very little is on record about the music of the Assyrians. The discoveries which have only been made in the present century, however, throw a flood of light on the subject,—in fact they form the only sources from which any substantial information can be derived. The discovered monuments, on which the musical instruments of the Assyrians are represented, consist of bas-reliefs. Most of these are now to be seen in the British Museum. They have been obtained from three extensive mounds near the Tigris, called the mounds of Nimroud, Khorsabad, and Kouyunjik. Nimroud, situated about 20 miles to the south of Mosul, was explored in 1847 and 1850 by Mr. Austen Henry Layard. Khorsabad, about 10 miles to the north-east of Mosul, was excavated by M. Botta, French Consul at Mosul. The mound of Kouyunjik, which is believed to contain the ruins of Nineveh, is situated in the immediate vicinity of Mosul on the opposite bank of the Tigris. Here, too, Mr. Layard made discoveries of some sculptures. Another series of slabs from this last place was obtained, later on, by Mr. Hormuzd Rassam, and by Mr. Loftus, who excavated the mound in 1853 and the two following years, under the direction of Sir H. C. Rawlinson, who was at that time British Consul-General in Bagdad. The most competent judges on Assyrian history assert that the period when these monuments were executed commenced about 1000 years B. C. The musical instruments carved thereon must, as a matter of course, be older, perhaps, by many centuries previous to that period. Considerations of an antiquarian kind establish clearly the fact that, among the Assyrians as well as the ancient Egyptians and Hebrews, not to mention the

Hindus, music attained to a degree of perfection very much higher than is observed in many of the nations of the present day. The monuments alluded to show not only that the Assyrians possessed a variety of pulsatile, wind, and stringed instruments, but also that they knew how to employ different kinds of stringed instruments in concert, either vocal or instrumental. Moreover, it would appear that they were acquainted with the use of the finger-board, by means of which they could obtain a great number of distinct notes on a few strings, like those on the guitar or mandoline. As the bas-reliefs chiefly represent historical events, religious ceremonies, and royal entertainments, it is more than probable that the Assyrians possessed several popular instruments, which, on account of their not having been employed on occasions under representation, do not find a place on the bas-reliefs.

One of the instruments noticed in the sculptures is the Harp. It is about four feet high and held before the breast of the performer, and played by him while standing or walking. The upper portion of the frame contains the sounding board; two sounding-holes, somewhat in the shape of an hour glass, are seen on one side. Below them are the screws, or tuning pegs, arranged in regular order. The strings run from these pegs down to the horizontal bar of the frame, round which they are fastened. Ornamented tassels were sometimes appended to the lower part of the frame. Representations of three kinds of lyre occur in the sculptures, differing in shape as well as in the number of strings. It would seem that in one case the performer carried the instrument before him by means of a band slung over his right shoulder, and that in all cases he employed both hands in twanging the strings, which was done with the plec-

trum as well as with the fingers. The Dulcimer, of which an imperfect representation was obtained, seemed to have been played with a plectrum held by the performer in his right hand. The left hand appears also to have been used either in twanging the strings, or, perhaps, with the view of checking any undesirable vibrations of the strings. There is another instrument found on the sculptures which, in the absence of any specific name, has been called the *Asor* owing to its resemblance to the Hebrew instrument of the same name. In this, the strings are placed horizontally one above the other at regular distances. The lowest string is the shortest, producing the highest note, and the uppermost string is the longest producing the deepest note. The front bar of the instrument is surmounted by a small hand which, some one conjectures, served as a stand to hold written music. The instrument is supported by a belt passed over the shoulder of the performer, whose hands were thus free for the execution of his music. The Assyrians had a kind of guitar with many frets which, for want of a name and on account of its similarity with the Egyptian instrument, has been designated the *Tamboura*. Mr. J Bonomi in his work "Nineveh and its Palaces", (London, 1853), describes a Syrian *Tamboura* which "has ten strings of small wire, forty seven stops, and is invariably highly enriched and inlaid with mother-of-pearl. Th Tamboura is in common use upon the shores of the Euphrates and Tigris." A specimen of the double-pipe is observed in the Assyrian sculptures Judging from the shortness of the length of the Assyrian trumpet, it would appear that it was suited for producing three or four notes belonging to the Triad, or common chord. The "bell" end of the instrument is clearly discernable in one of the representations. The drums met with on

the sculptures have this feature in common that they are covered with skin only on their upper part, and that they are beaten with the hands instead of with sticks. The Assyrians used bells of different sizes, probably to represent different scales or succession of intervals. They also used the Tambourine and cymbals. Some varieties of the latter were funnel-shaped. Captain Willock discovered in the ruins of Babylon, Birs-i-Nimroud, a little pipe of baked clay which he presented to the Museum of the Royal Asiatic Society. It is about three inches long, and has only two finger-holes, placed side by side, and consequently equidistant from the end at which it is blown. The opposite end has no opening. In this respect, the instrument resemble a whistle. If both finger-holes are closed, it produces the note C; if only one of them is closed, it produces E; and if both are open, it produces G. Travellers state that the Syrinx or Pandean Pipe is used at present in Syria and other Oriental countries, chiefly by the lower classes. Perhaps, it was known to the Assyrians of old, and from the fact of its having been a popular instrument, it did not probably find a place on the monuments. It is surmised that the Bagpipe and the Sistrum were also known to the Assyrians. It is said that the Assyrians invented the *Trigonum* or *Triangulum,* a stringed instrument of a triangular shape, played upon with a plectrum. From the nature of the instruments represented in the sculptures, it would appear that Assyrian music was soft and soothing, and devoid of the noisy element that is so intimately connected with percussion instruments. From the construction of their instruments, specially from that of the harps, the strings of which could be touched with both hands simultaneously at different parts, and from the use of the double-pipe, it would appear that the Assyrians were in the habit of producing together

different notes which seemed to them agreeable in concord. It would also appear that the pentatonic scale, which was in use among almost all ancient nations, was in favor. As the Persians were indebted to the Assyrians for their early civilization, it stands to reason that the former obtained from the latter the knowledge of the use of smaller intervals than semi-tones. That music was brought largely into requisition by the Assyrians in their religious ceremonies has been abundantly proved by the sculptures, and confirmed to some extent by the Scriptures as the following extract from Daniel III, 1-5, will show:—"Nebuchadnezzar the king made an image of gold, whose height was three score cubits, and the breadth thereof six cubits. Then an herald cried aloud, To you it is commanded, O people, nations, and languages, that at what time ye hear the sound of the cornet, flute, harp, sackbut, psaltery, dulcimer, and all kinds of musick, ye fall down and worship the golden image which Nebuchadnezzar the king hath set up." There is no positive evidence as to whether the Assyrians possessed a musical notation, but considering the progress which they made in music and other arts, it would not be surprising if they had. Perhaps, further discoveries may throw some light on this subject. Some hope of this is held out in the following remarks made by Professor Max Muller in his "Lectures on the Science of Language," London, 1862:—"In a letter dated April, 1853, Sir Henry Rawlinson wrote: 'On the clay tablets which we have found at Nineveh, and which now are to be counted by thousands, there are explanatory treatises on almost every subject under the sun; the art of writing, grammars and dictionaries, notation, weights and measures, divisions of time, chronology, astronomy, geography, history, mythology, geology, botany, &c. In fact, we have now

at our disposal a perfect cyclopædia of Assyrian science.' Considering what has been achieved in deciphering one class of cuneiform inscriptions, the Persian, there is no reason to doubt that the whole of that cyclopædia will some day be read with the same ease with which we read the mountain records of Darius."

PHŒNICIA.

Sanchoniathon, the historian of the Phœnicians, attributes the invention of music to a celebrated woman of this nation, named Sido. They had several musical instruments, one being called after their country, *Phœnices.* They had also the *Naublum* which was played upon at the feasts of Bacchus. A kind of flute was used at funerals. It was about a foot long, and produced a wailing, mournful sound, and was called, in their own language, *Gingre.* According to Herodotus, the Phœnicians had among them a popular song called *Maneros,* which is, perhaps, the prototype of the Corsican *Vocero*—a dirge lamenting the death of a beloved friend or relative. There are professional singing-girls in modern Egypt known as *'Awálim,* which term is derived from the Hebrew or Phœnician word *'Almáh* meaning 'a girl' and 'a virgin', particularly, 'a singing-girl'. Mr. Lane thinks it probable that in the olden times the most celebrated of the singing-girls in Egypt were *Phœnicians.*

ASIA MINOR.

In Asia Minor, the natives accompany their dancing with tambourines, which are either circular pieces of wood, or earthen pots, covered with skin, and played upon with the fingers. The *Doff* is the most elegant of the variety, and to this the women are said to dance in the

harems. The castanets also form one of their musical instruments. Some of the mendicants carry different kinds of horns and drums, which they sound before asking alms. The music of the Georgians is described by Sir R. Ker Porter as particularly rude. They have small double drums, and a kind of guitar which is played upon with a bow. The music produced by the combination of these has been compared to the noise of a water mill, but without its harmony.

PALESTINE.

The materials from which any reliable knowledge can be derived of the music of the Hebrews exist in the Scriptures. The first mention made there of either vocal or instrumental music after the Deluge and prior to the Exodus is the passage in Genesis XXXI, 26, 27, where Laban (who lived about 1700 B. C.) reproaches Jacob with stealing away from him secretly, instead of informing him of his intended departure, that he might have sent him "away with mirth and with songs, with tabret and with harp." As Laban was a Syrian, it has been contended by some that the passage refers to Syrian rather than Hebrew music. The next mention occurs in connection with the departure of the children of Israel out of Egypt, and the destruction of Pharoah and his host in the Red Sea. On this occasion, Moses composed the ode—said to be the earliest specimen of epic poetry extant (about B. C. 1491)—which is found in the 15th chapter of the Exodus. In rendering this ode, the Israelites were divided into two great choirs, Moses and Aaron being at the head of the men, and Miriam leading the women. After this period, the Bible makes frequent mention of music as connected with the religious ceremonies of the Jews; and it has been supposed that this music

was derived from Egypt, for Moses is said to have been "learned in all the wisdom of the Egyptians,"—"but above all in medicine and music." David effected great improvements in the science and art of music. From 2 Samuel, VI, 5, it would appear that "David, and all the house of Israel played before the Lord on all manner of instruments, made of firwood; even on harps, and on psalteries, and on timbrels, and on cornets, and on cymbals." He appointed four thousand of the Levites, according to Chronicles XXIII, 5, "to praise the Lord with instruments which he made to praise therewith." Asaph, Heman, and Jeduthun, were chiefs of the music of the tabernacle, under David. Solomon, the son and successor of David, "spake three thousand proverbs, and his songs were a thousand and five." He himself says—"I gat me men-singers and women-singers, and the delights of the sons of men, as musical instruments, and that of all sorts;" (Ecclesiastics ii, 8). Josephus, who lived in the first century of the Christian era, states that the number of musicians whom Solomon employed at the dedication of the temple was two hundred thousand. Considering that the length of the temple, according to 1 Kings VI, 2, was 60 cubits, its breadth 20 cubits, and its height 30 cubits, the statement of Josephus must be taken with a very liberal allowance of salt. The supposition that Solomon did not accomodate two hundred thousand musicians in the temple, but caused the same number of trumpets to be merely deposited in its vaults at the inauguration of the temple, is decidedly against the proverbial wisdom of that celebrated monarch. When Moses received the law on Mount Sinai, it was given to him not only with the sound of trumpets, but with songs also. The Jews are consequently prohibited from chanting the Bible in any other manner than as it was recited to them by Moses, the

tune of which is supposed to have been handed down from generation to generation until about the fifth century when Rabbi Aaron Ben Aser invented certain characters to represent the accent and true tone that were given to each word, by means of which the original chant has been preserved to this day.. The Scriptures abound in passages showing that the Hebrews also had military music, triumphal songs, love songs, funeral songs, convivial songs, music at bridal processions, and secular songs in various other forms. Two historical facts show the extent of the power of Hebrew music and how fully it was appreciated. These are, its use as a cure in nervous disorders, and its employment as a means of stimulating prophetic inspirations. King Saul became afflicted with attacks of a nervous malady,—"And it came to pass, when the evil spirit from God was upon Saul, that David took an harp, and played with his hand; so Saul was refreshed, and was well, and the evil spirit departed from him", (1 Sam. xvi, 16, 23). Elisha being required by the kings of Israel, Judah, and Edom, to prophesy before them, his request was for a musician. "But now bring me a minstrel. And it came to pass when the minstrel played, that the hand of the Lord came upon him. And he said, Thus saith the Lord, Make this valley full of ditches," &c. &c., (2 Kings, iii, 15). There were schools of the prophets in various places, in which music seemed to have been systematically taught. It is not unlikely that the Hebrews possessed written treatises on the principles and practice of music. A musical performance on a certain occasion in the Temple of Jerusalem is thus described in 2 Chron., v, 13:—"It came even to pass as the trumpeters and singers were *as one*, to make *one sound* to be heard in praising and thanking the Lord." This passage is interpreted by some authorities as

indicating the use of *unison*, and by others that of *harmony*, in Hebrew music. Those who suppose that *harmony* is meant argue that it is not likely that a performance in *unison* could be implied, for that would not be specially recorded if no other mode of *combining the voices and instruments* had been known.

Many were the musical instruments in use among the Hebrews of old, and mentioned in the Scriptures. But it is somewhat difficult to establish the identity of some of these. Some of the instruments mentioned in the Book of Daniel may have been synonymous with some which occur in other portions of the Bible under Hebrew names—the names given in Daniel being Chaldæan—which, according to Professor Max Muller, is the name " given to the language adopted by the Jews during the Babylonian captivity." "Though the Jews," observes he, "always retained a knowledge of their sacred language, they soon began to adopt the dialect of their conquerors, not for conversation only, but also for literary composition." The English translations of the Bible, again, give in some cases different names to the same instruments. The following is a fairly correct list classified under general headings.

1. The Harp.—It is difficult, however, to make out which of the Hebrew names of the stringed instruments mentioned in the Bible come under the designation of harp.

2. The Dulcimer.—Some conjecture the *Nebel*, others the *Psanterin* (mentioned in the Book of Daniel), to have been a kind of Dulcimer.

3. The Asor.—A ten-stringed instrument, played with the plectrum and supposed to have borne some resemblance to the *Nebel*.

4. The Lyre.—This instrument is represented on a Hebrew coin supposed to be of the time of the High-priest Simon Maccabæus. The *Kinnor*, the favourite instrument of king David, was most likely a lyre.

5. The Tamboura, or Guitar.—*Minnim, Machalath*, and *Nebel* are usually supposed to be instruments of the of the guitar or lute species.

6. The Pipe.—*Chalil* and *Nekeb* were the names of Hebrew pipes or flutes.

7. The Double Pipe.—Probably the *Mishrokitha* mentioned in the Book of Daniel.

8. The Syrinx or Pandean Pipe.—Probably the *Ugab*, which, in the English authorised version of the Bible, is rendered "organ." The Hebrew name is derived from a word *ugab* which means *to delight in.*,

9. The Bagpipe.—The word *Sumphonia* is supposed to denote a bagpipe. The Italian peasantry of the present day call the bagpipe by the name of *Zampogna*. Another Hebrew instrument, the *Magrepha*, which is generally described as a small organ, was more probably only a species of the bagpipe. Others state that the *Magrepha* was a kettle drum; some others, that it meant a fire-shovel. A kind of bagpipe represented on one of the terra-cottas of old was excavated in Tarsus, Asia Minor, by Mr. W. Burckhardt Barker. These remains are believed to be 2,000 years old, and they

give some idea of the nature of the instrument then in use.

10. The Trumpet.—Three kinds are mentioned in the Bible, *viz.*, the *Keren*, the *Shophar*, and the *Chatzozerah*. The first two were more or less curved, something like horns. The last mentioned instrument was a straight trumpet, about two feet in length, and sometimes made of silver. It has been already stated that the law was received by Moses on Mount Sinai with the sound of the trumpet. This instrument is supposed by Padre Martini to have been the *Buccina*, made of the horn of the ram, (or some other beast, for a ram's horn is not hollow). Moses was subsequently commanded by the Lord to make two trumpets of silver, (Numbers, x, 2), from which time, probably, these instruments were made of metal. The *Tuba*, called by the Hebrews the *trumpet of jubilee*, was a simple instrument made of metal.

11. The Drum.—Several varieties of the drum were used by the Hebrews. The *Toph* (translated in the English Bible as *Timbrel* or *Tabret*) appears to have been a tambourine or a small hand-drum. This instrument was specially used in processions, on occasions of rejoicings, and frequently by females. It was found in the hands of Miriam when she was celebrating in songs the destruction of Pharaoh's host (Exod., xv, 20) ; and in the hands of Jephtha's daughter when she went out to welcome her father (Judges, xi, 34). Almost synonymous with the Hebrew *Toph*, there exists now in the Oriental countries a small hand-drum called the *Doff* or *Dampha*.

12. The Sistrum.—Some authorities are of opinion that the *Menaaneim*, mentioned in 2 Sam. vi, 5,

P

signifies this instrument. The word is translated *cymbals* in the English Bible.

13. Cymbals.—The *Tzeltzelim*, *Metzilloth*, and *Metzilthaim*, seem to have been varieties of cymbals.

14. Bells.—The little bells on the robe of the high-priest were called *Phaamon*. At the present day, the Jews have, in their synagogues, small bells attached to the "rolls of the law," containing the Pentateuch,—a kind of ornamentation supposed to have been in use from time immemorial.

The *Jobel*, believed to have been derived from *Jubal*, the inventor of musical instruments, is classed with the trumpets. *Shalishim*, mentioned in 1 Sam. XVIII, 6, is said to denote a *Triangle*. The *Sabeka*, (mentioned in Daniel), which is believed to have been identical with the Greek *Sambuka*, was also an instrument of the triangle kind. Some say it was a species of the guitar. The terms *Nechiloth*, *Gittith*, and *Machalath*, which occur in the headings of some of the *Psalms*, represent, according to some, certain musical instruments, and, according to others, peculiar modes of performance, or certain favorite melodies to which the *Psalms* were directed to be sung. The *Machol*, mentioned in several portions of the Bible, is believed by some writers to have been a kind of flute, especially used for accompanying dances; by others, to mean the dance itself.

The Jews, since their dispersion as a nation, have been forbidden the use of instruments. Nathan, in his "Essay on the History and Theory of Music," remarks that "they have, with increased tenacity, preserved their ancient melodies." The *Shophar*, however, is still

retained. The Jews in Germany possess several hymn-tunes of an undoubtedly high antiquity. The "Penitential Hymn" which they sing is said to have been composed by King David. The "Blessings of the Priests" is said to be identical with the melody which used to be sung in the Temple by the priestly choir. Another favorite melody of the Jews, the "Song of Moses," is stated to be the same which Miriam and her companions sang after the deliverance from Pharaoh's host. The characteristic chanting, which musicians call *cantillation*, and which may he heard in every synagogue, bears a close affinity to certain vocal performances of the Arabs and Persians. Some of the Rabbins have attempted to discontinue the *cantillation* altogether, and to adopt simple hymn-tunes and part-singing instead. Even some of the tunes of the Protestant Church, the Chorales, have been adopted and are sung in some of the synagogues to the accompaniment of an organ,—innovations which, on the Continent of Europe, have contributed to divide the Jews into two parties, the reforming and conservative. In modern Jerusalem, there are several distinct Jewish communities. Among these, the Sephardic constitutes the largest. The Aschkenasim community consists of Jews from Germany, Holland, Russia, Poland, Bohemia, and other parts of Europe. They all understand the German language, of which they have created a strange dialect; while the Sephardic Jews, principally derived from Egypt, Tunis, Tripoli, Morocco, Algiers, India, and Persia, use the Spanish language. Dr. Frankl, who had stayed in Jerusalem for a long time, found the singing of the Sephardic Jews closely allied to that of the Arabs, "more rhythmical than melodious, shrill rather than soft, and closely bordering on snuffling." Still, he preferred it to the singing of the

Aschkenasim Jews, consisting of a kind of cantillation, which is usually called Polish singing. Burckhardt, in speaking of the Jews of Tabaria, or Tiberias, in Palestine, describes how the congregation imitate by their voice and gestures the meaning of some remarkable passages in the Psalms of David when they are recited by the Rabbin; for instance, when he says, "Praise the Lord with the sound of the trumpet," they imitate the sound of the trumpet through their closed fists. When a "horrible tempest" is spoken of, they puff and blow to represent a storm; or when "the cries of the righteous in distress" is mentioned, they all set up a loud screaming. Padre Martini has published, in his "Storia della Musica," a number of chants from synagogues in different European countries, some of the chants being nearly 300 years old. Mr. Weintraub observes that the oldest and most universally used chants are generally in the *Phrgyian* and *Mixolydian* modes. The Jews are limited in their choice of occupation for gaining a subsistence, by their religious, and, in many countries, by their civil laws. Hence their innate love and predilection for music, and hence the extraordinary talent which some of them have displayed for this art. It would be worth mentioning that the celebrated composers Halévy, Meyerbeer, and Mendelssohn were either Jews, or were of Jewish extraction. Their compositions bear evidence of the peculiarities of Hebrew music, among which are the use and frequent repetition of short melodious phrases, and passages of a peculiar rhythmical effect.

AFRICA.

NORTH-EASTERN AFRICA.

EGYPT.

THE first mention of music or musical instruments in the Bible is made in Genesis, where in connection with the enumeration of the posterity of Cain, it is said that "Jubal was the father of all such as handle the harp and the organ." Padre Martini supposes that Adam was instructed by his Creator in every art and science including music, and that he utilized his knowledge in praising and adoring the Supreme Being. The Genesis further informs us that in the days of Seth, about the period of the birth of Enos, (3664 B. C.), "men began to call upon the name of the Lord." Padre Martini considers this the first introduction of music into religious rites. The Alexandrian Chronicles say that the "sons of Seth did according to the angels, invoking in the angels' hymn." This is nearly all that is known of music before the Flood. According to Archbishop Usher, the Deluge took place A. M. 1656, and 2348 B. C. The sons of Noah, after the waters had passed from the face of the earth, first settled in the plains of Shinar, part of the ancient Mesopotamia, the

modern Diarbekr. The first migration of Noah's descendants took place about 2281 B. C., when several of the younger branches of the family of Ham, if not Ham himself, travelled towards the west and south, and settled in Phœnicia and Egypt, taking with them, as some say, Noah himself. Others, soon after, migrated to the east, and the empires of Assyria, Babylon, India, Persia, and China were founded. The Egyptians are generally supposed to be the fountain whence the arts and sciences were diffused over the greater part of Europe. Certain authorities attribute to them the invention of music amongst other arts. The earliest account of this country, as indeed of all ancient countries, is enveloped in a myth ; and if any records existed, as in all likelihood they did, they were destroyed by Cambyses, who conquered Egypt in about 525 B.. C., and overthrew the temples, where such records were likely to be deposited, and slew the priests. Some writers suppose that Noah reigned in Egypt, and identify him with Osiris, to whose secretary Hermes Trismegistus, the invention of the lyre is ascribed. It is said that owing to an overflow of the Nile, several dead animals were left on the shores, and, among others, a tortoise, the flesh of which was dried and wasted in the sun, and nothing remained within the shell but nerves and cartilages, which being tightened and contracted by the heat, became sonorous. While walking along the banks, Hermes happened to strike his foot against this shell, and felt so pleased with the sound produced, that he at once formed the idea of constructing the lyre. The first instrument of the kind he made was in the form of a tortoise, and was strung with the sinews of dried animals. Athenæus (a Greek grammarian born in Egypt in the third century after Christ) ascribes the invention of the flute to Osiris himself. Kircher. however, supposes that the Egyptians

very early formed flutes and pipes from the rushes which grew upon the shores of the Nile

The varieties of representation in sculptures and paintings as well as the specimens discovered give an idea of the musical instruments of Egypt. Among these are the following :—

The Harp.—The name of the harp was *Buni*, or *Beni*. In the Egyptian paintings the words *Sek an ben*, "scraper on the harp", have been found written in heiroglyphs over the figure of a harper. The number of strings vary in different specimens. Some of the harps were placed on the hand when played ; others were put on stands. Two harps, one mounted with 13, and the other with 10 strings, and both excellently carved and elaborately decorated, were first noticed by Bruce. These were painted in fresco on the wall of an ancient sepulchre at Thebes, which is supposed to be the tomb of Rameses III, who reigned about 1250 B. C. A drawing of one of these harps appeared in Dr. Burney's "History of Music." Soon after, engravings of both were published in Bruce's "Travels," Vol I. A kind of harp with twenty-one strings was discovered in a well-preserved condition and deposited in the Paris Museum. The absence of the front pillar is a peculiarlity common to all the specimens.

The Lyre.—These instruments also vary in shape and in the number of strings. The Hermean Lyre is said to have been mounted with three strings representing the three recognized seasons of the year, and producing an acute, a mean, and a grave sound,—corresponding, respectively, to the summer, the spring, and the winter. Some lyres were held perpendicularly.

The frame was frequently ornamented with the carved head of the horse, gazelle, or some other favorite animal. Dr. Burney, in his "History of Music,' gives a drawing of a *Trigonon* with ten strings, and observes that it is called by Sophocles a Phrygian instrument, and that one Alexander Alexandrinus made a great impression in Rome where he displayed his skill on it. "The performer", continues the Doctor, "being a native of Alexandria, as his name implies, makes it probable it was an Egyptian instrument upon which he gained his reputation at Rome." Amphion is said to have built the walls of Thebes by the music of his lyre.

The Tamboura.—Egyptian name, *Nofre*. It was played with a plectrum. Some specimens were provided with frets. A variety with a comparatively short neck resembled the modern guitar, or rather the Arabian *Oud*.

Specimens of certain peculiar stringed instruments of Egypt have been discovered and deposited in the British and the Berlin Museums.

The Pipe.—Small pipes have often been discovered, made of reed, usually with four finger-holes. The *Monaulos*, or single pipe, was used in the religious worship of the Egyptians.

The Flute.—The common variety was of considerable length. The Coptic name of the flute is *Sebi*, the word being often found in the heirglyphics with the representation of this instrument, and, as it is also the name of the leg-bone, it has been supposed that the *Sebi* was originally made of bone. The *Photinx*, or crooked flute, was shaped like a bull's horn.

The Double-pipe.—Egyptian name, *Mam*. This seems to have been a favorite instrument with the Egyp-

tians of old, as it occurs frequently in the representations of their musical performances.

The Trumpet.—This is supposed to have been the *Buccina*, which Festus describes as a crooked horn. Other varieties were made of brass or wood.

The Drum.—Three varieties are known. One of them resembles the small hand-drum beaten with the hands on both ends, and slung over the shoulder of the player. A specimen of another kind was excavated in 1823 at Thebes. It was beaten with two sticks slightly bent. The third variety is almost the same as the *Darabukkeh* of modern Egypt.

The Tambourine.—This instrument was generally played by the women. It was either round or square. The latter variety is supposed to have been the same as the *Toph* of the Hebrews and the *Doff* of the Arabians.

The Sistrum.—This consisted of a frame of bronze or brass, into which three or four metal bars were loosely inserted, so as to produce a jingling noise when the instrument was shaken. A few metal rings were sometimes strung on the bars to increase the noise. The top of the frame was sometimes ornamented with the figure of a cat. On the lower part was a handle by which the instrument was held. Virgil describes Cleopetra as using it for a signal. It sometimes did duty for a trumpet in war. The *Sistra* were generally used by females in religious performances. Villoteau, on the authority of Jablonski, believes *cencen* to have been the common name of the Sistrum, and he suggests that its present Ethiopian designation *Sanasel* (*Tzenacel* or *Cenacel*) and also the Hebrew *Tzeltzelim* may have been derived from the same name.

The Crotala.—This served to produce rythmical effects, like the Greek instrument of the same name or the castanets of the present day. The *Crotala* consisted of two balls or knobs, sometimes made to represent human heads, probably of metal, and hollow, to which were affixed handles, either straight or slightly curved. The name *castanet* is derived from *castana* (chesnut), of which it was usually made in Spain. One of the *Crotalas* was held by the player in each hand, and the heads were struck together, to mark the time in instrumental performances or in dances. The *Crotala* has its counterpart in India where it is called *Karatáli* or clapper.

Cymbals.—These closely resembled similar instruments of the present day. One of the pairs, out of two, deposited in the British Museum, was found in a coffin enclosing the mummy of Ankhhape, a sacred musician.

Bells.—Among the specimens to be found in the British Museum is one having on it a face with a protruding tongue, which represents Typhon, the evil spirit of the ancient Egyptians.

Two peculiar instruments of percussion are represented in the engravings. The one held with the left hand by a man, and accompanying the performance of two harpers, is most probably a kind of gong struck upon with a piece of ivory or wood. The other looks as if it was constructed of metal, with a view to produce, when beaten or shaken, a sound like a gong or bell; and, perhaps, some loose pieces of metal were attached to it to produce a jingling noise like that of the *Sistrum.*

This second instrument is represented as being played by one preceding another who is singing.

As already mentioned, the Egyptians were subjugated by Cambyses, about 525 B. C. Since then they have always been under a foreign yoke. After the establishment of the empire of the Ptolemies, the hieroglyphics, in which their ancient records were written, gradually became unintelligible to the Egyptians themselves; and the memory of their ancient greatness and learning was lost. The first three of the Ptolemies, Soter, Philadelphus, and Euergetes encouraged music to a considerable extent. But it was Grecian music, as the arts and philosophy of that people supplanted those of Egypt. In describing a Bacchanalian festival which was celebrated by Philadelphus, Athenæus states that more than six hundred musicians were employed in the chorus, and that there were no less than three hundred performers on the *Cithara.* He also states that it was in the time of the second Ptolemy Euergetes that Ctesibius, a native of Alexandria, invented the *Hydraulicon,* or water organ, an instrument which was played, or at least blown, by water, but the exact method of execution is not indicated. In the collection of antiquities bequeathed to the Vatican by Queen Christina of Sweden, there is a large and beautiful medallion of Valentinian, on the reverse of which is a representation of a hydraulic organ, with two men, one on either side, seeming to pump the water which plays it. It has only eight pipes placed on a round pedestal, and, as no keys or performers are visible, it is most likely that it was played by mechanism. During the reign of the seventh Ptolemy, there were never a people more skilled in music than those of Alexandria; "for," observes Athenæus in his rare and valuable work known as the *Deipnosophist,* "the

most wretched peasant or laborer amongst them is not only able to play upon the lyre, but is likewise a perfect master of the flute." Owing to his extreme fondness for the flute, the father of Cleopetra, the last of the Ptolemies, was called *Auletes*, or the *Flute-player*. The history of Egypt closed with Cleopetra and the Empire became a Roman Province. Since then, the cultivation of music was neglected and finally prohibited Strabo, who wrote his history about the time of Christ says, "the sound of instruments was not heard in their temples, but their sacrifices were made in silence." Herodotus (born 484 B. C.) relates: "among the many wonderful things I have met with in Egypt this one astonishes me specially, whence they can have obtained the song of Linus; for they seem to have celebrated him thus from time immemorial. The Egyptians call him Maneros, and they say that he was the only son of the first king of Egypt. Happening to die in the prime of life, he is lamented by the people in this dirge, which is the only song of the kind they possess in Egypt." Plato, who lived about 400 years B. C., and who is said to have sojourned in Egypt thirteen years and systematically studied the science of music, records a favourable opinion of the character of Egyptian music. Diodorus Siculus, who visited Egypt about 60 years B. C., speaks of the universal mournings of the Egyptians on the death of a king. On such an occasion the temples were closed, and all feasts and solemnities forbidden, for the period of seventy-two days. Men and women in large numbers walked about, twice a day, throwing dust upon their head, and singing mournful songs in praise of their deceased monarch. Dr. Samuel Birch, in his "Introduction to the Study of the Egyptian Hieroglyphs," gives in original and in translation the song of the thrashers to the oxen treading out the corn. This

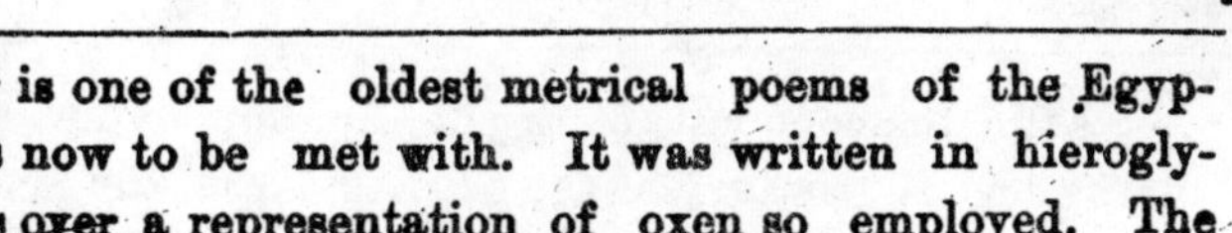

song is one of the oldest metrical poems of the Egyptians now to be met with. It was written in hieroglyphics over a representation of oxen so employed. The translation is reproduced below :—

Thrash ye for yourselves,
Thrash ye for yourselves, O oxen,
Thrash ye for yourselves,
The straw which is yours,
The corn which is your master's.

The following specimen of religious poetry, which was, no doubt, sung or chanted by the Egyptians,—the first stanza of a hymn to the Nile (taken from a papyrus in the British Museum)—is also reproduced from Dr. Birch's work :—

A HYMN TO THE NILE.

Incline thy face, O Nile,
Coming safe out of the land,
Vivifying Egypt,
Hiding his dark sources from the light,
Ordering his sources ;
The streams of his bed
Are made by the sun
To give life to all animals,
To water the lands which are destitute,
Coming all along the heaven,
Loving fragrance, offering grain,
Rendering verdant every sacred place of Phtha !

The dances of the Egyptians were characterised by lively figures, and rapid evolutions, and consisted of several varieties. Sometimes both sexes joined in the dances ; and these were, in some cases, accompanied nly by the rhythmical sounds produced by clapping the hands and snapping the fingers. From the accounts given by various classical authorities, it appears clear that the Egyptians possessed written treatises on the theory of music.

After the conquest of Egypt by the Mahomedans, in the seventh century of the Christian era, the arts and customs of the Arabs were introduced into this country along with their religion. The bulk of the present inhabitants of Egypt are Muslim-Egyptians (also called Arab-Egyptians), a mixed race, principally descended from the Arabs. The music of modern Egypt is more closely allied to that of the Assyrians and Chaldæans than to that of the Egyptians of old. There are, however, a few remains of the original instruments to be found in the country, and among those are the *Kissar* (the Nubian lyre), the *Darabukkeh,* and the *Sistrum.* The *Tamboura* and most other instruments are now observed in modified forms. The *Maraoveh,* a modification of the *Sistrum,* is used in their religious ceremonies by the Copts, who are descendants of the ancient inhabitants of the country and are a Christian sect, dispersed throughout parts of Egypt. The *Kemamgeh roumy* of modern Egypt is a violin said to have been introduced here from Greece. The musical scale of modern Egypt admits of *one-third-tones* like that of the Arabs, but the common people whose ear has not been specially trained to them do not, generally speaking, appear capable of distinguishing them. Hence the absence of *one-third-tones* in the popular melodies which Europeans have collected in Egypt. Mr. E. W. Lane, in his "Account of the Manners and Customs of the Modern Egyptians", (London, 1860), remarks :—"I have heard Egyptian musicians urge against the European systems of music that they are deficient in the number of sounds." Among the varieties of the modern drum are the *Baz* (or Dervish drum), the *Tabl Beledee* (or country drum), *Tabl Shami* (Syrian drum), and the *Davool* (or bass drum). The *Arghool* is a wind instrument of the "Double-pipe" kind, one of its tubes being consider-

ably longer than that of the other, and serving as a drone. The *Zummárah* is another variety of the Double-pipe, in which the tubes are of equal length. It is some sometimes played at weddings when the bride is being conducted through her apartments, and oftentimes by the boatmen. The singing of the boatmen on the Nile is one of the characteristic performances of the modern Egyptians. It usually consists of alternate *solo* and *chorus* in short phrases, and varies with the nature of the occupation in which the men happen to be engaged. For instance, one particular air is sung when they shift the sails; another, when the boat has struck on a sandy bank, and they are working to set it afloat again; a third when the wind is favorable; a fourth, when a village is approached; and so on. The male professional musicians of modern Egypt go by the name of *Aláteeyeh*; the professional singing-girls, by that of *'Awálim*. The common dancing-girls are called *Ghawázee*, who, according to Lane, "are descended from the class of female dancers who amused the Egyptians in the times of the early Pharaohs." Mr. Lane reproduces in his work, "Manners and Customs of the Modern Egyptians," the words and music of the "Call to Prayer" of the Muezzin, from the minaret of the mosque. The *Zikrs*, or religious dances of the Dervishes, have been frequently described by travellers in Turkey, Egypt, and other Eastern countries. The Dervishes assemble in the mosque, and perform their sacred evolutions to vocal and instrumental music,—the latter consisting generally of drums and pipes. The choruses, which are accompanied by those instruments, partake, in some instances, of the character of a short chant, which is several times repeated; in others, they most resemble the Christian hymn-tunes in rhythmical construction. The *Nay*, otherwise called the "Dervish Flute", which is one of the principal instruments accom-

panying the *Zikr*, consists, according to Lane, of "a simple reed, about eighteen inches in length, seven-eighths of an inch in diameter at the upper extremity, and three-quarters of an inch at the lower. It is pierced with six holes in front, and generally with another hole at the back. . . . . .The sounds are produced by blowing through a very small aperture of the lips against the edge of the orifice of the tube, and directing the wind chiefly within the tube. By blowing with more or less force, sounds are produced an octave higher or lower. In the hands of a good performer, the *Nay* yields fine mellow tones, but it requires much practice to sound it well." In his "Travels in Various Countries of Europe, Asia, and Africa", (London, 1810), Mr. E. D. Clark gives an interesting detailed description of the *Zikr*, a performance of which was witnessed by him in a mosque at Tophané, a suburb of Constantinople. The Egyptians are in the habit of honoring their celebrated Saints by an anniversary birth-day festival called *Moolid.* Villoteau witnessed a musical performance at the *Moolid* of *Seyyideh Zeyneb*, a female Saint and a grand-daughter of Mahommed the Prophet. The *Fakirs*, a class of Dervishes, executed a religious dance, singing at the same time a short air. The melody was sung by the *monched*, or leader, and the bass part by the whole chorus. The words of the air were simply the phrase "La Ilahi Illulla."

ABYSSINIA.

Perhaps, the kingdom next in antiquity to Egypt is Abyssinia or Habesh. Here the pentatonic scale of old seems to have been retained on some of the musical instruments. The lyre of the Abyssinians is, as regards

the mounting of the strings, constructed on the same principle as some of the Assyrian lyres, *viz.*, that the strings are tied round the bar so as to allow of their being pushed upwards or downwards with a view to raising or lowering their pitch. Some of the lyres had the two sides of the frame made of the horns of animals, or of wood formed in imitation of horns. The traveller Bruce states that formerly they were made of the horns of a kind of goat called Agazan, about the size of a small cow and common in the province of Tigré—a State in the N. W. portion of Abyssinia. He saw in that country several of these lyres "elegantly made of such horns, which nature seems to have shaped on purpose." The Abyssinians have a tradition, according to which the *Kissar* was introduced into Ethiopia from Egypt by Toth, or Hermes, at a very early period. A *Kissar* from Abyssinia, deposited in the East India Company's Museum, is so far different from the ordinary Nubian *Kissar*, that its body is square, without sounding holes, and it has ten strings which rest upon a large wooden bridge. A plectrum, made of horn, about 3 inches long, is affixed to the instrument by a leathern thong. According to Villoteau, the *Bagana*, or the ten-stringed lyre of the Abyssinians, has only five different notes, but each note has its octave. By the name of *Sanasel*, the *Sistrun* is used by the priests of a Christian sect in Abyssinia. Its sound is supposed by them to drive away the evil spirits, and it was specially employed by the ancient Egyptians for the like purpose. Its Egyptian name was *Seshesh*. Mr. Mansfield Parkyns, in his "Life in Abyssinia," (London, 1853), describes the *Wattas* of the present day who are "musicians and buffoons, sometimes attached to the courts of the chiefs of Abyssinia, but also frequently itinerant in their habits, making professional tours, something

after the manner of ballad-singers." Similar to the *Tarantula* dance which is suposed to cure a person bitten by the Tarantula spider, the Tigritiya dance is believed to exercise a curative effect in a mysterious nervous disorder, known as Tigritiya, to which females are almost exclusively prone. With some patients it is necessary to have recourse to music before the real cause of this complaint can be discovered. If her illness be of an ordinary kind, she will of course beg the musicians to desist; but if possessed, she will jump or fall from the couch, and keep dancing in time with the music and going through various evolutions with a velocity and power of endurance that would be surprising even in a person of an ordinarily strong constitution. "On her dancing and singing", observes Mr. Parkyns, "is supposed chiefly to depend her chance of recovery." The traveller Nathaniel Pearce mentions that the Abyssinian Christians regard St. John as the patron of dancing. Hence it is supposed that the Tigritiya was originally a religious performance like the famous St. John's dance which was so much in vogue among the pious people of the Netherlands and Germany during the fourteenth century. Mr. Bruce mentions that the Abyssinians believe that the flute, kettle-drum, and trumpet (which along with the Tambourine are used in war), were brought from Palestine by Menelek, the son of their Queen of Saba, by Solomon, who was their first Jewish king. Mr. Bruce describes their trumpet as being made of a piece of cane, to which a round piece of the neck of the gourd is affixed, which is, on the outside, ornamented with small white shells. It is all covered over with parchment and produces only one note, E, in a loud and hoarse tone. The guitar is sometimes seen in the hands of Mahomedans in Abyssinia. It is said to have come here from Arabia. The

Right Revd. Samuel Gobat gives, in his "Journal of a Three Years' Residence in Abyssinia", (London, 1847), a specimen of an Abyssinian dirge, which is reproduced below :—

Alas ! Sebagadis, the friend of all
Has fallen at Daga Shaha, by the hand of Oubeshat.

Alas ! Sebagadis, the pillar of the poor,
Has fallen at Daga Shaha weltering in his blood !

The people of this country, will they find it a good thing
To eat ears of corn which have grown in the blood ?

Who will remember Michael * of November ? †
Mariam, with five thousand Gallas, has killed him.‡

For the half of a loaf, for a cup of wine :
The friend of the Christians has fallen at Daga Shaha !

NUBIA.

Nubia is the modern name of Ethiopia of old. *Kissar*, the principal musical instrument of this country, is a lyre, the body of which consists of wood, hollowed in the form of a bowl, and covered with sheepskin. The cover is generally pierced by three sounding-holes equidistant from each other ; sometimes there are more. The *Kissar* has five strings made usually of the intestines of the camel. The strings rest on a kind of bridge made of wood which is placed near the end of the body.

* St. Michael.
† *i. e.*, to give alms.
‡ Him, *i. e.*, who remembered to give alms.

The instrument is played with a small plectrum, made of a piece of leather or horn, and fastened with a cord to the instrument. The plectrum is held in the right hand, and the strings are struck with it, while the performer twangs some strings with his left hand, using the plectrum and his fingers either alternately or together. Sometimes the body of the instrument is made square instead of circular, and sometimes six or even more strings are used. But five is the usual number, as the *Kissar* is supposed to produce the pentatonic scale. The first string is tuned a fifth from the second string which has the principal interval or tonic of the songs. The modern Egyptians call this instrument *Qytarah Barbaryeh,* which indicates that this is considered the national instrument of the Barabras or Berbers (Sanskrit *Barbara,* which means, *uncivilized ?*) who are believed to be descendants of the original inhabitants of Egypt. Niebuhr says that he saw in the hands of a Barbari, or an inhabitant of Dongola, (one of the territories in Nubia), a sort of harp which he does not specify by name, but which, from the description given, cannot be any thing else but the *Kissar.* The songs sung to the accompaniment of the *Kissar* are called by the Nubians *Ghouna.* Some of these songs have nothing in common with the Arabic language; some others contain not only Arabic but also corrupted Italian words. Dr. E. Ruppell witnessed in Nubia the performance of a dance resorted to by the people with a view to relieve a young man from a malady from which he was suffering for a long time. The patient, who was made to dress well, was placed on a raised spot in the middle of a circle formed by the dancers. The object may have been to benefit the low-spirited sufferer more by the cheering influence of the scene than by any pretended power of effecting a radical cure.

NORTHERN AFRICA.

ALGERIA.

THE Arabs in Algiers, the capital of Algeria (ancient *Numidia*), have a composition called *Nouba*, which is a kind of fantasia upon popular melodies in a certain prescribed form. The Revd. J. W. Blakesley, who visited a Jewish synagogue in Algiers, was surprised to find that "the air to which the Psalms were chanted coincided almost exactly with one of the 'Gregorian tones." The instruments in use in Algiers are chiefly the *Kuitra* (a kind of guitar), the *Gunibry* (*Kuniberi*, something like the Banjo and having its body made of tortoise shell), the *Rebab* (a two-stringed violin, shaped like a fish), the *Raita* (oboe), the *Gasba* (fife), *Bendir* (drum), and *Tar* (Tambourine).

MOROCCO.

The *Tabla* (a sort of kettle-drum), the Triangle, the *Erb'eb* (an instrument akin to the Grecian lyre, but having only two strings), and a rude kind of flute, are described as the principal instruments used in Morocco. In Tangier, one of the chief towns of Fez, the music is chiefly confined to bagpipe players, who are said to have no fixed airs, and play only from memory. Mr. G. J. Cayley being invited to a Jewish wedding in Tangier, found a company, including about 36 young Jewesses, singing, clapping hands, and dancing to the music of a

Kemangeh which the chief Rabbin, an old man, played upon. The Revd. Thomas Debary describes the ceremony of the circumcision of a little Jew boy in Tangier during which the Psalms were chanted.

TUNIS.

The Revd. Mr. Blackesley describes a Jewish custom which he observed in Tunis on the 1st of May, on which occasion a kind of bower, composed of flowers and wax-candles, is carried in procession to the synagogue, the people all the while chanting and the females uttering the peculiar sound of *ly-ly-ly*, in the manner of the Mahomedan women at weddings and funerals. After the arrival of the singers at the synagogue, the whole building is decorated with flowers and the wax-tapers are lighted.

FEZZAN.

Fezzan is chiefly inhabited by the Arabs, Moors, and Negroes.

The following lines are taken from the "Narrative of Travels and Discoveries in Northern and Central Africa," by Denham and Clapperton ; London, 1826 :—

AN ELEGY OF THE FEZZANEES ON THE DEATH OF A HERO.

Oh ! trust not to the gun and the sword !
The spear of the unbeliever prevails.
Boo Khaloom, the good and the brave, has fallen !
Who shall be safe ?

Even as the moon amongst the little stars,
so was Boo Khaloom amongst men !
Where shall Fezzan now look for her protector ?

Men hang their heads in sorrow, while women
wring their hands, rending the air with their cries!

As a shepherd is to his flock, so was Boo Khaloom
to Fezzan.
Give him songs! give him music! What
words can equal his praise?

His heart was as large as the desert!

His coffers were like the rich overflowings from the
udder of the she-camel, comforting and nourish-
ing those around him.

Even as the flowers without rain perish in the
field, so will Fezzanees droop; for Boo
Khaloom returns no more!

His body lies in the land of the heathen.
The poisoned arrow of the unbeliever prevails.
Oh! trust not to the gun and the sword!
The spear of the heathen conquers!
Boo Khaloom, the good and the brave, has fallen!
Who shall now be safe?

WESTERN AFRICA.

WESTERN Africa is chiefly inhabited by the Negro races, and is divided into three portions, *viz.* Senegambia, Upper Guinea, and Lower Guinea. The following are the principal musical instruments of Western Africa :—The Trumpet, which is simply the hollowed tusk of the elephant ; the *Zanze* (in different parts of Africa known also by the names of *Ambira, Marimba, Ibeka, Vissandschi*) consisting of a wooden box on which a number of sonorous slips of wood, or tongues of iron, are fixed in such a position as to admit of their being made to vibrate by pressing them down with the thumb or with a stick ; the *Boulou* or *Ombi*, a kind of harp the strings of which are made from a kind of creeping plant, or from the fibrous root of a tree ; the *Balafo*, which is a species of harmonicon ; and the *Valga* (also known as *Wambee, Kissumba*, &c.) which is somewhat like the *Sancho*, a small stringed instrument also in use in this part of the country. The neck of the *Valga* consists of several canes, generally five, which are stuck into the holes in the underpart of the body of the instrument, and can be pushed in or drawn out independently of each other. As each string is affixed to the extreme end of one of the canes, it can be tightened or slackened by drawing the cane further out, or pushing it deeper in ;—by which way it is tuned. The strings are made of the same materials as those of the *Boulou*. The

Negroes of Senegambia and Guinea have a class of musicians called *Guiriots*, or *Griots*, who are poets as well as singers, and whose calling it is to recite the ancient legends and war-songs of the people, and to improvise either panegyrics or satires upon others.

Major A. L. Laing (who, in 1826, succeeded in accomplishing what Europeans for three centuries had failed to do, *viz.*, in penetrating to Timbuctoo, but who was murdered on his return homewards), had jotted down his experiences of African music in his work "Travels in Timanee, Kooranko, and Soolima Countries in Western Africa", London, 1825. He found that music formed a prominent part in all the public ceremonies of these people. Some songs were improvised on the occasion of his visit. At Seemera, in the Kooranko country, the King Bee Simera sent him his *Griot* to play to him and sing a song of welcome. This man performed on a sort of fiddle, the body of which was formed of a calabash, in which two small square holes were cut. It had one string, composed of many twisted horse-hairs, and only four tones could be got out of it. At Soolima, the Major was treated by the King Yarradee to a military spectacle, and while the warlike movements were going on, about a hundred musicians kept playing on drums, flutes, *Balafos*, and other instruments. Two of the large drums used on the occasion were shaped like a chess-castle turned upside down. An *extempore* dialogue was then chanted between one of the *jellé*-men (minstrels) and some females, who, towards the close of the performance, sang a song in honor of the king. They also sang a warsong which was composed in honor of a great victory that Yarradee obtained over the *Foulahs* (an amiable Negro race widely diffused through Western Africa), and which was always

rehearsed before him on all public occasions. This war-song is reproduced below from Major Laing's work :—

Shake off that drowsiness, O, brave Yarradee !
thou lion of war !

Hang thy sword to thy side, and be thyself !

Dost thou not behold the army of the Foulahs ?

Observe their countless muskets and spears,

Vying in brightness with the rays of the departing sun !

They are strong and powerful, yea, they are men; and they have sworn to the Alkoran that they will destroy the capital of the Soolima nation.

So shake off thy drowsiness, O brave Yarradee, thou lion of war ! hang thy sword to thy side, and be thyself !

The brave Tahabaeere, thy sire, held the Foulahs in contempt ; fear was a stranger to his bosom. He set the firebrand to Timbo, that nest of Islamites; and though worsted at Herico, he scorned to quit the field, but fell, like a hero, cheering his war-men.

If thou art worthy to be called the son of Tahabaeere—shake off thy drowsiness, O brave Yarradee ! thou lion of war ! hang thy sword to thy side, and be thyself !

Brave Yarradee stirred ; he shook his garment of war, as the soaring eagle ruffles his pinions. Ten times he addressed his greegrees, * and swore to them that he would either return with the sound of the war-drum, † or with the cries of the Jelle.‡

The war-men shouted with joy—Behold, he shakes from him that drowsiness, the lion of war ! he hangs his sword to his side, and is himself again !

"Follow me to the field !" exclaimed the heroic Yarradee ; "fear nothing ; for let the spear be sharp, or the ball swift, faith in thy greegree will preserve thee from danger."

* Amulets. † *i. e.*, in triumph.

‡ The Jelle, or Jellekes, are employed to sing at the death of any great man.

"Follow me to the field! For I am roused and have shaken off my drowsiness. I am brave Yarradee, the lion of war! I have hung my sword to my side, and am myself!"

The war-drum sounds, and the sweet notes of the balla * encourage warriors to deeds of arms. The valiant Yarradee mounts his steed; his head men follow. The northern gate of Falàba is thrown open, and a rush is made from it with the swiftness of leopards. Yarradee is a host in himself. Mark how he wields his sword! They fall before him—they stagger—they reel!—

Foulah men, you will long remember the day; for Yarradee has shaken off his drowsiness, the lion of war! he has hung his sword to his side, and is himself!

The daughter of a Negro chief of Ngumbo, a District in Western Africa, south of the Equator, having seen a young English traveller, gave forth her feelings in the following *extempore* effusion:—

In the blue palace of the deep sea
Dwells a strange creature:
His skin as white as salt;
His hair long and tangled as the sea-weed;
He is more great than the princes of the earth;
He is clothed with the skins of fishes,
Fishes more beautiful than birds.
His house is built of brass rods;
His garden is a forest of tobacco.
On his soil white beads are scattered
Like sand grains on the sea-shore.

The following "Song of a Negro mother to her babe" appeared in "Savage Africa," by Winwood Reade, London, 1863:—

* Balla, or Balafo.

Why dost thou weep, my child ?

The sky is bright, the sun is shining: why dost thou weep ?

Go to thy father; he loves thee; go, tell him why thou weepest.

What! thou weepest still? thy father loves thee; I caress thee; yet still thou art sad.

Tell me then, my child, why dost thou weep ?

Mr. T. E. Bowdich, the author of "Mission from Cape Coast Castle to Ashantee," London, 1819, mentions that in the Empoongwa country, he came across a Negro performer (from the interior country of Imbeekee), who had a harp, formed of wood, and mounted with eight strings. After running through a variety of notes, he burst forth in the notes of the *Hallelujah* of Handel. Mr. Bowdich remarks—"To meet with this chorus in the wilds of Africa, and from such a being, had an effect I can scarcely describe, and I was lost in astonishment at the coincidence."

Various kinds of dances are in vogue among the tribes in Western Africa, as indeed among all savage nations. The Apono tribes have a peculiar dance called Ocuya, or giant dance, which is performed by a man who enacts the part of the giant and raises himself to the necessary height by means of stilts. The moon-dance which is performed by the Fan tribes is accompanied by the playing on a drum and an instrument called the *Handja*, a kind of harmonicon, which goes by the name of *Balonda* in Senegambia and *Marimba* in Angola. The Fans are described as having some ear for music and possessing some pretty though rudely constructed airs.

UPPER GUINEA.

ASHANTEE.

With the Ashantees, the singing is almost all in the form of the recitative, and this is the only part of music of which the women partake; they join in the choruses, and, at the funeral of a female, sing the dirge itself. The men employed in the canoes have, like the gondoliers of Venice, a natural talent for music. Their airs, which Mr. Bowdich says, "have a sweetness and animation beyond any barbarous composition," are said very much to resemble the chants used in Christian cathedrals. Some of the Ashantee airs are very old; indeed, one of them, according to the statement of the natives, "was made when the country was made." Their instrumental music is executed in the most rapid manner. Their flutes are made of a long reed, and pierced with only three holes. They have a kind of bagpipe, the drone of which is scarcely audible. Their drums are made of hollow trunks of trees covered with skins, and struck upon with sticks. The most highly esteemed of the drums are covered with leopard skin, and played like a tambourine with two fingers. The instruments called the Fetish drum and trumpet are used as accompaniments to the sacrifice of human beings. The bands of the caboocees (noblemen) are principally composed of horns and flutes playing in concert. Mr. Bowdich remarks that "all the superior captains have peculiar flourishes or strains for their

horns, adapted to short sentences, which are always recognized, and will be repeated on enquiry by any Ashantee you may meet walking in the streets, though the horns are not only out of sight, but at a distance to be scarcely audible. These flourishes are of a strong and distinct character. . . . The king's horns go to the market-place every night, as near to midnight as they can judge, and flourish a very peculiar strain, which was rendered to me 'King Sai thanks all his captains and all his people for to-day.'" Mr. Bowdich further states that whenever the king drank, his royal band played, while the executioners (who decapitate victims destined for human sacrifice on certain public festivals) holding their swords with their right hands, covered their noses with their left, whilst they sung his victories and titles. About half a dozen small boys stood behind his chair, and finished the whole with a hymn.

The Fantees are a Negro tribe in the Ashantee country and on the Gold Coast. Their musical instruments are much the same as those of the Ashantees. Regarding their flute, Mr. Bowdich observes that its "tone is low at all times, and when they play in concert they graduate them with such nicety as to produce the common chords." Their music is described as wild and irregular, and scarcely amenable to the rules of harmony, and yet characterised by a sweetness and liveliness beyond that of most barbarous nations. Remarking on a dirge of the Fantees which Mr. Bowdich has set to notation, he says—"I must add, that in venturing the intervening and concluding bass chord, I merely attempt to describe the castanets, gong-gongs, drums, &c., bursting in after the soft and mellow tones of the flutes; as if the ear was not to retain a vibration of the sweeter melody."

The dances of the Fantee tribe are rather peculiar. Two dancers stand opposite each other, and stamp on the ground with each foot alternately. The stamping becomes faster and faster, until it is exchanged for leaping, and at every jump the hands are thrown out with the fingers upward, so that the four palms meet with a sharp blow. The couple go on dancing until they fail to strike the hands, and then they leave off and make room for another pair.

DAHOMEY

Mr. Richard F. Burton, in his " Mission to Gelele, King of Dahomey," London, 1864, states that as the people of Dahomey have no written language, anything that happens in the kingdom, from the arrival of a stranger to an earthquake, is formed into a kind of song, and being taught to professional men is thus transmitted to posterity. Commander F. E. Forbes relates in his work " Dahomey and the Dahomans," that on one occasion when he found the king was drinking before his people in the capital of his kingdom, Abomey, " there thundered forth a salute of guns almost drowned by the shouts of the multitude. The ministers and cabooceers danced, and the eunuchs and ladies held cloth before the king. Men must not see the kings eat or drink." The natives of Dahomey possess a great aptitude for remembering foreign tunes which they once hear. One man Attah is said to have played all the old Scotch airs in a creditable manner. The king retains an army of female warriors who, on certain public solemnities, extol the greatness of their master and their country. The following *extempore* song of the Amazons of Dahomey appeared in Commander Forbes' work :—

1. When the wolf goes abroad,
   The sheep must fly.

2. Gezo is king of kings!
   While Gezo lives we have nothing to fear,
   Under him we are lions, not men.
   Power emanates from the king.

3. Let all eyes behold the king!
   There are not two, but one,
   One only, Gezo!
   All nations have their customs,
   But none so brilliant or enlightened
   As of Dahomey
   People from far countries are here:
   Behold all nations, white and black,
   Send their ambassadors!

4. When we go to war, let the king dance,
   While we bring him prisoners and heads.

BENIN.

The musical instruments of the people of Benin consist of drums of different sizes, covered with skins of beasts. They have, besides the instruments in use in other parts of Upper Guinea, a kind of harp, strung with five or six reeds. The performance on this is accompanied by singing and dancing.

LOWER GUINEA.

CONGO.

The natives of Congo have a lute of a rather peculiar kind. The body and neck resemble those of the European lute; but the belly, *i. e.*, the part where the rose or sound-hold has place in the European variety, is of very thin parchment. The instrument is strung with

the hair of an elephant's tail, or the bark of the palm-tree. The strings extend from one extremity of the instrument to the other, and are fastened to rings. Small iron and silver plates are fastened to these rings, and when the whole is put in motion by thrumming the strings, it produces a murmuring harmony, not altogether disagreeable to the ear. The *Zanze* appears in Congo under the name of *Vissandschi* The Negroes of Congo have a rude kind of bagpipe, which emits a shrill and piercing tone. A curious stringed instrument from the Congo River has been deposited in the American Museum of Natural History in New York. It has a narrow wooden body, ornamented at the upper end with two small horns, and mounted with five strings of vegetable fibre.

CENTRAL AFRICA.

THE Karague, a tribe of the lake region of Central Africa, have a kind of flageolet, as also certain reed instruments made in telescopic fashion. They have also a kind of guitar in which six of the seven strings agree perfectly with the diatonic scale of Europe, the seventh only being discordant. In his "Journal of the Discovery of the Source of the Nile," Captain John H. Speke gives a picture of one of the concerts of the Karague tribe, in which seven performers are represented as taking part:—one playing upon a harp with seven strings, a second upon the flute, a third upon a trumpet, a fourth upon the *Miramba*, a fifth upon a large kettle-drum, and the sixth and the seventh each beating a pair of smaller drums.

Mr. J. G. Wood, author of the "Uncivilized Races of Men", mentions a curious instrument of the Shillooks of Central Africa, which was in his collection and which, for want of a better word, he calls a flute. It is made of some hard wood, and is rudely covered with a spiral belt of iron and leather. Inside the flute is fitted an odd implement which may be called the cleaner: it is composed of an ostrich feather with the vanes cut short. The sound produced by the flute is described as being of "a wailing and lugubrious character."

The *Sansa* is one of the most popular instruments of the Batoka tribe in Central Africa. The principle of the *Sansa* is exactly that of the musical boxes of

Europe, the difference being that the teeth or keys of the latter are steel, and that they are sounded by little pegs, and not by the fingers as in the case of the former. The best form of the *Sansa* is that in which the sounding-board is hollow (which increases its sound), and the keys are made of iron instead of wood,—which produces a really musical sound The instrument is enclosed in a hollow calabash which has the effect of intensifying the sound, and both the *Sansa* and the calabash are furnished with bits of steel and tin, which make a jingling accompaniment to the music. The *Sansa* is used in accompanying songs. Dr. Livingstone mentions that a genuine native poet attached himself to the party, and composed a poem in honor of the white men, singing it whenever they halted and accompanying himself on the *Sansa*. At first he modestly curtailed his poem as he did not know much about his subject, but as, day by day, his knowledge extended, the poem became at last quite a long ode. There was an evident rhythm in the piece, each line consisting of five syllables. Another poet is ʟ cribed as having been in the habit of amusing himself every evening with an *extempore* song in which the deeds of the white men were enumerted. The *Marimba* is also in use among the Batoka tribe. A similar instrument is made with strips of stone, the sounds of which are superior to those produced by the wooden bars. It might be mentioned here that the *Marimba* has been introduced into England under the name of "Xylophone."

The Felatas of Central Africa appear to belong to the same stock as the Foulahs of Senegambia. From the country of the latter races, the former nation originally wandered out with their flocks and herds in

small companies and in the former times never resided in towns. Now the Felatas are the ruling race of a good part of Negro land. The bulk of the Felatas are Moslems but many hordes are still pagans. The chiefs are accompanied by many personal followers (both horse and foot), some of whom form a band. The *Barca Gana,* or head general of the Shiek of Bornou, when visited by Major Denham, had close behind him five mounted performers, who carried a sort of drum hung round their necks, and beat time, when they sang *extempore* songs. One carried a small pipe made of a reed ; and another blew loud blasts on a buffalo's horn. This band sung some *extempore* verses when the Major joined them. The following is a literal version of the stanzas sung on the occasion :—

" Christian man he come,
Friend of us, and sheikhobe ;
White man, when he hear my song,
Fine new tobe give me.

Christian man all white,
And dollars white have he ;
Kanourie like him come,
Black man's friend to be.

See Felatah, how he run ;
Barca Gana shake his spear
White man carry two-mouthed gun,
That's what make Felatah fear."

The Felatahs have, among other instruments, some long pipes, like clarionets, ornamented with bells; and trumpets from twelve to fourteen feet long, which are made of pieces of hollow wood, with brass mouth-pieces.

SAHARA.

In his account of "Travels in the Interior of Africa," 1820, Mr. G. Molliens mentions that the Moors

of Sahara have a rude kind of guitar, the music of which, as also that of their songs, partake of the character of Spanish music. As both the Spanish and Moorish music were derived from the same source namely Arabia, this coincidence is easily explained.

SOUDAN.

Soudan, or, as it is also called, Nigritia, is inhabited principally by Negroes of various tribes as the Felatahs, Mandingoes and Arabs The Niam-Niams and Monbuttoo of the Soudan have large signal drums. Some of the smaller drums are shaped like an hour-glass or a double *Darabukkeh,* and provided with a head of iguana skin. The Mittoo of the Soudan have a rude lyre which greatly resembles the Nubian Kissar. The Negroes of the Soudan have a kind of cymbals which consist of two plates of iron, with leather handles, which are used to accompany the beating of their drums, which are called by the same name as that of the ancient Egyptians, namely *Dhaluka,* and are almost identical. The *Nanga* of the Soudan, which is a composite of the lute and the harp, is also a characteristic instrument of Egypt. The Niam-Niams of the Soudan have a class of professional bards or minstrels, called *Nzangah,* who use a combination of harp and mandolin as an accompaniment to their recitatives. These bards are looked upon with contempt by their hearers, as is indicated by the name *Hashash* (buffoon) applied to them by the Arabs of the Soudan.

BORNOU.

Bornou is one of the most powerful kingdoms of Central Africa. The people of Bornou, as well as the Mosees, Mollowas, and other natives from the more

remote parts of the interior, have a rude species of violin, the body of which is a calabash and the top covered with deer-skin. Two large holes are cut in it for the sound to escape. It has only one string composed of cow's hair; the bow used is like that of a violin. There is another instrument in use called the *Oompoochwa*, which is a box, one end of which is left open, two flat bridges are fastened across the top, and five pieces of thin carved stick, scraped very smooth, are attached to them, and (their ends being raised) are struck with some force by the thumb. The Sheik of Bornou expressed great wonder at the musical snuff-box, which was shown him by Major Denham, and his feelings were completely overcome when he heard the celebrated Swiss air "Ranz des Vaches." He covered his face with his hand, and remained in silence, and when a man near him broke the charm by a loud ejaculation of wonder, he struck him a blow and put to terror all his followers. He asked if one twice as large would not be better. On being told that it would be twice as dear, he exclaimed it would be cheap if it cost a thousand dollars.

The following *ex tempore* song of the Negro bards of Bornou in praise of their Sultan, is taken from the "Narrative of Travels", by Denham and Clapperton :—

Give flesh to the hyenas at day-break :
Oh ! the broad spears !
The spear of the sultan is the broadest.
Oh ! the broad spears !

I behold thee now—I desire to see none other.
Oh ! the broad spears !
My horse is as tall as a high wall.
Oh ! the broad spears !

He will fight against ten ; he fears nothing.
Oh ! the broad spears !
He has slain ten ; the guns are yet behind.
Oh ! the broad spears !

The elephant of the forest brings me what I want.
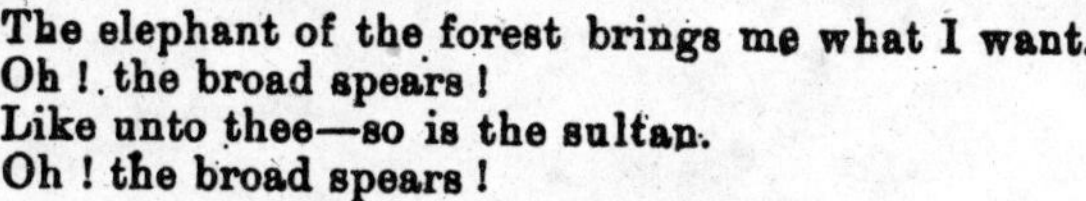
Oh ! the broad spears !
Like unto thee—so is the sultan.
Oh ! the broad spears !

Be brave ! be brave, my friends and kinsmen !
Oh ! the broad spears !
God is great !—I wax fierce as a beast of pray.
Oh ! the broad spears !
God is great !—To-day those I wished for are come.
Oh ! the broad spears !

SOUTHERN AFRICA

THE melody of the vocal music of the Bechuanas is simple enough, consisting chiefly of descending and ascending by thirds. Two-part harmony is sometimes used. The instrumental music of the tribe consists mainly in blowing a reed pipe called "Licháka", which emits only one note, repeated as often as the performer chooses to play on it. These pipes can be tuned to any required note by pushing or withdrawing a movable plug which closes the reed at the lower end. They run through a scale of some eleven or twelve notes. Blowing a penny whistle, or a key, produces a correct imitation of the instrumental music of this tribe. In his "Travels in the Interior of South Africa," Mr. James Chapman mentions that the Bechuanas have "a musical bow with a hollow calabash attached to one end, on which is stretched a twisted string made of sinews, on which the performer strikes with a thin stick, *modifying the tones with his fingers by running them along the string*" The sound produced by this instrument is said to be audible only to the player, as one end of the bow being constantly between his teeth, "the sounds vibrate powerfully to his own ears, and are lost on the bystanders." The dance of the Bechuanas is described as a very fatiguing affair. Each dancer is at liberty to take any step he chooses, and to blow his reed pipe at any intervals that may seem most agreeable to him.

The Damaras spend their evenings at home in singing and dancing Their principal instrument is the bow, the string of which is tightened and then struck with a stick in a rhythmic manner. The Damara musician thinks that the chief object of his performance is to imitate the gallop or trot of the various animals. Great skill is usually displayed in doing so, the test of an accomplished musician being the imitation of the clumsy canter of the baboon. The dances of the Damaras are remarkable, as would appear from the following account which appeared in Mr. Baines's work :—"At night, dances were got up among the Damaras, our attention being first drawn to them by a sound between the barking of a dog and the efforts of a person to clear something out of his throat, by driving the breath strongly through it. We found four men stooping with their heads in contact, vying with each other in the production of these delectable inarticulations, while others, with rattling anklets of hard seed-shells, danced round them. By degrees the company gathered together, and the women joined the performers, standing in a semi-circle. They sang a monotonous chant, and clapped their hands, while the young men and boys danced up to them, literally, and by no means gently, 'beating the ground with nimble feet,' raising no end of dust, and making their shell anklets sound, in their opinion, most melodiously. Presently the leader snatched a brand from the fire, and, after dancing up to the women as before, stuck it in the ground as he retired, performing the step round and over it when he returned, like a Highlander on the broad sword dance, without touching it. Then came the return of a victorious party, brandishing their broad spears ornamented with flowing ox-tails, welcomed by a chorus of women, and occasionally driving back the few enemies who had the audacity to approach them."

U

The Makololo tribes usually show their joy and work off their excitement in dances and songs. "The dance," says Dr. Livingstone, "consists of the men standing nearly naked in a circle, with clubs or small battle-axes in their hands, and each roaring at the loudest pitch of his voice, while they simultaneously lift one leg, stamping twice with it, then lift the other and give one stamp with it; this is the only movement in common. The arms and head are thrown about also in every direction, and all this time the roaring is kept up with the utmost possible vigour. The continued stamping makes a cloud of dust ascend, and they leave a deep ring in the ground where they have stood."

KAFFRARIA.

The Kaffirs are generally believed to be of the Negro race, and are of a dark brown color. They have no written characters, but their language is sonorous, resembling Italian. They are divided into hordes, and governed by hereditary chiefs who exercise absolute rule. It is said that after the death of her husband, the Kaffir wife meets with other women in some open space of the village, where they sing together, at the same time beating the ground softly with their feet. The following "Kaffir Widow's Lament" appeared in the "Narrative of an Exploratory Tour to the North-East of the Colony of the Cape of Good Hope," by Arbousset and Daumas; London, 1852:—

Women. We are left outside;
We are left to sorrow;
We are left to despair,
Which increases our miseries.

Widow. Oh, that there were a refuge in heaven !
That *there* was a pot and fire !
That *there* were found a place for me !
Oh, that I had wings to fly thither !—
Why have I not wings to fly to heaven ?
Why does there not come down from heaven
a twisted rope ?

I could cling to it, I would mount on high,
I would go and live there.
Oh, foolish woman that I am !
When evening comes I open my window,
I listen in silence, I watch,
I fancy that he returns.

The sentiments expressed in the above tally with the remarks made by Dr. Prichard in his "Natural History of Man," that the Kaffirs believe in the immortality of the soul and also in the attendance the souls of their deceased relatives, whose aid they occasionally invoke.

The whistle is considered a valuable instrument in the limited orchestra of the Kaffirs. The *Marimba* is also in use among the Kaffirs. They have a curious instrument of the stringed kind, which is a bow mounted with a string of twisted hair, and having a gourd attached to the frame-work. Without the gourd, this instrument looks exactly like the *Pináka* of India, which is described as being the invention of the Hindu God *Mahádeva,* and the father of all stringed instruments. It is not unlikely that the *Pináka* made its passage to South Africa, from the Northern regions, the people of which, the Egyptians in particular, were in constant commercial communication with India; or it might have found its way to Egypt, or the Barbary States, the land of the *Barbaras,* (Sanskrit name for uncivilized races), where the *Yaduvansa,* the relations of the Hindu God Krishna,

are said to have settled after the family skirmishes. This instrument is played with a small stick and emits a rather feeble sound. It is held much in favor among both men and women, and is sometimes played by the hour together.

The songs of the Kaffirs are characterised by a wild and quaint sort of melody, and by a strict regard for timing. The Kaffir singer invariably squats on the ground when singing, and delights in strong contrasts, now using a high falsetto and now dropping suddenly into a deep bass. The hunting dance of the Kaffirs takes place, by order of the chief of the tribe, after a successful hunt has been made. This dance consists of the hunters arranging themselves in regular lines, advancing and retreating with the precision of trained soldiers, beating their shields, brandishing their weapons, and working themselves up to a surprising pitch of excitement. The leader of the dance, who faces them, leaps, stamps, and shouts with the energy of a maniac, while the chief sits still, drinks his beer, and occasionally expresses his approval of the proceedings. The following is the translation of a war song of the Kaffirs composed in honor of Tchaka, or, as some say, by the renowned chief himself, when he had made himself master of the whole of Kaffirland:—

Thou hast finished, finished the nations !
Where will you go out to battle now ?
Hey ! where will you go out to battle now ?
Thou hast conquered kings !
Where are you going to battle now ?
Thou hast finished, finished the nations !
Where are you going to battle now ?
Hurrah ! Hurrah ! Hurrah !
Where are you going to battle now ?

The sentiment contained in the above is somewhat like that which Alexander the Great expressed when he lamented that there were no more worlds for him to conquer.

HOTTENTOTIA.

The people called by Europeans Hottentots and Bushmen are said to have among themselves the national appellation of Saabs or Saaps. Quaiquæ is another name which belongs to them generally, and one syllable or rather a portion of this word enters into the epithets of particular tribes of Hottentots, as Namaaqua, Gonaaqua. The word Hottentot is supposed to be a corruption of Houteniqua, the name of a particular tribe now extinct, or at least unknown. Some authors wrote the name of these people Hodmadods, instead of Hottentots. There was a tribe formerly termed Sonquas, and the Bushmen were termed in some old accounts Sonqua Hottentots. The Bushmen (or Bosjesmen) are a branch and sub-division of the Hottentot race, and not a distinct nation as some suppose.

Singing and dancing constitute the chief amusements of the Hottentots, and these are invariably performed at night. The songs of the Hottentots and Bushmen are evidently derived from the same source and their melodies are identical There is this difference in the words of the songs that in the case of the Hottentots the words have some meaning, while in that of the Bushmen, they have not even the semblance of any signification. The subject of the Hottentot's song is generally some adventure which has happened to themselves and its burden is the words " Hoo ! Hoo ! " A peculiar dance prevails among the young Hottentot girls, which goes by the name of the "Melon Dance," on account of a melon being thrown up and caught by the dancer in the course

of her dancing. If another girl catches it, the dancer has to make room for her, and she goes through the same manœuvres, and thus the sport continues till the dancers are tired, when the dance is given up. The dance of the Bushman is also of a singular character. One foot remains motionless, while the other dances in a quick, wild, and irregular way. When one foot is tired out, the second one comes forward to take its place and goes through similar evolutions. The dancer uses the word "Wawa-koo" repeatedly, while the spectators respond with the word "Aye O," separating the hands at the first syllable, and bringing them sharply together at the second.

Herr Lichtenstein, who lived for several years in South Africa, states that the Hottentots produced on the *Gorah,* their favorite national instrument of old, the interval of a *third* standing between the major and minor third of the European scale; a *fifth* between the perfect and diminished fifth; and a *seventh* between the minor seventh and superfluous sixth. He adds that the Hottentots stuck to these intervals in their songs as well. The fondness of the Hottentots for music and their susceptibility for harmony have been mentioned by several writers. The missionaries mention that whenever they taught the Hottentots a simple hymn or psalm tune, they instantly added the *second* of their own accord as if by natural instinct. The men are generally possessed of a tenor voice. Mr. W. L. Burchell gives a description and some specimens of the songs of the Bushmen in his "Travels in the Interior of Southern Africa." These songs, which are also dances, consist of one part which is sung by the dancer, of a second part sung at the same time by the spectators, and of a rhythmical accompaniment of the water-drum, which, at the performance at which Burchell was present, was beaten

with the right fore-finger by an old woman. The water-drum is a bamboo or wooden jug with a piece of wet parchment strained over the top, and containing water to keep the parchment wet. The *Gorah,* mentioned above, is a slender stick, with a string of cat-gut, drawn from end to end, so as to give it a slight curve like the bow of a violin. To the lower end of this string, a flat piece of an ostrich's quill, about an inch and a half long, is attached, which connects that end of the string with the stick. This quill, being applied to the lips, is made to vibrate by strong inspirations and respirations of the breath; and whilst the principle upon which its different tones are produced may be classed with the trumpet or French horn, the tone itself, in the hands of a master-player, approaches to that of the violin. At time of playing, the performers sometimes put one of their fore-fingers into their left nostrils, holding the instrument with that hand, and the other into their right ear. The Hottentots have contrived to construct a rude kind of violin, having ecome acquainted with that instrument through the Dutch boors who settled among them. A modified form of the *Goura* (or *Gorah*), under the name of *Joum joum,* is used by the women, who do not play upon it by the breath, but strike it with a stick. On account of the portable size of the Jew's harp (whose tone the *Goura* resembles), the Hottentots and the Bush-men have latterly shown a preference for it. There are two more musical instruments used by these people, one being a guitar called *Rabouquin,* (which looks somewhat like the Banjo of the Negroes), and the other a drum designated the *Romelpot,* which is made of a hollowed log, over one end of which a piece of tanned skin is tightly stretched, and which is beaten sometimes with sticks and sometimes with the fists Among the offshoots of the Hottentots is a tribe called

Kora, Koraqua, Korans, or Korannas, of whom the Missionary Moffatt has expressed a very high opinion. They were found by him impatiently desirous of gaining knowledge. While he was one day engaged in teaching some of the young Korannas the rudiments of learning, some of the young people came dancing and skipping towards him and insisted upon being taught the A B C with music—a discovery which they had made through one of his boys. "The tune of *Auld Lang Syne*," says Mr. Moffatt, "was pitched to A B C, each succeeding round was joined by succeeding voices until every tongue was vocal and every countenance beamed with heartfelt satisfaction. The longer the song, the more freedom was felt, and *Auld Lang Syne* was echoed to the farthest end of the village."

ZULULAND.

In his work, "Missionary Labors and Scenes in Southern Africa," London, 1842, the Missionary Robert Moffatt describes a dance of the Zulu firs in which the king himself acted as director. Moselekatse (the king) took his stand in the centre of an immense circle of his soldiers, numbers of women being present, who, with their shrill voices and clapping of hands, took part in the concert. About thirty ladies from his harem marched to the song backward and forward. War songs, and one composed on the occasion of the visit of the strangers, were sung under the guidance of the king. After the performance was over, he sat down on his shield of lion's skin, and asked Moffat if it was not fine, and if he had such a thing in his own country. The Zulus have the musical bow, which they call the *Gubo*; but, unlike the variety in use among the Kaffirs, it has no gourd resonator attached to it.

EASTERN AFRICA.

THE Revd. Dr. Lewis Krapf in his "Travels, Researches, and Missionary Labors," London, 1860, makes mention of a singular kind of telegraph by means of drums, made by the people of Kaffa, a district in Eastern Africa :—"At given distances drummers are placed near a tall tree, any one of whom upon sighting an enemy immediately climbs the tree and signals the event by so many beats of the drum, which is taken up by the next drummer also mounting his tree for the purpose, and so on to the end of the line. They have various other signals, all well understood." The Kaffirs in Eastern Africa use a kind of rattle for the purpose of expelling a malady. Captain Burton describes the *Sange* of the medicine-men and rain-makers of the Kafirs on the coast of Zanzibar, as "a hollow gourd, of pine-apple shape, pierced with various holes, prettily carved, and half filled with maise, grams, and pebbles ; the handle is a stick passed through its length, and secured by cross-pins." A person suffering from illness is believed to be visited by an evil spirit, called *p'hepo*, and the *Mnganga*, or medicine-man, is expected to heal the patient by expelling the unwelcome guest by means of his mysterious chants and rhythmical noise. The airs of the natives of Mozambique have a deal of liveliness in them. The *Ambira* is popular among the people of Mozambique. The inhabitants of the East use a "huge bassoon of black wood," which goes by the name of *Siwa*. The *Zeze* (*Tzetze*) or Banjo is one of the most

v

important instruments of the East Coast. The Wajiji, an East African tribe, have a rude tom-tom made, as Captain Burton says, of "a pair of foolscap-shaped plates of thin iron, joined at the apices and connected at the bases by a solid cross-bar of the same metal." This drum is beat with a muffled stick. The drums used in Mombassa are covered on the head with snake skin.

MADAGASCAR.

MADAGASCAR is inhabited by Malagasies, Hovas, and other tribes of Papuan, Malay, Arabian and Kaffir origin. The Malagasies have some knowledge of musical sounds and are known to have invented some instruments which are far superior to those of the African tribes. One of the best is the violin. Another instrument of Madagascar is the *Lokanga* which is a guitar with four strings and a wooden body grotesquely carved, painted and decorated with feathers. The Rev. William Ellis relates that he has often seen more than a hundred men dragging a single tree past his house, "keeping time with the *Lokanga* played on the way before them."

EUROPE.

GREECE.

ANCIENT PERIOD.

IT is stated that Cadmus landed in Greece, at the head of a Phœnician colony, and founded the kingdom of Thebes, about two years before the Exodus of Israel (B. C. 1493). He is said to have first brought to that country letters and music. This account is, perhaps, not altogether correct; for it would appear from the Oxford marbles, that Hyagnis, a native of Celænæ (the capital of Phrygia), who flourished 1506 B. C., invented the flute, or pipe, and the Phrygian mode, as well as the *nomes* or airs that were sung to Cybele, the mother of the gods, to Bacchus, to Pan, and to other deities. It may, therefore, be concluded, that the Greeks derived their music partly from Phrygia, partly from Phœnicia, and partly from Ætolia, Ionia, and Doris, after which countries their principal modes were subsequently named. According to some authorities, Harmonia, the wife of Cadmus, introduced the *Monaulos* or single pipe, into Greece: according to others, the invention of this instrument is attributable to Minerva, who is said to have substituted it for the Syrinx or pipe of Pan. Pan was led to the invention of this pipe from noticing the effect of the wind rushing through and over a bundle of reeds which he clasped in his arms, instead of the

nymph Syrinx, she being changed into reeds when flying from his embraces. The *Syrinx* consisted of a number of reeds, of unequal lengths, tied together. It was played upon by blowing into them, one after the other, moving the instrument backwards and forwards to admit the wind into each tube. It was for long a popular instrument with the shepherds, and was subsequently improved by the use of *foramina* or holes and stops. The Greeks who lived by the sea-shore, very likely, used shells as musical instrument; and this fact would account for the representation of the Tritons blowing their conches before the chariot of Neptune. They also had pipes, formed out of oaten reeds, called *Avena*. The *Tibia* was originally a pipe made of the shank or shin-bone of an animal. After the discovery of the art of boring had been made, the flutes were made of box.tree, laurel, brass, silver, and sometimes of gold. Sometimes the flute had a horn attached to the end of it, by which it took the shape of a lituus, or clarion, which was the characteristic of the Phrygian flute. To Mercury is attributed the invention of the lyre. He is said to have retired with some oxen (which he had stolen from Apollo), to the foot of a mountain in Arcadia where he found a tortoise which he killed and ate. While amusing himself with the shell, he noticed the sound it emitted from its concave fig on which he cut several thongs from a bull's hide, fastened them tight to it, and thus invented a new kind of music. The art of playing upon the lyre is ascribed to Apollo, well known in Greece as the great patron of music. At the Pythian games (which were instituted in honor of his killing the serp nt Python), music and poetry formed subjects for prizes. Some of the earliest specimens of Grecian poetry are hymns to this deity. Contemporary with him was Marsyas, the reputed inventor

of the double flute. Among the other musicians of the fabulous period were the Muses, Bacchus, and the Sirens. Bacchus was celebrated for performing on the flute The Muses added the string called *mesè*, or A, to the lyre which had up to that time consisted of three strings, *viz.*, *Hypate meson* (E), *Parhypate meson* (F), and *meson Diatonos* (G) The most celebrated Greek musicians of the ancient period were (1) Orpheus (B. C. 1300), who wrote several hymns, improved the flute, and added to the lyre the strings named *Hypate* (B), and *Parhypate* (C), and who is reported to have attracted wild beasts by the charms of his music; (2) Linus, (the pupil of Orpheus and tutor of Hercules), who added one string to the lyre (D); (3) Musæus, the son or pupil of Orpheus; (4) Thamyris, to whom Orpheus taught the use of the lyre; (5) Chiron, the tutor of Achilles; (6) Amphion, (the son of Jupiter and Antiope), to the music of whose lyre the rocks danced, and the stones arose and formed themselves into the walls of Thebes, and to whom the in ention of the Lydian mode is attributed.

In the Iliad and Odyssey, Homer mentions not more than three instruments, *viz.*, the *Lyre*, the *Flute*, and the *Syrinx*; from this it may be justly concluded that no others were known at the time of the Trojan war. From his w ks it would also appear that the bards or rhapsodists, who sang their poems *extempore* in the streets or palaces, were treated with the greatest respect. The Greeks had special songs suited to their different trades and rural occupations. Homer describes Calypso weaving and singing, thus:—

> While she with work and song the time divides,
> And through the loom the golden shuttle guides.
>
> *Odyssey* (Pope's Translation)

Again, when the companions of Ulysses approached the palace of Circe —

> "Now on the threshhold of the dome they stood,
> And heard a voice resounding through the wood
> Placed at her loom within, the goddess sun "

In Book IX of the Iliad, Homer mentions a *Phorminx* (a kind of lyre) made of silver :—

> "The well-wrought harp from conquer'd Thebæ came;
> Of polish'd silver was its costly frame."

The Greeks had blind mendicants singing and soliciting alms from door to door. The singer carr d on his hand a raven (Greek name, *Corone*,)—a bird sacred to Apollo. The following is the first stanza of a song of one of these beggars which Athenæus has preserved from Phœnix of Colophon, an iambic poet :—

> Ye who to sorrow's tender tale
> With pity lend an ear,
> A tribute to Corone bring,
> Apollo's favorite care.

These mendicants were called Coronistæ, and their songs Coronismata. During the period which is being described, the Olympic, the Pythian, the Nemean, and the Isthmian games were instituted, at all of which, and at the Pythian games particularly, a considerable impetus was given to the cause of music. It is stated by Lucian that at one of these games a young flute-player, named Harmonides, who appeared there for the first time, began a solo with so violent a blast that he breathed his last breath into the instrument and died on the spot.

Of the Greek lyrists, Alcman, Stersichorus, Alcæus. Sappho, Simonides, Ibycus, Bacchylides, Anacreon, Callistratus, Arion, and Pindar are the most

celebrated. They extended over a period of over two hundred years, and enriched with their compositions three out of the four dialects of Greece.

Several eminent musicians flourished in Greece during the interval between the time of Homer and that of Sappho (B. C. 600); and among these are Thaletes of Crete (870 B. C.), an excellent singer and flute-player; Archilochus (700 B. C.), the inventor of lyric poetry, and of that kind of composition, which, now called the "the recitative accompanied", was afterwards adopted by the dithyrambic and tragic poets; Olympus, the Phrygian, (697 B. C.), who is said to have been descended from the first Olympus and whose attainments are highly spoken of by Plato, Aristotle, and Plutarch; Terpander (650 B. C.), who invented the notation, who is considered one of the earliest writers of the *Scholia*, or convivial songs of the Greeks, and who is said to have been the first Greek musician to use 7 strings on the lyre; Tyrtæus, who was contemporary to Terpander, and whose songs were very popular; and Mimnermus of Smyrna, who flourished at the beginning of the 6th century before the Christian era.

From the time of Pindar (522 to 400 B. C.) to the conquest of Greece by the Romans may be reckoned the classic age of that country. It was during this age that the following celebrities lived and wrote:—Æschylus, Sophocles, Euripides, Herodotus, Thucydides, Xenophon, Pythagoras, Plato, Aristotle, Aristoxenus, Euclid, Theocritus, Callimachus, &c., &c. It was during this era that the drama was invented and its combination with music contributed to the progress of both. All the tragedies were set to music. The poets themselves were musicians. They adapted airs to their own pieces, which they recited to the lyre. The Greek drama consisted

of soliloquy, dialogue and choruses. The first two were declaimed to a kind of recitative, while the last were sung in the time of Æschylus by 50 persons, the number being subsequently reduced by law to 15. The leader of the chorus was called *Coryphæus*. Each of the principal odes or choruses was divided into (1) *Strophe*, which was sung by the chorus moving to the right, (2) *Antistrophe*, while moving to the left, and (3) *Epode*, after these two evolutions were performed, the choristers standing still. Among the musicians of this era were Timotheus, Phrynis, Antigenidas, Philoxenus, Arion, Dorion, Ismenias, Telephanes, and Lamia (a female flutist). Of the eminent musical theorists of ancient Greece, Lasus, a native of Hermione (a city of Peloponnesus), was one of the earliest (B. C. 548.) Another celebrated theorist was Pythagoras, the Samian philosopher, who died about 497 B. C., at the age of 71. He considered numbers as the principles of every thing, and was the first who applied them to the theory of music. He appears to have been the first who attempted to give a theory of sounds: he supposed the air to be the *vehicle* of sounds; and its agitation, produced and accompained by a similar agitation of the sounding body, to be the *cause* of it. He was the first of the Greeks who entertained the notion of the music of the spheres : he taught that the seven planets, and the sphere of fixed stars, united in harmonious concert, and he apportioned different tones to each planet, according to their distance from the earth. He invented the harmonical canon, or *monochord*, of a single string, furnished with moveable bridges and contrived for the measuring and adjusting the ratios of musical intervals by accurate divisions. It is stated that on his death-bed he recommended this instrument as the musical investigator,—the criterion of truth. He is said to have added the eighth string to the lyre, and according

to some, to have devised the musical notation of the Greeks, and to have introduced a diatonic order of intervals, consisting of two disjunct tetrachords. Aristoxenus (B. C. 394), who learned philosophy and music under Aristotle, wrote several treatises on the latter subject. Euclid treated of music as well as of mathematics.

Of musical instruments, the Flute appears to have been in high favor in ancient Greece. The Lacedemonians had a song which said that "a good performer on the flute would make a man brave every danger, and face even iron itself." They played an air called *Adonion* on the Flutes called *Tibiæ Embateriæ* (Flutes to march to), when on the point of attacking an enemy. Immense prices were sometimes given for Flutes. It is said that Ismenias (the celebrated Theban musician) gave three talents, (or £581,5*s*) for one at Corinth, and that Theodorus, a flute maker of Athens, made considerable money by selling this instrument. The Lyre also was held in so high an estimation that it was said in derision that Greece was governed by the Lyre, as Egypt was called the country of Sistrums. There were several varieties of the Lyre, *viz.*, the *Phorminx, Cithara, Chelys, Testudo,* &c. Quintilian remarks that "among the stringed instruments, you will find the *Lyre* of a character analogous to masculine, from the great depth, or gravity and roughness of its tones; the *Sambuka* of a feminine character, weak and delicate, and, from its great acuteness, and the smallness of its strings, tending to dissolve and enervate. Of the intermediate instruments, the *Polypthongum* partakes most of the feminine; but the *Cithara* differs not much from the masculine character of the *Lyre*." Other instruments were in use in Greece, such as the *Nabla*,

the *Barbiton*, the *Trigonon*, the *Magadis*, and others The first three were stringed instruments, and it is doubtful whether the *Magadis* was a stringed or a wind instrument. A Greek vase deposited in the Munich Museum has depicted on it the representation of Polyhymnia with a harp. This valuable relic dates from the time of Alexander the Great. The instrument is represented as having thirteen strings which are being touched by Polyhymnia with both hands, the right hand being used for the treble and the left for the bass. The *Sambuka* of the Greeks (which is believed to have been identical with the *Sabeka* of the Chaldæan people) is described by some writers as of a triangular shape, and mounted with four short strings; according to others, it was boat-shaped. Drieberg believes it to have been a kind of guitar. Pythagoras, the Zacynthian, invented a curious instrument called the Tripodian Lyre. It resembled in shape the Delphic Tripod; the three legs supported a vase, which served as a sound-board, and the strings were placed between the legs; thus forming, in fact, three Lyres which were tuned to the Doric, Lydian, and Phrygian modes, and played with such dexterity (by striking the strings with the fingers of the right hand, using the plectrum in the left, and turning the instrument round with his foot), that those who did not see him supposed that three persons were performing. Athenæus says that after the death of Pythagoras, no other instrument of the kind was ever constructed. The harpers received large sums for giving performances. It is stated that one Amœbæus received one talent, or £193, 15*s*, for a single performance at the theatre. Besides the Flute, the Greeks had other wind instruments, *viz.*, the Syrinx, the double-pipe, and latterly the trumpet, bagpipe (*Askaulos*), and wind-organ. The trumpet was not in use in the Trojan war, the first

signals of battle being lighted torches to which succeeded shells of fish, the conch, or *Buccina*. The knowledge of the trumpet is said to have been derived by them from the Etruscans, in the time of the Heraclidæ. With reference to instruments of percussion, the Greeks had the *Tympanum, Parvum Tympanum*, or *Tympanolum*, or varieties of the Drum; *Cymbalum, Crotalum*, or Cymbals; and *Campanum*, or Bells. The *Crotali* resembled the Egyptian instrument of the same name. Anacreon mentions the *Ascarus. Nyagale*, which was a percussive instrument, a cubit square every way, and, when struck, produced a sound like the *Crotala*. It is severally called an invention of the Troglodytes, Libyans, and Thracians. Several other instruments are described by classical authors, but there are no means of identifying or describing them in an accurate way. Most of the instruments which the Greeks possessed, and specially the stringed varieties, were derived from Asia. In conjunction with this may be taken the fact that many of the noted musicians of Greece were natives of Asia Minor, or of some island adjacent to it. Marsyas, who was contemporary to Apollo, was a Phrygian, and Olympus, his pupil and the reputed inventor of the old Enharmonic scale, was a native of Mysias, also in Asia. Terpander, Arion, and Sappho were natives of the island of Lesbos. It was this Olympus who, according to Plutarch, brought into Greece the practice of touching the strings of the Lyre with a quill, for before his time they were vibrated with the fingers.

The most ancient musical system of the Greeks appears to have been the "old Enharmonic genus," the invention of which, as mentioned above, is attributed to Olympus of Mysias (B. C. 1250); the scale of which resembled the ancient Scottish scale in the minor key, omitting the fourths and sevenths. Dr. Burney states

that "the cast of the old national Greek airs was much like that of the old Scots music." How long this "old Enharmonic" system prevailed, it is impossible to ascertain. It was succeeded first by the *Diatonic* genus (or tetrachord, proceeded by a semi-tone and two tones); next by the *Chromatic* genus, which consisted of semitones and minor thirds; and then by the *Enharmonic* genus which consisted of two quarter-tones and a major third. The *Chromatic* genus was invented by Timotheus, the Milesian, (who was born 346 B. C.), and was contemporaneous with Alexander the Great. It is stated that Timotheus was banished by the Senate from Sparta, for, among other innovations which he introduced in the music of the country, "rendering melody infamous, by composing in the Chromatic, instead of the Enharmonic," (the "old Enharmonic genus" of Olympus). The new Enharmonic genus was introduced about the time of Eratosthenes, who died B. C. 194. There were five principal modes in Grecian music, *viz.*, the *Dorian*, *Lydian*, *Phrygian*, *Ionian*, and *Etolian*,—all the names being derived from Asiatic countries. The *Dorian* was the gravest, the *Phrygian* was in the middle, and the *Lydian* the acutest. The *Ionian* was placed in point of character between the *Dorian* and the *Phrygian*, and the *Etolian*, between the *Phrygian* and the *Lydian*. The *Dorian* was grave and magnificent, neither too diffusive, gay, nor varied; but severe and vehement; exciting and spirit-stirring, "such as raised to height of noblest temper heroes old, arming to battle." The *Ionian*, was neither brilliant nor effeminate, but rough and austere, with some degree of elevation, force, and energy. The *Phrygian* was consecrated to religious ceremonies. The *Etolian* was grand and pompous; and the *Lydian*, mild and soothing. The Greek system of music included Sounds, Intervals, Muta-

tions, Melopœia, and Rhythm. *Sounds* meant the elements of music; *Intervals*, the difference between sounds, the least of which was the Enharmonic diesis or fourth of a tone; *Mutations* signified the changes in genus, mode, time, or air; Melopœia, the art of composition, and, in a strict sense, included Intervals, Mutations, and *Rhythm*, or the measurement of time, which was very different from the modern rhythm, being, with the ancients, prescribed by the long and short syllables of the poetry, and had no other variety than that allowed by its metrical laws. Several authorities on music agree in remarking that the Greeks possessed the knowledge of harmony, or counterpoint, though not exactly in the modern acceptation of the term.

Before Terpander invented his system of notation, the Grecian melodies, like those of the Egyptians and Hebrews, were handed down traditionally from generation to generation. Terpander's method consisted in using the alphabets to denote musical sounds. There are only four specimens of ancient Greek music in their supposed original notation that have come down to the present age. Three of them are hymns addressed to Calliope, Apollo, and Nemesis, which were found among the papers of the Archbishop Usher. The fourth was found in a monastery, near Messina, by Kircher. It consists of the first eight verses of the first Pythic ode of Pindar, set to musical characters corresponding to those attributed by Alypius to the Lydian mode.

MODERN PERIOD

As in the classical times, rhapsodists abound in modern Greece, some of whom are blind, who go from village to village and from fair to fair, singing songs to the accompaniment of a stringed instrument. The songs embrace a variety of subjects,—historical, nuptial, domestic, topical and others. The funeral song, called *Myriologia*, is of very high antiquity. Homer describes the whole family of Priam as mourning over the corpse of Hector ; and the custom has come down to the modern Greeks. The *Myriologues* are sung by women only, and are always *extempore*. These elegiac songs are sung to music which, in its general character, closely resembles the Gregorian chant ; but they have this peculiarity that while other songs generally end in a low note these terminate in a high one. The character of Greek songs is exceedingly simple, and the music seems more nearly allied to plaintive chants than to the music of other European nations. The air is frequently comprised in a single verse, usually in two, but never in more. It is often lengthened by the arbitrary introduction of words between the verses, in the shape of burden. M. Fauriel states that he heard many songs sung to Italian airs, long since forgotten in Italy. The music of modern Greece does not bear much resemblance to that of ancient Greece. At a dinner given at the Mansion House, London, in October, 1824, four young Greek gentlemen, who were among the guests, were asked by the Lord Mayor to entertain the party with their national music. The melodies they sang on the occasion were founded on the modern Diatonic scale and

did not partake of the character of their ancient music. This shows that the Chromatic and Enharmonic systems that prevailed in the country in the olden times have now been lost. Dodwell describes the music of the modern Greeks as being in general "harsh and offensive to the ear," while other authorities speak of it in glowing terms. The only foreign tune they have any relish for is, according to Dodwell, the "Malbrouke," which was introduced into Constantinople by the Franks, and is sung in many of the Greek towns. As they did in Homer's time, the Greeks frequently dance as they sing. The *Romaika* and *Syrto* of the modern Greeks and Albanians are generally supposed to have been derived from the Pyrrhic dance. Rochlitz relates that on one occasion he played on the piano a Greek dance-tune to a young Greek who was visiting Leipzig. To this Rochlitz played an accompaniment very commonly used in piano-forte music. Having listened for some time, the young Greek recognized the melody of his country, and on its being repeated grew enthusiastic over it, but he could not reconcile himself to the accompaniment. The player then tried whether a substitution of detatched chords, struck *arpeggio*, would prove more agreeable. This appeared somewhat more to the taste of his hearer, though not altogether to his satisfaction, as he remarked :—"It is so, and is not so." The Church music of the modern Greeks is described as very monotonous and as being soporofic in its tendency. The invention of the characters of the musical notation of the Greek Church is generally attributed to St. John of Damascus, while Fétis holds that this notation belonged to ancient Egypt, the characters resembling the demotic or popular characters of that country. The Greeks have now made considerable improvements in the art of teaching music. The system is now so simplified that it may be taught in two years,

whereas formerly it could not be mastered, it is stated, in less than thirty years, owing to the large number of arbitrary characters used in the notation, to which each professor gave his own interpretation.

Among the instruments used in modern Greece are the *Cavonto* and *Bouzouki* which are of the *Tamboura* class and played with a quill, the *Lyra* (the *Kemangeh* of the Turks, played with a bow), the *Floyera* (shepherd's pipe), and varieties of the flute and clarionet.

The following "Farewell of a dying chieftain" is a specimen of the songs of modern Greece :—

The sun was sinking in the west,
When Demos thus his sons address'd :—
"My sons, your evening meal provide,
Then come and seat ye at my side.
Thou, Lamprakis, hope of my race,
There ! take my arms and fill my place.
My sons, my much loved sabres take,
Cut boughs a verdant couch to make ;
And when upon it I am laid,
Go, call the priest my soul to aid.—
Full fifty years my land I served,
Nor ever from my duty swerved.—
Prepare my tomb, and mako it large ;
Place me in act the foe to charge ;
And in it leave a passage free,
Where spring's sweet bird may visit me,
And nightingales, whose notes may bring
The tidings of returning spring."

TURKEY.

THOUGH Mahomedans form the ruling race of this country, they represent about a fourth of the population, the remainder consisting of Romans, Greeks, Slavonians, Armenians, and Jews. There is, therefore, no *national* music of this country, in the usual acceptation of the term ; but each nation inhabiting it practices its own. Dr. Frankl visited on a Sabbath in Constantinople the Jewish Synagogue Bene Hamikra, belonging to the Karaites. He describes what he saw and heard as follows :—"A handsome boy, about twelve years of age, in a green caftan, with a red fez and yellow slippers, walked up to the elevated table covered with a beautiful carpet, which was brought into the middle of the Synagogue. He fell down on his knees, and, like a Mussalman at prayers, touched the pavement with his forehead, and then stood up and sang with a beautiful clear voice a song of praise to God ; the congregation sang the concluding verse as a chorus. The boy sang a similar song between the customary bending of the knees and the head after the *thora*, a book of parchment (there are no rolls among the Karaites), had been read." The *Zikrs* of the dervishes (referred to in the previous pages of this book) have been frequently described by travellers in Turkey, Egypt, and other Eastern countries. Mr. E. D. Clark, who witnessed a performance in a mosque at Tophané, a suburb of Constantinople, gives as follows

a circumstantial account of it, in his "Travels in Various Countries of Europe, Asia, and Africa", London, 1810 :—

"As we entered the mosque we observed twelve or fourteen dervishes walking slowly round, before a Superior, in a small space surrounded with rails, beneath the dome of the building. Several spectators were stationed on the outside of the railing ; and being, as usual, ordered to take off our shoes, we joined the party. In a gallery over the entrance were stationed two or three performers on the Tambourine and Turkish pipes. Presently the dervishes, crossing their arms over their breasts, and with each of their hands grasping their shoulders, began obeisance to the Superior, who stood with his back against the wall, facing the door of the mosque. Then each in succession, as he passed the Superior, having finished his bow, began to turn round, first slowly, but afterwards with such velocity that his long garments, flying out in the rotatory motion, the whole party appeared spinning like so many umbrellas upon their handles. As they began, their hands were disengaged from their shoulders, and raised gradually above their heads. At length, as the velocity of the whirl increased, they were all seen with their arms extended horizontally, and their eyes closed, turning with inconceivable rapidity." (During this exhibition, the music consisted of a chorus of voices accompanied by pipes and drums. One of the dervishes, dressed in a green pelisse, walked in the middle of the circle formed by the dancers, and regulated the ceremony with the utmost watchfulness and care. This lasted about fifteen minutes). "Suddenly, on a signal given by the director of the dance, unobserved by the spectators, the dervishes all stopped at the same instant, like the wheels of a machine, and, what is more extraordinary, all

in one circle, with their faces invariably towards the centre, crossing their arms on their breasts, and grasping their shoulders as before, bowing together with the utmost regularity at the same instant, almost to the ground. We regarded them with astonishment,—not one of them being in the slightest degree out of breath, heated, or having countenance at all changed. After this they began to walk as at first, each following the other within the railing and passing the Superior as before. As soon as their obeisance had been made they began to turn again. This second exhibition lasted as long as the first, and was similarly concluded. They then began to turn for the third time; and as the dance lengthened, the music grew louder and more animating. Perspiration became evident on the features of the dervishes; the extended garments of some among them began to droop; and little accidents occurred, such as their striking against each other. They nevertheless persevered, until large drops of sweat falling from their bodies upon the floor, such a degree of friction was thereby occasioned that the noise of their feet rubbing the floor was heard by the spectators. Upon this the third and last signal was made for them to halt, and the danee was ended. This extraordinary performance is considered miraculous by the Turks. By their law, every species of dancing is prohibited, and yet, in such veneration is this ceremony held, that an attempt to abolish it would excite insurrection among the people."

A collection of some of the tunes sung in connection with these dances was made by a gentleman at one time attached to the Austrian Legation in Constantinople, who had frequent opportunities of witnessing these performances, and being himself of a musical turn of mind, took great care to render the music as correctly as possible in notation.

The following are the principal stringed instruments in use among the Turks :—(1) The *Kanoon,* the favorite among the ladies of the upper classes. The instrument is mounted with 72 strings of gut, in sets of 3, producing 24 distinct tones. It is played with a plectrum of tortoise shell, or silver. (2) The *Santir,* strung with 72 strings in sets of 4, and played with two wooden hammers. (3) Varieties of the *Tamboura,* of which the largest in shape is called *Tanbour Kebyr Tourky*—these are mounted with wire strings, furnished mostly with frets of gut, and played with a plectrum. (4) The *Kemangeh,* a violin mounted with three strings of gut and wire. (5) The *Fellahee,* a rude instrument strung with strings of coarse gut. The body is of wood cut into the shape of an octagon. The wind instruments consist of the *Ghaida* (Bagpipe), the *Zourna* (Oboe), and varieties of the *Nay* (Flute). The *Gele-masha,* or *Bell-tongs,* a kind of cymbals, comes under the class of instruments of percussion. The drums include the *Darabukkeh,* the *Dervish drum* (which is made of brass), and the *Daira* (which is a tambourine of an octagonal shape and decorated on the sides with looking glass).

Up to the time of the Greek revolution, the ablest musicians of Turkey were Greeks of Constantinople and Smyrna. The favorite singer of the Sultan Mahmud was a Greek named Chiveli-Oglou Zorgaki. Many of the popular songs of modern Turkey are of Greek composition. The favorite songs of Turkey relate either to love or war. The love songs are invariably accompanied by the *Tamboura Bouzourk.* Instrumental music within doors is exclusively performed by female slaves whose value increases according to their musical attainments A special group of percussion and wind instruments are used for the military or *Janissary* music of the Turks ;

and among these are the "Mohammad's standard,"—the national instrument of the Turks, which consists of a brass frame with numerous bells, carried on a long perpendicular pole, the point of which is surmounted by the crescent and streamers of horse-hair; an elongated roll-drum, a big drum, a triangle, metal clappers, piccolos, oboes, horns, and trumpets. The dancing dervishes of Constantinople are well known for their skill in playing upon the *Nay* which accompanies the *Zikr*. Fétis relates that they were once banished from Constantinople because they had introduced music into Moslem worship; but they were subsequently restored by the Sultan, on their explaining that the Koran contained no injunctions against the use of song or of the flute in connection with prayer or exercises of religion.

Guiseppe Donizetti, a brother of the celebrated composer Gaetano Donizetti, was director of the Sultan's band in Constantinople, where he died in 1856. He was the composer of the Turkish "March of Mahmud II."

Some account is given below of the music of Roumania and Servia which form Tributary States of Turkey.

ROUMANIA.

The music of Wallachia (a Sub-division of Roumania) is marked by a predilection for the *superfluous second*. The *Hora* is a characteristic dance of the Wallachians and the modulation of its tune is of a peculiar kind. The instruments usually employed in a Wallachian band are three or four violins, a Pandean pipe, and a kind of guitar, or rather lute, called *Kobsa*. The effect of embellishments given to their melodies is described as

charming. The Wallachian lullaby is noted for its simplicity. The words for one of these songs run as follows :—*Nan-i pan-i pui-u mam-i.* The *Tambouritza* is a modern instrument used in Roumania. The body and handle are made of three different kinds of wood. The instrument is mounted with four wire strings.

SERVIA.

Unlike the tunes of European nations which generally end in the tonic, those of the Servians frequently conclude with the interval of the *second.* One of the national dances of the Servians is called *Kolo,* and in these melodies a preference is given to the *minor seventh.* The famous Servian march and song, " Rise, Servians, rise to arms !" is said to exercise the same fascinating power upon the Servians as the Marseillaise upon the French, and the Rákotzy march upon the Hungarians. The drinking songs of Servia are set to music of the gravity and solemnity of devotional songs. When a Servian entertains his friends at his table, he lifts his glass, pronounces a couplet or two in honor of his guests, and proceeds to sing what may be called a Drinking Hymn, in which the whole party joins. The music seems to be comparatively modern since it does not exhibit much of the peculiarities of construction that characterise the old melodies. The following are the words of one of the Drinking songs :—

Worthy friends, my welcome guests !
Worthy friends, my welcome guests !
Heav'n be thank'd that we are met
Here in social fellowship !

AUSTRIA.

THE Austrian national hymn "Gott erhalte [Franz] den Kaiser" is a composition by Joseph Haydn which was suggested to him by the effect which "God save the King" had on public and solemn occasions in England where he had been on a visit. This hymn was for the first time performed at the celebration of the birth-day of the Emperor Franz on the 12th February, 1797, at the theatre in Vienna. The poetry was by L. Leopold Haschka. Subsequently, in the reign of the Emperor Ferdinand, other words were substituted, written by Baron Zedlitz. The air is said to be thoroughly German in its character.

The *Streich Zither* is an instrument of modern Austria. It is strung with four wire strings. It is placed horizontally upon a table and played with a bow.

HUNGARY.

The Hungarians who, like the Russians, the Poles, the Bohemians, &c., originated from Scythia, settled in Europe about the ninth century, bringing with them the instruments which they used in their native country, and which consisted almost exclusively of wind instruments. It appears that in 1192 of the Christian era, a person was sent to Paris to learn French music ; but it was not till the reign of Corvinus, who was proclaimed King of Hungary at the age of 15, in 1458, and reigned till 1490,

that any improvement was effected in the music of the country During this rule, vocal music attained to so much excellence that the Pope's nuncio, who visited Buda in 1483, said in a letter to His Holiness that "the singers of this prince's chapel are the best of all those I have ever heard." Though music was studied and its interests were promoted under his successors, Ladislaus VI and Lewis II, it did not come up to the standard maintained by Corvinus in regard to the grandeur of musical establishments and in the number of bands kept. The Magyars form nearly one-half of the population of Hungary; their music may, therefore, justly be taken as the national music of Hungary. It partakes largely of the character of the people—being sad and plaintive. The original music of the Magyars has been to some extent affected by the gipsies by whom it is even now chiefly cultivated in Hungary. The repeated introduction of the *superfluous second* contributes much to the plaintive and impressive effect of the Hungarian songs. The *catch* occurs most usually in the middle of a bar, and specially towards the end of a section. Modulations from a major key into a minor key frequently occur in the music of the Hungarians, and of some Slavonic nations. The patriotic songs of the Hungarians often produced a surprising effect. It is related that at a repast given by Attila, the Enckesius, or director of the music, had a seat on the right hand of the throne; and after the service two men sang verses in honor of Attila's victories. A portion of the audience shed tears, while the rest waxed furious and expressed a wish to be led to battle. Two stanzas of these songs have been preserved in their original language and also in Latin. The following translation of them appeared in Rees's *Cyclopædia* :—

Let us ever remember those ancient domains,
Which our ancestors left, when they flew
To a climate more mild, from the Scythian plains,
Where dread mountains of snow are in view.

To Hungary they hast'nd, with God for their guide,
And chose Transylvania for home ;
Be their force and their courage for ever their pride,
But, like them, let us ne'er again roam.

The Rákotzy march, which is the most widely known of all Hungarian tunes, fairly represents the characteristics of Hungarian music. There are, however, some older compositions extant, bearing the name of Rákotzy, and dating from the beginning of the eighteenth century, when the Transylvanian prince Franz Rákotzy unsuccessfully opposed the power of Austria. The prohibition by the Austrian Government of the performance of the Rákotzy march on public occasions, and the confiscation of the printed copies in the music shops, seem to have added a stimulus to the preservation of the cherished tune in the hearts of the people. "When I hear the Rákotzy," a Hungarian gentleman was once heard to exclaim, "I feel as if I must at once go to war to conquer the world. My fingers convulsively twitch to seize a pistol, a sword, a bludgeon, or whatever weapon may be at hand,—I must clutch it and march forward!" The present Austro-Hungarian Government (that of Francis Joseph) have given a great impetus to the cause of music by holding under their patronage an International Musical and Theatrical Exhibition, in Vienna, in the year 1892. The famous composer Franz Liszt was born at Raidings in Hungary, October 22, 1811, and died July 31, 1886. The well known violinist Remenyi, born in 1830, is also a native of Hungary.

BOHEMIA.

The natural capacity fcr harmony of the country people in Bohemia is considerably nourished in the village schools, where the children are often taught to sing together two-part songs. The practice thus begun in early life enables them to unite their voices very effectively in performing their favorite national airs when they come of age. Two old dances of the country people have been published in which bars of different measure occur in a distinctly symmetrical order. A large variety of dances prevails in Bohemia.

DALMATIA.

The traveller J. G. Kohl describes the singing of the Morlacchi in Dalmatia as consisting entirely of "chains of shakes."

GALICIA.

The Jews in Galicia adapt their sacred chants, at banquets, to secular words. When passing at midnight through the streets of Stanislawow, a small town in Galicia, Kohl was surprised to hear from a wine-house a chorus of male voices, which appeared to him exactly like the usual chanting of the Psalms of David in the services of the Synagogue. On entering the wine-house, he found a company of Jews who were drinking and singing.

TYROL.

Several European nations are known to cultivate *extempore* performances. The Italians, for example, have their Improvisatori; the Welsh their Pennillion singing; and the Southern Germans their Schnodahupferln. These last are short epigrammatic stanzas which the peasants of Tyrol, Styria, and other neighbouring

countries adapt to one or other of their favourite dan tunes in $\frac{3}{4}$ time. Sometimes they introduce unmeaning syllables into their popular poetry chiefly for the sake of the music.

STYRIA.

Kohl speaks very highly of the Landler dance of the Styrians, which he describes as the most elegant and charming of all similar performances that he witnessed in the European countries. The sentimental and graceful attitudes of the Styrians in their Landler are exactly in keeping with the emotions expressed in the music of this dance. These dances, like the Fandango of the Spaniards, the Csárdás of the Magyars, and the Mazurka of the Poles, are especially noted for the picturesque spectacle which the dancers in their national costume present in the performance.

RUSSIA.

THE Slavonians, the ancestors of the modern Russians, were noted for their passionate fondness for music. Even when within sight of their enemies, they indulged themselves in singing and merry-making. It is related that in the year 592, when they were attacked by a Greek General, they were so engrossed by their amuse. ments, as to be defeated before they could attempt a defence. There are many Russian couplets still current in which the gods of the Danube and of paganism are celebrated. Russian music is more usually vocal than instrumental. Their songs are simple recitations, ancient or modern, on the subjects of love and nature, and sometimes based on tales of chivalry. On Sundays and holidays, very good vocal music is heard in their churches, which is sung by singers expressly taught, and mostly by the people in the Ukraine, who are of a very musical disposition. Rochlitz remarks that the songs of the lowest classes of the Russians are usually confined to the compass of a *fifth.* He had the opportunity of hearing many of the songs through the *serfs* (servants) of the Russian merchants who annually visited the Leipzig fair. He found that the tonic and the dominant were by far the most prevalent intervals ; the intermediate notes of the diatonic minor scale being generally skipped through. There are many Russian tunes which commence in major, and continue in that key until towards the end, when they modulate into the minor key in which they close. It is rather singular that

the music of the Russians,—a people said to be of a remarkably cheerful disposition,—should be characterised by so much melancholy and plaintiveness as are evidenced by the features of some of the airs from the Ukraine, where the character of the national music has been preserved more intact than in the environs of St. Petersburg. A German musician gives an account of the part-singing of a band of fifteen Russian soldiers. Two of them sang soprano; while another began with a solo somewhat of the nature of the recitative. The voices of these men were very powerful, and the enthusiasm of the singers seemed always to increase during the performance, which sometimes extended over six hours without any intermission. Sometimes the singers formed a double line; each man grasped the hands of his opposite neighbour, and having placed one of their officers upon their arms, they tossed him into the air with much ease and regularity in time with the singing. Some of the melodies sung were accompanied by the chorus with a few chords, the staccato-notes being rendered very short, and the accentuation being very precise. A number of German songs, translated into the Lettish language, were introduced amongst the peasants in Courland, where, after a certain period of time, the pieces underwent a remarkable change :—what were originally in the major were now sung partly in the minor key, a rude kind of accompaniment being superadded.

The principal national instrument of the Russians is the *Cow-horn,* which is a kind of cornet, from one to four feet long, made of wood, or the bark of trees. The *Balalaika* is a very ancient instrument in common use amongst the Russians, and is said to have been derived originally from the East. The body is an oblong semi-

circle, about a span in length, with a neck or finger-board. It has only two strings, one of them giving a monotonous bass and the other playing the air. A larger number of strings may be found in other varieties of the instrument. The *Gudok* is a violin mounted with three strings, and is supposed by Fétis to be the prototype of all European stringed instruments of the violin kind. The *Rilek* is an ordinary kind of Lyre. The *Gussli* was originally a five stringed instrument of the harp kind played with the fingers, and popular with the Russian peasantry. At present it's wire strings embrace from two to three octaves. It is one of the old national instruments of the Russians. The *Torban* is an instrument of modern Russia mounted with 30 strings of gut and wire (14 from side, 12 from handle, and 4 from projection above handle). The body is oval and of a rich reddish wood. Varieties of the *Tamboura* and *Tar* may be found in parts the country. The *Dutka* is made with two parallel reed pipes, each with three holes, differing in their notes up to an octave, so that it appears as if two persons were performing.

A peculiar kind of music, called the hunting, or horn-music, was first introduced into Russia about the middle of the eighteenth century. At the suggestion of Marshal Kirilowitsch, M. Maresch, then director of music at the Russian Court, undertook to bring it to perfection. He formed at first a system of three semi-tone octaves, by means of hunting horns of different sizes; each of which performed only one note. The system was afterwards extended to four octaves, with the interval of a fourth more, with all the semi-tones comprised in that compass; and, finally, the sounds of the three upper octaves were doubled by the addition of thirty-seven other horns. The Emperor and Empress first heard this music at the

castle of Ismailor near Moscow, in 1757, on the occasion of a great hunt given by the Marshall. By improved drilling, the performers were subsequently enabled to perform an entire opera. Guiseppe Sarti was appointed by the Empress Catherine to the office of chapel-master in St. Petersburg. He made his *debut* by giving a sacred concert, composed of the music for Good Friday, with some Psalms in the Russian language. The band which rendered this music consisted of 66 singers and 100 Russian horns, in addition to the usual number of wind and stringed instruments. In a *Te Deum,* which was performed after the taking of Ocksakow, Sarti made use of the firing of cannon, of different calibres, placed in the court-yard of the castle, by way of bass in certain parts of the performance. In 1768, Bortniansky was one of the court-singers under Empress Catherine. She sent him to Italy where, under Galuppi, he made extraordinary progress in music. The capital has now its musical clubs. Private concerts are numerous; and sacred music is performed in the chapels in an effective style. Plain song was introduced into Russia by some chorus singers sent by the Patriarch of Constantinople to the Grand Duke Vladimir. The Russians have now adapted the rhythm of Italian music which received considerable improvement at the hands of Bortniansky, and another composer named Bérézoosky. Madame Catalini is said to have preferred the compositions in church music of the former to any other with which she was acquainted. The celebrated Opera-singer of Russia, Dapja Nichailowna Leonowa, died in March 1896.

A curious account of the nuptial ceremony of a rich Jew in the province of Podolia is related in a musical journal of Leipzig. The band consisted of four Hebrews playing on two violins, a dulcimer, and a violoncello.

They commenced the performance with a soft and sentimental *adagio*, and gradually went on to louder and more passionate music, the object being to touch the heart of the bridegroom so as to make him cry before the whole company, for, in accordance with an old custom, he should exhibit signs of repentance for his former sins, before he could be allowed to enter into the matrimonial world. As soon as the musicians, with the verbal assistance of his relations, had succeeded in making him shed tears, the whole company formed a procession to escort the happy pair to the wedding ceremony.

The following "Song of a Russian Peasant girl" appeared in Talvi's "Historical View of the Languages and Literature of the Slavic Nations," New York, 1850 :—

Nightingale, O nightingale,
Nightingale so full of song,
Tell me, tell me, where thou fliest,
Where to sing now in the night ?
Will another maiden hear thee
Like to me, poor me, all night
Sleepless, restless, comfortless,
Ever full of tears her eyes ?
Fly, O fly, dear nightingale,
Over hundred countries fly,
Over the blue sea so far ;
Spy the distant countries through,
Town and village, hill and dell,
Whether thou find'st any one
Who so sad is, as am I.
O, I bore a necklace once,
All of pearls like morning dew ;
And I bore a finger-ring,
With a precious stone thereon ;
And I bore deep in my heart
Love, a love so warm and true.
When the sad, sad autumn came,
Were the pearls no longer clear ;
And in winter burst my ring,
On my finger, of itself !
Ah ! and when the spring came on,
Had forgotten me my l ve.

The Russian hymn dates from the year 1830, when the Emperor Nicholas ordered it to be performed in concerts and representations at the theatres. Its composer is Colonel Alexis Lwoff, who was born in Revel, Esthonia, in 1799. The tune appears to have been suggested by the Sicilian Mariner's' Hymn, and possesses little of the characteristics of the popular music of Russia.

POLAND

Poland was formerly a part of an independent kingdom. After undergoing many changes in its government it has now been absolutely incorporated with the Russian Empire. It is now called the Vistula Province. The Poles have a national melody peculiar to their own country. What is called a *Polonese*, or *Polacca*, in the rest of Europe, is always in triple time, and is like the English hornpipe in that measure, except that the conclusion is on the second note of the bar, instead of the first. The Mazurka, the well-known dance of the Poles, has seldom any definite conclusion. The celebrated musician Francois Frederic Chopin (1809-1849) was born in Zela Zowa Wola, a village six miles from Warsaw, in Poland.

FINLAND

The Finns preserved for a long time a specimen of the Oriental harp. They called it *Kantele*, or *Harpu*, and it was the instrument which, according to their mythological accounts, the Finnish god Wainamoinen (or Vainamoinen) invented, and played, like Orpheus, with such irresistible effect that men and beasts became alike enchanted; trees did not venture to move their branches; the brook retarded its course, and the wind

its haste; and even the "mocking echo" approached stealthily and listened with the utmost attention to the heavenly sounds. Traditions referring to the wonderful effect of his performances are still extant in the national poetry of the Finns. Up to the beginning of the nineteenth century, there existed in Esthonia, (a Government of Russia), wandering minstrels who accompanied their old songs and improvisations on the *Kantele*. The last popular minstrel, much respected and everywhere welcomed as the "old singer," died in 1812, at an advanced age, and with him the Oriental harp of the Finns appears to have become extinct. Another national instrument of the Finns, called the *Kantele*, is still often found in Finland and sometimes in the hands of the Lapps in Lapland, who belong to the Finnish or Ugrian races. It consist of a wooden box over which five strings of metal are stretched. The strings are played with the fingers and cannot be shortened in playing, as those of the guitar or violin, the instrument having, like the Dulcimer, no finger-board. This instrument bears no resemblance to the *Kantele* of old. It is considered highly probable that the five strings were originally tuned according to the five intervals of the pentatonic scale. They are now tuned thus,—G, A, B Flat, C, and D. The intervals from which the Finnish songs are chiefly constructed are exactly the same; indeed, in many of the airs the compass does not extend above the dominant. The old *Runo* songs of the Finns extend only from the tonic to the fifth. Simple tunes are most in use in Finland; sometimes the *Runos* are composed in $\frac{5}{4}$ and $\frac{7}{4}$ measures.

The following "Song of a Finnish Maiden" appeared in Dr. E. D. Clarke's "Travels in Various Countries," London, 1810:—

If my well-known should come,
My often-seen should appear;
I would snatch a kiss from his mouth,
If it were tainted with wolf's blood;
I would seize and press his hand,
If a serpent were at the end of it.
If the wind had a mind,
If the breeze had a tongue
To bear and bring back the vows
Which two lovers exchange:
All dainties would I disregard,
Even the vicar's savoury meat;
Rather than forsake the friend of my heart,
The wild game of my summer's hunting,
The darling of my winter's taming.

LAPLAND.

Lapland belongs partly to Russia and partly to Norway and Sweden. The *Kantele* of modern Finland is also in use in Lapland. The singing of the nomad Lapps is described as a "fearful yell." When singing, they strain their lungs so as to cause a spasmodic convulsion of the chest, which, Dr. Clarke says, produces a noise like the braying of an ass. Their songs consist of five or six words repeated over and over. One that Dr. Clarke heard ran as follows:—

Let us drive the wolves!
Let us drive the wolves!
See they run!
The wolves run!

Joseph Acerbi, in his "Travels through Sweden, Finland, and Lapland," London, 1802, publishes another song of this description:—

Accursed wolf! far hence away!
Make in these woods no longer stay:
Fly hence! and seek earth's utmost bounds,
Or perish by the hunter's wounds!

Acerbi remarks it would be no wonder that if the wolf be within hearing when these songs are sung, he should be frightened away by the hideousness of the noise which characterised the singing.

SCANDINAVIA.

NORWAY.

IN his "Narrative of a Journey through Norway, Sweden, and Denmark," Derwent Conway says—"In Norway, generally speaking, musical talent is at a lower ebb than I have found it in any other mountainous country. There are few facilities in any part of Norway—none in the interior—for the encouragement of knowledge in instrumental music; and the climate scarcely admits of great vocal excellence; and although many of the airs possess considerable beauty, and a certain kind of wild attractiveness, yet they are, in general, so indifferently executed, that I should incline to attribute by far the greater portion of the enthusiasm, or feeling excited by the songs, to the poetry." The *Lure* is a wind instrument of the Scandinavians, consisting of pieces of wood fixed tightly together. In Norwegian dances there frequently occurs an additional bar, which, as it disturbs the rhythmical symmetry, must evidently have suggested itself chiefly for the sake of the conclusion. Melodies in the minor key occur in some of the popular dance-tunes of the Norwegians which gives them a plaintive character. In others, a great deal of sprightliness is observed, as for instance, in the *Halling*, which derives its name from the district Hallingdal, its original home. It is said to exercise a powerful charm on all those who are acquainted with these lively

tunes. "You feel yourself," observes a traveller in Norway, "as it were, raised from the floor, and wish, like the practised Halling dancer, to touch the rafters of the ceiling with your toes. The dancer jumps up as light as a feather, turns round in the air, and descends again standing on one leg; on the floor he curves, also resting on one heel, whilst his jacket describes a circle round him like a bell; them he makes a jump to the opposite side of the room, and goes on as before." In his "Travels through Sweden, Norway, and Finmark," London, 1823, De Capell Brooke relates that he heard the watchmen at Trondhjem (or Drontheim), a fortified sea-port of Norway, sing, as each hour elapsed during the night, a different kind of exhortation to prayer, of which the following is the translation of a specimen:—

Ho, the watchman, ho!
The clock has struck ten,
Praised be God our Lord!
Now is it time
To go to bed,
The housewife and her maid,
The master as well as his lad.
The wind is south-east.
Hallelujah! praised be
God our Lord.

SWEDEN.

Among the Swedish highlanders, the shepherdesses blow a kind of trumpet, made of birch bark, and called a *Mir*. It measures sometimes four yards in length, has a strong but musical sound, and, in calm weather, can be heard at a great distance. It is generally used to frighten away wild beasts. In Sweden, music is held in great esteem, as one of the most polite accomplishments, especially, among the ladies. Professors of music are held in high repute; and their calling is considered so

honorable that persons of the highest rank are solicitous of their company and acquaintance. There was, 60 years ago, an opera at Stockholm, but the pieces performed were of French or Italian, or of some other origin. In 1772, a Royal Academy of Music was founded at Stockholm by Gustavus III. Some of the popular tunes of the Swedes resemble tunes of other nations. The Swedish song "En gang i bredd med mig," for instance, is something like an English Christmas Carol. Another ballad of the Swedes, called "Sven i rosengard," is somewhat a modification of an old Scotch ballad. This tune also prevails among the Finns, under the name of "Welisurmaaja," and may have been received by them from the Swedes, who for several centuries, had dominion in Finland. The Swedes have a dance called "Polska," and another called "Neckens Polska," the Necks of the Scandinavians being water-sprites, who are musically disposed and believed by the peasantry to be fallen angels hoping some day for forgiveness. One of the Necks was heard near Hornbogabro, in West Gothland, singing to a sweet melody, "I know, I know, I know that my Redeemer liveth," and another was said to have wept bitterly when some boys once said to him, "what good is it for you to be sitting here and playing, for you will never enjoy eternal happiness." One of the sacred dances prevailing in the country is the solemn bridal dance with which the Protestant clergyman in the rural districts of Sweden (as well as in some parts of Finland where Swedish customs have been preserved from former times) opens the ball immediately after the wedding-dinner. This custom, however, has greatly fallen out of use.

DENMARK.

THE national songs of the Danes bear a close resemblance with the old English ballads, both as regard the nature of the poetry and the airs to which they are sung,—both being of Teutonic origin. Dr. Crotch, in his "Specimen of Various Styles of Music," has pointed out a Danish tune, the beginning of which is the same as that of the Welsh song "Of noble race was Shenkin." The tune of "Ar hyd i wos," one of the most popular songs of Wales, is also current in Denmark, especially among the peasants in Jutland. It is believed that Jutland was in the olden times inhabited by the same race as is found in Wales. But it is not definitely known whether the tune originated in Denmark or Wales. The Danish ballad "Svend i Rosensgaard," like that of the Swedes, seems to have had its origin in an old Scotch ballad which commenced—"Quhy dois zour brand sae drop wi' bluid!" Again, the old Danish tune "Kong Regners Vise" claims, as far as its rhythmical construction is concerned, a relationship with the English "God save the King." The patriotic song of the Danes, "Kong Christian stod ved hoien mast," commemorates in its first verse the bravery of Christian IV, their favorite king, and in the subsequent verses those Danish heroes who, like that king, distinguished themselves in naval battles. The poetry is by Ewald, and the music by a German composer, Johann Hartmann, who in 1768 settled in Copenhagen where he died in 1791. The song being introduced into an Operetta called *Fiskerne* (The Fisher-

men) written by the same composer, was received with enthusiasm, and soon became popular all over Denmark. The piece shows some similarity with "Rule Britannia." There are many instances on record regarding the resemblance of Danish music to that of the Anglo-Saxons. King Alfred (849—901) is known to have assumed the guise of a harper, passed into the Danish camp, and entertained his enemies with his music, which he could not have done, without arousing any suspicion, if his performances had differed from those of the Danes. When Alfred had defeated the Danes, he permitted them to settle in Northumberland and incorporated them with his subjects. In Mr. Halliwell's "Dissertation on Popular Rhymes and Nursery Tales", the identity of several English and Scottish children's ditties has been pointed out. The *Reel* is a Danish as well as a Scottish national dance. It was formerly popular in England too, and its name (from the Anglo-Saxon *Hreol*, or *Reol*) points rather to Denmark or Northern Germany as its original home, than to Scotland. Several of these dances, still extant in some districts of Denmark, bear in construction a strong resemblance to the old popular dances of Great Britain.

HOLLAND.

LEWIS Guicciardini, who was contemporary with Palestrina and died before him in 1589, states that in his time, it was the practice in the Netherlands, and had been a custom there of long standing, to supply Europe with musicians.

In some of the principal towns in the Netherlands, music is cultivated with much perseverance and success, though not to the same extent as it was before the seventeenth century. Amsterdam possesses a Harmonic Society, a Dutch Opera, and a French Opera, where the best compositions are produced. At Rotterdam, ecclesiastical music, during the first quarter of the present century, was at a low web. In the Protestant churches, the singing was then entirely in unison. The concerts given there are reported as respectable and well attended. The kingdom has nowadays made satisfactory progress in the cultivation of the Science and Art.

BELGIUM.

UNDER the Counts of Flanders, Belgium was independent and flourishing. It was afterwards added to the domains of the House of Burgundy, and in 1477 to those of Austria. It was overrun by the revolutionary armies of France in 1792, and in 1795 it was annexed to that country. At the peace in 1814, it was united with Holland into the kingdom of the Netherlands; but in 1830 it separated itself and elected as its king Prince Leopold of Saxe-Coburg, whose son, Leopold II, is the present king. At one time Belgium produced a race of eminent artists in music, painting, and architecture, who formed what was called the "Flemish School." In the fifteenth century, music made great progress in this country, and it met with considerable encouragement at the court of the Duke of Burgundy In the latter part of the fifteenth, and the beginning of the sixteenth century, the Flemish musicians were to be found in every court of Italy. The most celebrated Flemish musicians of the period were, Gilles Binchois, Caron, Regis, Dufay, and Brasart, who preceeded John of Okenheim, the master of Jasquin Des Pres, one of the most celebrated contrupuntists of his day; and who, even anterior to Palestrina, invented many ingenious modulations of harmony. Philip Verdelot, whose works all bear date previous to 1550, is mentioned as one of the best composers of the beginning of the

sixteenth century. Nic. Gombert, Clement von Papa, Cyprian Rose, Orlando di Lasso, Hobrecht, the master of Erasmus, Philip de Monte, Jacob de Kerl, Cornelius Caris, and Josquin Barton, were among the other Flemish musicians of the period.

"At Antwerp", says Dr. Crotch, "no temporal business interferes to stop the daily performance of that class of music which, in our Protestant country, is eagerly sought after by amateurs in the various holes and corners of our metropolis which furnish Catholic chapels—places in which the imagination can but ill conceive the pompous celebration of the Mass as it takes place in the vast churches of the continent, where music, painting, architecture, blending together, form, like colors when combined, another material, and produce in the mind poetry."

His Majesty, the present King of Belguim, is a great patron of the polite arts and encourages the study of music in a liberal manner. The Royal Conservatoire of Music in Brussels contains a splendid assortment of musical instruments collected from various countries, and affords the student considerable facilities for the cultivation of the subject. Francois Auguste Gevaert, the Director of the Conservatoire, was born July 31st, 1828. He received the Order of Leopold, for his cantata 'De Nationale Verjaerdag' composed in honor of the 25th anniversary of King Leopold's reign. He is a musician of a very high order. Chevalier Victor Charles Mahillon, the Honorary Curator of the Museum of the Conservatoire, was born in Brussels, March 10, 1841. He is the author of important works on accoustics and musical instruments. He has contributed several articles on wind instruments in the ninth edition

of the *Encyclopædia Britannica*. He has caused to be reproduced many rare instruments among which are the Roman Littius and Buccina. His services to the Inventions Exhibition of 1885 have been very highly appreciated.

GERMANY.

THE national music of the Germans (who form a branch of the Teutons, or Goths) has been preserved by the wandering minstrels from the time of Charlemagne (Charles the Great), who was born in 742 and died 814. It was about 1066 when Magister Franco, who was a scholar of Leige, first developed the principles of modern rhythm and invented the time table. The minnesingers (corresponding with the minstrels of England and the troubadors of France) were the earliest poets of Germany. They used the vernaculars of the country, their songs being written in the High German or Suabian dialect, and the Nether German or Upper Saxon. The subjects were principally love and war. In the reign of Louis Le Debonnaire, son of Charlemagne, their compositions had become so very popular in the convents, that this monarch had to issue an edict to the German nuns with a view to check their passion for erotic songs. In the twelfth and thirteenth centuries, the minstrels were very liberally patronized in Germany, and particularly during the reign of Frederic Barbarossa. In the fourteenth century, the Church regained its power over the people in consequence of which poetry and music received a sad shock. In the fifteenth century, however, music made much progress both in Germany and the low countries. It was in the sixteenth century that Pierre de la Rue, a celebrated contrupuntist, resided in

Germany; that Casper Krumbhorn, who was born at Lignitz in 1542 and had become totally blind at the age of three years from the effects of small-pox, made proficiency on the flute, violin, and harpsichord; and that the famous composers Reincke, Maurice, and Landgrave of Hesse Cassel, flourished. The principal theorists of the period were Martinus Agricola (of Magdeburg) and John Kepler (of Wiel). It was about this time that the organ was built and generally adopted in the German churches. This instrument was improved by Bernhard, in 1480, by the invention of the pedal. The Reformation in Germany did not cause much change in the solemn musical services of the church. Luther (1483-1546) is said to have been passionately fond of music, and, in conjuction with his friend Melancthon, to have framed a ritual. Several hymns composed by Luther are still in existence. Calvin (1509-1564) introduced, in lieu of the impressive chorus and the simple plain-song, the metrical psalmody, which is now in general use in the reformed churches of the continent. Charles V (1500-1558) was an excellent musician and had a regular band which played during dinner and at other periods; and it is generally understood that vocal concerts had their first rise in Flanders, about the middle of the sixteenth century, when this sovereign held his court in Brussels. The compositions chiefly sung were of the madrigal species, and were for three or more voices. German music showed a falling off during the thirty years' war, when the empire was traversed by five several armies in different directions. The Emperor Leopold, who ascended the throne in 1657, revived the art, and introduced Italian music into Germany. The Italian opera was established in Germany in 1660 by Santinelli, an Italian nobleman, whom Leopold appointed as his chapel-master. The opera *Gli Amori di Orfeo ed Euridici*, which Santinelli

composed in honour of the marriage of his royal patron, is said to have been superior to any then existing, and was thought so much of in Vienna, that an Italian opera was established there, which has been supported ever since. The first German opera was performed at Hamburgh, in 1678. It was called *Orontes*, and the music was by Thiel, the chapel-master of that city. Keyser, who was born at Leipsig in 1673, is, however, generally considered as the founder of the lyric theatre in Germany, by his operas of *Basilius* and *La Pastorale d'Ismene*, performed in 1692. He composed 113 musical pieces for the stage, which served as models for Handel (1685-1759) and his successors in the German school. It is related that the performers, specially at Hamburgh, were all tradesmen or handicrafts. Matheson, Handel, Cousson, and telemann were all composers for the Hamburgh theatre. Their compositions being of a sober, solemn, and majestic cast, they did not become popular among the masses. Hence the introduction of lighter compositions based on Italian models, by J. T. Agricola, Graun, Hasse, and others. The eighteenth century gave birth to some of the most celebrated composers that Germany had ever produced; among these were Gluck, (1714-1787), the family of the Bachs, Haydn, Mozart, and Beethoven. Francis Joseph Haydn was born in March, 1732, and died on the 26th of May, 1810. He was a distinguished composer of secular and ecclesiastical music. His oratorios, specially *The Seasons* and *The Creation*, are deservedly popular among all who can appreciate eminence in musical efforts. His symphonies are the highest pattern of instrumental music. Wolfgang Amadeus Mozart was born on the 27th of January, 1756. It is said that before he was six years old, he was capable of playing difficult com-

positions; and that when little more than eight, he wrote his *Sinfonia* in England whilst his father was ill and confined to the house. Mozart is distinguished as much for his performances as for his compositions for the church and the stage. His principal operatic productions are *Idomeneo, La Clemenza di Tito, Le Nozze di Figaro, Giovanni,* and *Der Zauberflote.* He died in December, 1792. Ludwig Von Beethoven was born in 1770. He did honor to his masters, Neefe, Hadyn, and Albrechtsberger, by his voluminous and remarkable compositions in instrumental music. For some years before his death, Beethoven was afflicted with an incurable deafness, which infirmity, however, produced no effect upon his talents. He died on the 26th of March, 1827, in Vienna. Next in eminence to Beethoven was Carl Maria von Weber, who was born, 1787. His principal operatic compositions are *Oberon, Euryanthe,* and the celebrated *Der Freischutz.* The enthusiasm with which the last-mentioned piece was received in England (where it was brought out in 1825) caused Kemble to engage Weber as director and composer for the Covent Garden Theatre. Weber died in England in the following year. Among the later German composers were F. P. Schubert, the only great composer native to Vienna (January 31, 1797—19th November, 1828); Mayer (the composer of the popular opera *Medea),* who was born 1799, and died 1862; Gyrowetz, who finished an opera called *the Blind Harper* in January, 1829, he being then in his 75th year; Schumann (1810-1856); Ludwig Sphor (1784-1859), the composer of the operas *Faustus* and *Jessonda;* Mendelssohn, who was born in 1809, and died in 1847; Giacomo Meyerbeer (1794-1864), the composer of *Il Crociato in Egitto*; and Wilhelm Richard Wagner (January 22, 1813—February 13, 1883). Besides composers, Germany has produced a number of instrumental and vocal performers

BB

whose merits have raised them to the very first rank in their profession ; and among them may be named Wilhelmine Shroder-Devrient, a highly-gifted dramatic singer, also called the "Queen of Tears," who was born at Hamburgh, December, 1804, and died January 21st, 1860. The greatest scientific musician of the latest times was Professor Hermann Ludwig Ferdinand Helmholtz. He was born at Potsdam, August 31, 1821. He began by teaching Medicine, Physiology, and Natural Philosophy. He was the author of the "Treatise on the Sensations of Tone as a Physiological Basis for the Theory of Music," (1863), and was noted for his valuable inventions and discoveries in relation to the art.

The *Laute* (Lute), *Pfeife* (pipe), the horn, and *Harfe* (harp) are among the musical instruments of Germany. The guitar has hardly been known in this country for more than a century and a half. The inhabitants of some mountainous districts had, however, from time immemorial, a somewhat similar instrument called *Zither*. There is another German instrument called *Hackbret*, or *Cimbal*, which is a kind of Dulcimer. It consists of a trapeziform or square box, about 4 feet and 18 inches broad, which contains the sounding board, at the right and left of which are the iron screws for tuning. The compass embraces about three octaves. The strings are of wire, and two or three of them are in unison for each note. The instrument is played with two little sticks having small oval knobs at each end. One side of the knob is covered with soft leather or felt and is used in *piano* passages. The *Clavicimbel*, (called in French *Clavecin* and in Italian *Cembalo*,) was a kind of spinet, now out of use. Some of J. S. Bach's concertos are written "a due cembali." Among the stringed instruments of the 18th century

are mentioned the *Taschengeige* (*Pochette*), and the *Nagelgeige* (Nail-Violin), which is a circular frame of wood in which are set 66 iron pins, and played with a bow. The *Fagott* is an old wind instrument of the Bassoon kind.

Several national songs of the Germans have undergone changes in tune and time in their passage through different districts. For instance, "Feinsliebchen" is sung in one way in Hanover, and in the manner universally adopted in Germany, in another way in the province of Silesia in Prussia, and in a third way in Bavaria. The drinking song "Rheinweinlied" was sung in 1776 in a manner different from the one it is sung now. And so is the "Prince Eugenius." This song, which is very popular even in the present time, contains a relation of the military exploits of Prince Eugene against the Turks before Belgrade (1717), and is said to have been made—both as regard music and words—by a common soldier who served under him. Some of the national airs end with the interval of the third instead of the tonic. Sometimes the bar of an air is repeated in order to give greater effect to the words, or to render a certain favorite motive more prominent. The huntsman's song "In sein Horn" is a case in point. The well-known "Dessaur Marsch" is of Italian origin. After Prince Leopold had stormed Turin (1706), the conquered Italians met him with this march to do him homage. The melody so pleased the German soldiers that their trumpeters soon began to blow it upon their instruments. When it had been transmitted by them to Germany, the people soon germanised its Italian flourishes. Handel's Pastorale in the "Messiah" owes its origin to a song of the Italian Pifferari (Calabrian peasants), who, according to an ancient custom, appeared in Rome every year about

Christmas to perform their pastoral melodies before the shrines of the Holy Virgin. Mendelssohn is indebted for the theme of the admirable *Scherzo* in his Symphony in A minor to a popular Scottish melody. In the vicinity of Minden, and in some other districts of Westphalia, remains have been found of an old German ballad which, in the opinion of Jacob Grimm, was probably made at the time of Charlemagne. It is rather remarkable that the tune to which it is sung is in the minor key, as this key is rarely met with now in the national songs of Germany. Many of the old German Church hymns were compiled from hunting-songs, love-ditties, and similar secular poems. Some of the tunes also were adopted and the words changed so as to give them a spiritual signification. For example, the ardent pursuer of the stag and roe in one of the hunting-songs has been transformed into a zealous Christian following after Faith and Charity, and the lover in a love-ditty complaining that he must depart and wander from the town where his sweetheart abides, is converted into a man exclaiming " O world, I must leave thee." These verbal alterations were made mostly at the time of the Reformation. But subsequently entirely new hymns were in most cases written to the old tunes.

In his " Airs of the Rhine," Mr. Edward Taylor observes :—" The peculiarity which strikes an Englishman in Germany is the general sensibility to vocal harmony. If he hears a party of country girls singing in a vineyard, or a company of conscripts going to drill, he is sure to hear them sing in parts." Mr. Planche, in his " Descent of the Danube," also notices the skill with which the Bavarians sing in parts. The peasants in Bavaria have a dance which they call " Der Zwiefache," or " Gerade und Ungerade" (*Even or Uneven*). The

tempo is taken very fast, and the tune is repeated at least half a dozen times. In the part-singing which prevails among the German country people, the singers, in some cases, accompany the melody with the tonic, the dominant, and with a series of thirds. Even a three-part harmony may sometimes be heard in the vocal performances of the peasants in Hanover and in some other districts of North Germany, generally during harvest-time, when, in the evening, the field labourers are returning home from their work singing in chorus. In the German villages and small towns may be heard every hour during the night until four o'clock in the morning the blowing of the watchman's horn, or the springing of his rattle, followed by a song, containing some religious or moral sentiment in keeping with the hour of the night. The song is so curious in its conception that no apology is needed for reproducing the following translation of a specimen from William Howitt's "Rural and Domestic Life of Germany," London, 1842 :—

1. Hear, my masters, what I tell,
Ten has struck now by the bell !
Ten are the Commandments given
By the Lord our God from Heaven.
Human watch no good can yield us ;
God will watch us, God will shield us :
May He through His heavenly might,
Give us all a happy night !

2. Hear, my masters, what I tell,
It has struck eleven by the bell !
Eleven were the Apostles sound,
Who did teach the whole world round.
Human watch no good, &c.

3. Hear, my masters, what I tell,
Twelve has struck now by the bell !
Twelve did follow Jesus' name,—
Suffered with him all his shame.
Human watch no good, &c.

4. Hear, my masters, what I tell,
One has struck now by the bell!
One is God, and one alone,
Who does hear us when we groan.
Human watch no good, &c.

5. Hear, my masters, what I tell,
Two has struck now by the bell!
Two paths before our steps divide,
Man beware, and well decide!
Human watch no good, &c.

6. Hear, my masters, what I tell,
Three has struck now by the bell!
Threefold is what's hallowed most,
The Father, Son, and Holy Ghost.
Human watch no good, &c.

7. Hear, my masters, what I tell,
Four has struck now by the bell!
Four times our lands we plough and dress,
Thy heart, O man, till'st thou that less?
Human watch no good can yield us;
God will watch us, God will shield us;
May He through His heavenly might,
Give us all a happy night!

The English hymn "God Save the King" has been adopted in several German courts. In Prussia it is called. "Heil Dir im Siegerkranz." It was first sung there in 1796 at the Berlin National Theatre.

The famous national air "Holde Nacht" had, in the years 1813 and 1814, a considerable influence upon the Prussian soldiers. It is said that many who sang it were plunged into profound melancholy; so that Blucher and Gneisenau found it necessary to forbid its being sung. The effect has been ascribed partly to the music, and partly to the words and to the recollections associated with the song.

The cultivation of music is probably more general in Germany than in any other part of the world. Even

in charity schools this art is taught; and it is stated that no schoolmaster is allowed to exercise his profession, unless he is able to teach the elements of music and some instruments. Under such circumstances there can be little wonder that Germany has produced so many eminent composers and practical performers, whose name and achievements have not only been appreciated at home, but honored and perpetuated also in England and other foreign countries. Handel had a statue erected to him in the Vauxhall Gardens, in the reign of George II, of England; and even now the Handel Festival is held there periodically and with due *eclat*.

SWITZERLAND.

THE Swiss are said to love music as much as they love their mountains and their liberty. The composer Spohr, while sojourning among the peasants in Switzerland, observed that the people sang, as a rule, the interval of the *third* slightly higher, that of the *fourth* still higher, and that of the *minor seventh* considerably lower than in the diatonic scale; whence he concludes that this intonation is the most natural to the human ear when it has not been accustomed from infancy to the *tempered* tonal system.

The *Alphorn* is the national instrument of the Swiss. It is made of fir and is a hollow tube, four or five feet long, of a moderate size, bent at its thickest and lowest extremity, and terminating with a basin similar to that of a trumpet to which instrument its compass may be compared. Professor Wysz, in his preface to a collection of Swiss national airs, observes, that "the compass of the Alphorn is nearly the same as that of a trumpet; as on that instrument, and on the horn, the upper *F* is not an exact *F*, neither is it an exact *F-sharp*; for the former it is too sharp, for the latter too flat." The Professor pointed out to a Swiss herdsman that it would be an improvement if by some contrivance, the instrument could be made to produce a proper *F-Natural*. He was told in reply that the present interval was preferred because it had a more pleasing and soothing effect than *F-Natural*. The *Alphorn*

is first mentioned by Conrad Gessner, in his *Account of Mount Pilate* which was published in 1555. The instrument is now getting out of use. Mr. S. W. Stevenson states in his "Tour in France, Savoy, Northern Italy, Switzerland, &c," that it is played upon in all the mountainous districts of Switzerland, and serves to summon the shepherds and cow-keepers to their employments, and to call the cattle themselves to pasture in the morning and to re-enter their stables in the evening."

The Swiss music is characterised by a soothing sweetness and a wild simplicity; and the varied and rapid transitions from one note to another, from the tones below the break of the voice to those above, and from above to below, (which the Swiss express by the term *yodlen*), are said to produce a very pleasing effect. It is difficult to acquire the art of making these changes perfectly, unless one practices it from early youth; it is a wild interchange of guttural sounds with those of the *falsetto*; and is introduced in the part-songs of the Swiss and Tyrolese peasantry and substituted for an instrumental accompaniment.

Dr. John Forbes, in his work called "A Month in Switzerland," London, 1849, states that in the town of Stein there is in nightly use a chant to which an interesting history is attached. Sometime in the fourteenth century, when there were frequent contests between the towns and the feudal lords of the country, a treacherous plot was concocted to deliver Stein into the hands of the enemy. The night of attack came, and it was arranged that the enemies would be admitted by the traitors at two o'clock in the morning, the watchword agreed upon between the parties being "Noch a Wyl" (*Noch eine Weile—Yet a while*). A shoe-maker

who happened to overhear the whispered signal gave the alarm, frustrated the nefarious plan, and saved the town. Ever since, the nightwatch of Stein, when he calls the hour of two, must chant out the old words "Noch a Wyle! Noch a Wyle!"

The celebrated national air of the Swiss, the *Ranz des Vaches* (which literally means, the march or procession of the cows) is either sung or played on the *Alphorn*. It has often been described, and possibly it may have happened, that the Swiss soldiers in foreign regiments have been forbidden, under heavy penalty, to sing or even to whistle this air, because it affected them to tears, induced them to desert, or made them home-sick and unfit for service. Mr. Stevenson, who heard it sung in 1828, thus describes it:—"Its commencement is slow and heavy; but the burden is in a quicker movement, and a more lively strain. The melody is ordinary enough, and the words uninteresting; yet the character being that of unmeasured simplicity and mournful wildness, its effect is by no means destitute of influence, even over a stranger's feelings." According to Professor Wysz, it ought to be heard at a certain distance, in order to modify the rudeness of sounds that proceed from a powerful breast and are uttered with energetic force. "It requires to be sung," adds the Professor, "with the whole heart and soul, by a shepherd, who is calling together his scattered flock, or descending gaily with his load from the mountains. Ignorant of all the rules of art, and guided by his fancy alone, he utters such sounds as produce the most harmonious effects in the distance, and are attended with an indescribable charm."

ITALY.

ANCIENT PERIOD

ACCORDING to Strabo (B. C. 54—A. C. 24 ?), the public music of the Romans, specially that used in sacrifices, was derived from Etruria ; and Dionysius Halicarnassus says that the Etruscans obtained their musical knowledge from Argos, though it is more likely that it came from the Eastern countries. The earliest mention of Roman music is made in connection with the triumph of Romulus over the Cæninenses (B. C. 749). Numa, who began his reign about 715 B. C., in dividing the people into tribes according to their different occupations, gave musicians the first rank as they were employed in affairs of religion. It was in the reign of this Emperor that mention is made of the *Salii*, who were dancers and singers of hymns in praise of the war-god. Servius Tullius, who began to reign in 578 B. C., formed the people into classes or centuries, and he ordered that two centuries should consist of "trumpeters, blowers of the horn, &c., and of such as, without any other instruments, sounded the charge." By the laws of the ten tables, which were enacted 450 B. C., the number of flute-players to be used at funerals was limited to ten. The drama was first introduced into Rome in 364 B. C., on the occasion of a plague. To appease the incensed deities who were supposed to have sent the visitation upon the city, the games called

Scenici were instituted. In this amusement, actors, who were sent for from Etruria, danced to the flute. Subsequently satires, accompanied with music set to the flute, were recited with appropriate gestures. Some years afterwards, Livius Andronicus wrote plays with a regular and connected plot. Hitherto the authors were actors in their own pieces, and Andronicus was the first who gave the singing and dancing to two different persons. Music was for a long time confined to the religious ceremonies. Horace (B. C. 65-8) calls music "a friend to the temple," and Maximus Tyrius, "the companion of sacrifices." It was after the conquest of Antiochus the Great, king of Syria (B. C. 237 to 187), that the custom was introduced in Rome of having *Psalteriæ*, or female musicians, to attend and perform at feasts and banquets. Vitruvius, the first Roman author who treated of music, says that "the science of music, in itself obscure, is particularly so, to such as understand not the Greek language." From this it would appear that the music of Rome was chiefly Grecian. The orators in Rome were sometimes accompanied on the flute while they harangued. The *Ambubaiæ* were a class of strolling minstrels who played on the *Tibia*, or flute, and danced in public places. The odes of Horace are supposed to have been sung by himself, and these became as popular in Rome as the songs of Anacreon in Greece. The soldiers had their war-songs and lampoons which they sung on all public occasions. In the time of Ovid (B. C. 43—A. C. 18), the music of the theatre was very simple in its construction. Cicero (B. C. 106—B. C. 43), however, remarks that the composers were acquainted with one great principle in the science,—the art of contrast with the advantages of light and shade, and of swelling and diminishing sounds. He also mentions that it was

the custom of people of rank to retain a band of musicians as part of their domestic establishment. Music received much encouragement at the hands of the Emperors, and specially of Nero (37 A. C.—68), who is said to have kept 5000 musicians at his expense and to have himself mounted the stage at Naples, as a public singer, (63 A. C.). He used to compete at the Olympic games and travel in Greece, playing upon the *Cithara* and singing. He used to compel people to listen to his performances. "Nero fiddling, while Rome is burning" is a well-known proverb indicating the passion which he had for music. After the death of Nero, the art sensibly declined till its introduction into the Christian church later on.

The musical instruments of the Romans were similar to those of the Greeks, and embraced a wider variety. Among their wind instrument were the *Tibiæ pares,* or equal flutes ; the *Tibiæ dextræ* or right-handed flutes ; the *Tibiæ sinistræ,* or left-handed flutes ; and the *Tibiæ impares,* or unequal flutes. As many of the flutes were without perforations, it is surmised that they were modulated with the mouth, as in the case of the trumpets and horns. They were all played on by blowing into the top, like the clarionet. In the Farnese collection in Rome, there is the figure of a female bacchanal blowing a double flute, the tubes of which are of unequal length and are furnished with keys or stopples.

The best account of the music of the period is to be found in the work of Aristides Quintilianus, a Greek musician, who flourished about 103 A. C. He defined music to be the art of the beautiful in bodies and movements, though he subsequently confined it to the culti-

vation of the voice and accompanying action. The following are the principal divisions of the art as given in his work which is the most complete of all on ancient music :—

- Music.
  - Contemplative.
    - Natural.
      - General.
      - Arithmetical.
    - Artificial.
      - Harmonic.
      - Rhythmic.
      - Metric.
    - Sounds. Intervals. System. Genera. Tones. Mutations. Melopœia.
  - Active or Eruditive.
    - Usual.
      - Melopœia.
      - Rhythmopœia.
      - Poetry.
    - Enunciative.
      - Organic.
      - Odic.
      - Hypercritic.

By contemplative music was meant that part of the science which defined the principles, and enquired into the causes of the effects produced ; *i. e.*, the theory ; while active music, which applied those principles already developed, denoted the practical part. Quintilianus distinguished the three genera, the Diatonic, the Chromatic, and the Enharmonic, each of which comprised a number of notes, represented by different marks, varying with the various modes, and in the formation of which no analogy was attended to. As regards rhythm and metre, music was entirely subservient, in these respects, to poetry ; and composition was almost entirely confined to vocal pieces.

MODERN PERIOD.

The cultivation of music declined after the death of Nero, and the art took shelter with the early Christians. In the first ages of the church, music formed an im-

portant item of divine worship, and it is supposed that it was the solemn music of the Temple, derived from the ancient Jews, and communicated, with the psalms, to the Christians, by the first teachers of the religion. During the reign of the Emperor Constantius, son of Constantine the Great, the antiphonal singing was adopted in the Christian churches. St. Ambrose, who presided over the see of Milan (from 374 to 398), in the reign of Theodosius, instituted in his Cathedral a peculiar kind of singing called *Cantus Ambrosianus*. He is said to have used four authentic or principal modes, *i. e.*, the Dorian, from D to d ; the Phrygian, from E to e : the Æolian, from F to f ; and the Mixolydian, from G to g. These modes were also distinguished by the Greek numerical terms, *Protos* (first) ; *Deuteros* (second); *Tritos* (third); and *Tetartos* (fourth). St. Ambrose is credited by some authorities with the authorship of the *Te Deum*, one of the most ancient specimens of ecclesiastical music yet extant. The style of sacred chanting established by St. Ambrose was succeeded by a more gay and florid one which went by the name of *Canto Figuranto*, which was supplanted by the *Canto Fermo* (or the Plain chant), introduced by Pope St. Gregory (who was born about 550). He substituted the Roman letters in place of the Greek notes and added four modes (called *plagal*, or *relative*, or *collateral*) to those adopted by St. Ambrose. It is said that Pope Vitalian introduced the organ into the Romish church about 670 A. C. About this time, the Gregorian chant or plain-song began to be organised for voices, in the manner which was afterwards called *discant*, and which, in the infancy of counterpoint, implied a double chant, or melody. This mode of singing was, at first, practised only with the organ, but it was soon after adopted for vocal performances only ; and from two voices extended to three, four, &c, and the

terms *triple, quadruple, motet, quintet, quartet,* began to be introduced and applied to musical compositions. Dancing appears to have formed a part of the religious ceremonies of the early Christians. Father Menestrier remarks that the word *choir* was originally derived from a Greek term which meant a dance, or a company of dancers. Subsequent to St. Gregory, many changes were effected in the notation of the chants. Points and accents, and various marks were adopted to denote the elevation or depression of the voice. In the tenth century, lines were used (8 or 9 in number) ; between which the syllables of the psalm or hymn were written. Their place on these lines was denoted by an alphabetical letter placed at the beginning of each ; capitals for the grave sounds, and small letters for the acute. Sometimes the notes were written over the words, and connected with the latter by ligatures. Gerbert Scholasticus, who was elected Pope (Sylvester II) in 999, and who died 1003, is said to have brought the organ to perfection by means of blowing it with warm water, and to have paved the way for the discoveries of Guido Aretinus, a native of Arezzo (in Tuscany), where he was born in 990. Guido converted the Greek tetrachords into hexachords, *i. e.,* a diatonic ascent from the key note to its sixth, and to these six sounds he applied the syllables, *ut, re, me, fa, sol,la,* the initial syllables of a hymn written by Paulus Draconus, in 770, for the festival of St. John. This is what is called *solmization.* Guido simplified notation, by reducing the number of letters used to denote sounds, from fifteen to seven, and instead of placing them at different heights above each other, he wrote them at the commencement of the line, using a point where they were to be repeated. In course of time the letters were discontinued

and the points only retained. He was the first that used the intervals between the lines to denote degrees; placing the points in those intervals, as well as in the lines themselves. The lines were of different colors. The stave of five lines (or of four for church music) was simplified, if not invented, by him. He settled the use and distinction of clefs. Some authorities ascribe to him the invention of *counterpoint* (the term being derived from *contrapunctum*, or point against point: the notes in each stave being placed in opposition to each other).

The improvements effected by Guido were introduced into the monastery of the Benedictines at Arezzo, as also in Rome, and other parts of Italy, but after his death (about 1050), music advanced by slow degrees in the country. For several years the art was confined to the church and to bands of wandering minstrels. Dante (1265-1321) mentions one Castelli as a musician in his *Divina Commedia*. Scochetto, a friend and contemporary of Dante, set some of his poetry to music. Dante speaks of two different species of song which prevailed in his time; *viz.*, the *Canzone*, signifying a song composed on grave and tragic subjects, and *Cantinela*, a comic or buffo composition. He also speaks of the *Madrigal*, or *Madriale*, which term was originally applied to hymns addressed to the Virgin. It would appear from the accounts given by Boccacio (1313-1375) that in the fourteenth century the *Laudi spirituali* were performed at Florence in 1310 by the Philharmonic Society of that city. The instruments chiefly in use at this period were the viol and the lute. In the fifteenth century a famous organist, named Antonio, lived at Florence. The Neapolitan school of music was founded by John Tinctor of Brabant between 1450 and 1490

The church compositions of this period were chiefly the productions of foreigners. Gafurius, otherwise called Franchinus, who was born about 1451 at Lodi (in Italy), published works on the theory of music in which he speaks only of five characters of time, *viz.*, the *maxima*, the *long*, the *breve*, the *semi-breve*, and the *minim*. In the early part of the sixteenth century, the *crotchet*, *quaver*, and *semi-quaver* were used in the compositions. The *Fugues* came to be in use at this period, but no trace is found of the inventor or the place of invention of this kind of composition. Giovanni Pierluigi da Palestrina was born at Palestrina in the campagna of Rome in 1528 or 1529. He died in 1594. On account of the magnificence of his church compositions, he was called the "creator of modern church music." At this time various classes of secular music were brought into use by eminent masters of the different schools. The most ancient secular music, in parts, is to be found in Naples, and consists of the rustic and street tunes of that place, which go by the names of *Arie*, *Canzonette*, *Villote*, and *Villanella alla Napolitana*. Among the many theoretical musicians of the century might be named Zorlino (1540-1589), who was a practical composer, too, of great celebrity. Concert music and oratorios were first introduced into Italy during this century. The latter probably were derived from the Mysteries and Moralities of the Middle Ages.

Though the application of music to the secular drama was attempted in Italy in previous centuries, it was upon the close of the sixteenth century that an opera in the modern form, in which the recitative was adopted on the lines of the ancient Greek declamation, was brought out. *Dafne*, which is the name of the piece, was written by Rinuccini (the best poet of the age),

between 1594 and 1597, and represented in the latter year, in the palace of Count Giacomo Corsi who took an active part in putting the opera on the stage. The music was composed by Giocomo Peri, the most celebrated musician of the period. The performers were the author and his friends ; a harpsichord, a viol da gamba, a harp, and a lute, formed the accompaniment ; and the recitative (there was no attempt at air) was merely a kind of measured intonation. Rinuccini afterwards wrote the *Euridici* and *Ariadne*. The former was the first piece of the kind performed before the public, its representation taking place at the theatre, Florence, in 1600, on the occasion of the marriage of Henry IV of France with Mary de Medicis. The lyric drama made its appearance in the seventeenth century first at Florence, next in Rome, and then at Venice, where the *Orfeo* of Claude Monteverde was performed in 1667 Giacomo Carissimi (who was born in 1604, or according to some in 1582, and who died in 1674) improved the recitative in the form in which it is now presented. He greatly improved the lyrical drama and introduced the viols and bass viols into the service of the church. Domenicho Mazzochi, one of the Roman school, about 1638, improved the composition of madrigals, and invented the characters of *crescendo, diminuendo, piano, forte,* and the *enharmonic sharp*. Gregorio Allegri (1580-1652) was the composer of the famous *Miserere*, which was held in so much esteem that it was forbidden to be copied, under pain of ex-communication. Mozart, however, succeeded in noting it down when the choir were performing it. It has since been printed in England, under the supervision of Dr. Burney who is said to have obtained a copy of it though Santarelli the singer. Alessandro Stradella (1645-1681 ?) improved the oratorio, and was a great performer on the violin. It is related of him that two

bravos, who were sent to Rome by a Venetian nobleman to assassinate him, were so charmed by his singing (at St. John Lateran); that they abandond their purpose, and allowed him to escape. Alessandro Scarlatti (1659-1725), a pupil of Carissimi, vastly improved the opera. He made the overture (which had previously been a meagre obligato symphony) a species of musical prologue, or programme of the action, and perfected the obligato, or accompanied recitative, and introduced the *da capo*, or ritornel of the symphonies, into recitatives of strong passion. Corelli (1653-1713) was the founder of the Roman or the ancient school of violinists, and was the first composer who brought the violin into repute. Nicolo Amati (the last of the celebrated family), who was born on September 3, 1596, and died August 12, 1684, together with his pupil, Antonio Stradivari (born 1649 or 1650 and died December 1737), were the well-known violin-makers of Cremona of this period. Cantatas first came into fashion in Italy about 1618. The invention of this kind of composition is attributed by Sir John Hawkins to Barbara Strozzi; a Venetian lady, who, in 1653, published vocal compositions under this title. Among the eminent musicians who flourished in Italy in the eighteenth century were the following :—Logroscino, a celebrated composer of the *opera buffa*; Galuppi, or Il Buranello, as he is commonly called, (1703-1805), one of the finest composers of the comic opera; Niccola Piccini (1728-1800), the composer of over 300 operas and one of the first to introduce into operas concerted pieces and finales ; Giovanni Battista Bononcini (1670 ?-1752), famous for his competition with Handel; Sebastiano Nazolini (1768-1799), a dramatic composer ; Giovanni Battista (commonly called Padre) Martini (April 25, 1706-1784), the most celebrated scientific musician ; and Guiseppe Tartini (April 12,

1692, February 16, 1770), the composer of "Il Trillo de Diavolo," or "the Devil's Sonata." Metastasio, "the last poet of Italy," who was born in Rome, January 3, 1698, and who died, April 12, 1782, was a player on the harpsichord and a singer. He was considered as the originator of a real improvement in the musical drama. His cantatas afforded ample themes for the exercise of the talents of a great many musicians of the century. Vocal music was carried to a very high pitch of perfection at this period. The greatest musician of Italy of the nineteenth century was Gioachio Antonio Rossini. He was born on February 29, 1792, and died on November 13, 1868. He was the composer of a large number of successful operas, and his attainments and execution are the theme of admiration of almost all musicians of the present age. Among the other distinguished musicians of the ninteenth century were Nicholas Zingarelli, a Neapolitan, born April 4, 1752, and died 1837; Salvatore Cherubini, a Florentine, born September 14, 1760, and died May 15, 1842; Gaetano Donizetti, (November 29, 1797-1848); Nicolo Paganini, the most famous of violin virtuosos (February 18, 1784, May 27, 1840); Antonio Tamburini, an eminent lyric artist, bari-tone singer, born March 28, 1800, died November 9, 1876; and Guiseppe Verdi, born October 19, 1813. At the present day, there are musical academies in almost all the important cities of Italy, and the country maintains the reputation which it has, for so many centuries past, achieved in musical excellence. The Italian Opera, all over the civilised world, is the resort of people who love and can appreciate the higher forms of music, and is considered the repository of the time-enduring productions of the master-composers whose name and fame will last so long as music will continue to be regarded as the most ennobling of all the polite arts.

252c

The calascione is an instrument formerly held in high favor by the peasantry in Southern Italy, the two catgut strings of which extending over a long neck with frets, are played with a plectrum. The instrument somewhat resembles the Assyrian Tamboura. It has latterly fallen out of use. The bag pipe goes by the name of *Zampogna* among the Italian peasants. Varieties of the Mandoline, Lyre, and Harp are in use in Italy. The *Terzina* is strung like the modern guitar, but tuned a third higher. The *Guitar Battente (chitarrah Battente)* is mounted with five pairs of wire strings. The modern variety of this instrument is used by the peasants of Apulia.

The Tarantella is a South Italian dance which derives its name from Taranto, in the old province of Apulia. The music is in $\frac{6}{8}$ time, played at continually increasing speed, with irregular alternations of minor and major. It is generally danced by a man and a woman, but sometimes with two women alone who often play Castanets and a Tambourine. It was formerly sung, but this is seldom the case now. This dance has obtained a fictitious interest from the idea that by performing it one can get cured of a kind of insanity which is attributed to the effects of the bite of the Lycosa Tarantula, the largest of European spiders. A certain disease (something like hysteria) known as Tarantism prevailed in South Italy in the 15th, 16th, and 17th centuries, and it was believed that it could be cured only by means of the continued exercise of dancing the Tarantella. It is doubtful, however, if the real cause of the malady could be the bite of the spider, as recent experiments have shown that it is no more poisonous than the sting of the wasp. The different forms which the disease assumed were cured by means of

different airs, to which the Tarantists (patients) were made to dance, until they dropped down with sheer exhaustion. Most of the songs, both words and music, which were used to cure Tarantism, no longer exist. Kircher, who has preserved a few specimens, says that the Tarantellas of his day were rustic extemporisations, and these bear no resemblance to the tripping melodies of the modern dance. Auber and Mendelssohn have made use of the Tarantella in some of their compositions. Several musicians have composed allegros in the form and character of this dance, among which may be mentioned the last movement of Weber's sonata in E minor.

SICILY.

SICILY claims the honor of producing one of the eminent musicians of the nineteenth century. Vincenzo Bellini was born at Catania, the capital of Sicily, November 3, 1802. He was contemporaneous with other celebrated composers of Italy; among them, Donizetti and Mercadante. He died September 23, 1835.

The music of Sicily is mostly that of Italy. The Sicilian Mariners' Hymn is a favorite air of the Gondoliers in Venice, who sing it in solemn chorus, it is said, especially on the morning of St. Mary's Day.

SARDINIA.

THE national instrument of the people of Sardinia, called the *Lionedda*, is a kind of double pipe, which bears a greater resemblance to instruments of this kind used among the Eastern nations of old than to any now found in other European countries. The fact of this country having been at one time colonized, as Corsica was, by the Phœnicians, may account for the presence of this instrument in Sardinia.

SPAIN

THE Saracens invaded Spain in the beginning of the eighth century, and were subdued about three hundred years later by the Moors. It was not until the beginning of the seventeenth century (under the reign of Philip III) that the Arabs were entirely expelled from Spain, which, with the exception of some small districts in the north-west, had been for several centuries under their rule. The Arabs remained in Spain for a sufficiently long period to exercise a sensible influence over the music of the country; and nowhere more strongly than in the province of Andalucia, where the character of Arabian music has been preserved intact. The Spanish popular melodies derived from the Arabs are generally founded upon a series of intervals partaking of the character of the Phrygian and Mixolydian modes of the ancient church music. The church music of Spain, however, did not appear to have been so much influenced by Arabic music. The Jews had come over to Spain with the Moors, and the oriental character of their music bore a close affinity to that of the Arabic music. Even in the Synagogical hymns of the Sephardic Jews, who were expelled from Spain at the end of the fifteenth century, distinct traces of Moorish music are still preserved. The church music of Spain is based on the Italian model. In 1068, under Alexander II, the Gregorian chant was introduced into Arragon and Catalonia. The people, however, evinced a liking for the Gothic service, which had become amalgamated with the

Arabian melodies, and obtained a footing in the early Christian churches of the country. But Gregory VII succeeded in abolishing it and establishing the Roman form in its stead.

The Spanish ballads have become known all over the civilized globe. They are called by the natives *Canciones, Romanzes,* and *Coplas.* The oldest of them are termed *Las Coplas de la Zarabanda,* and are chiefly vulgar songs of an amorous, satirical, or humorous character. These are supposed to be as old as the twelfth century. Alphonso, king of Castile, who reigned from 1252 to 1284, endowed a professorship of music in the University of Salamanca, and was himself a poet and a musician. The *Decidores,* or *Trobadores,* of Spain flourished in the fourteenth and fifteenth centuries. Francis Salinas, Christopher Morales, and Tomaso Ludovico da Vittorio (the last two being attached to the Pope's chapel), were among the celebrated musicians of the sixteenth century. In the seventeenth century, the melodrama was introduced into Spain by Lopez de Bueda, in whose time the performers sung, behind the scenes, the old airs called *Romanzes,* without any accompaniment. The musical dramas seem to have appeared in Spain during the reign of Charles II (1661-1700). On the occasion of H Majesty's marriage with Maria Anna of Newbourg, dramas were represented with Lully's music,—the first being *Armida.* Soon after, Italian music and singers were imported from Milan and Naples; and subsequently, Italian operas were established in some of the chief cities. Among the composers of the present century might be named Doyague (of Salamanca), Nielfa (of Madrid), Sor, Aquado, and Ochoa (also professors on the guitar), and Carnicer (the only Spaniard who devoted his talents to theatrical composition). There are several

kinds of the musical drama of the Spanish nation. The *Saynette* is an interlude opening and interspersed with music. The *Zarzuelas* are lyrical dramas, something like the comic operas of France. The *Tonadilla*, originally a simple and popular song, combining the characters of the *Saynette* and *Zarzuela*, now frequently represents an entire action, embracing a whole scene, or sometimes, a whole act.

The guitar, of which there are several varieties including the *Mandora*, is the most celebrated of the instruments used in Spain. It is to the accompaniment of this instrument that the young man serenades his mistress, and the laborer, on return home from the day's work, exercises his voice. The *Bandurria* is a kind of half guitar and a truly national instrument of Spain. It is played with a plectrum of tortoise-shell, called in Spanish "Pua." The Spaniards are singers from nature. They possess an accurate ear, and their songs are characterised by simplicity and feeling, partaking more of intellect and fancy and of romantic and refined sentiment, than of bacchanalian or comic expression. They are very fond of introducing embellishments into their melodies, particularly in descending the diatonic scale, not only in their instrumental performances, but even in their songs. The *Bolero*, *Fandango*, and *Seguidilla*, all varieties of the Spanish dance, are executed to the music of the guitar and the rhythmic sounds of the *castanets*. Spohr, Weber, Gluck, and Mozart have made use of these dances in some of their operatic compositions. The Spanish watch-man's call is musical, and the following are the words of one of them as heard at Seville:—"Ave Maria purissima! las diez anda. Sereno!" It is related in the "Travels of H. R. H. Prince Adalbert of Prussia," London, 1849, that in Cadiz, sometimes the students,

during their holidays, walk through the streets entertaining the people with music and dances:—"after which, like common street-singers, they go round among the crowd of gaping spectators to beg the money which is to pay for their education."

PORTUGAL.

THE music of Portugal is derived from the same source and partakes of the same character as that of Spain. The Portuguese have in their possession many songs of antiquity and excellence, some of them being the compositions of their kings Dionysius and Peter I, who died, respectively, in 1325 and 1367. The *Laudums* and the *Modinhas* (*i. e.*, little tunes) are the national airs of the country. The latter differ from the popular melodies of other nations by the peculiar features in their modulation. These airs are described as being singularly simple and beautiful and expressive of some erotic, pathetic, or melancholy sentiment. They are often sung to the accompaniment of the guitar. Among the Portuguese composers of the present century are DaCosta, Franchi, and Schiopetta. Jaos Domingo Bomtempo, a celebrated musician and composer of Portugal, was born 1775. As instructor of the Royal family he was made Knight of the Order of Christ, and chief director of the court band. He established a Philharmonic Society in Lisbon about 1822. He died August 13, 1842. The music as practised in private society at the present day is more that of Italy than that of Portugal.

The following four varieties of the guitar are used in parts of the country; *viz.*, *Machete de Braga* (with 4 gut strings); *Machete Rajao* (made of Spanish mahogny and having 5 gut strings); *Viola de Arame* (made of Madeira cedar and having 6 pairs of wire strings); and *Viola Franceza*

(or Spanish guitar having 3 strings of wire and 3 of gut). These four instruments form a perfect quartet corresponding to first and second violins, *Viola*, and *Cello*. The *Guitarra* has 12 wire strings strung in pairs. The *Castanholas* are castanets made of very old *Til* wood (*Laurus Foeteus*). The *Pandeiro* is a tambourine having a wooden frame in which are inserted copper jingles, among which, in some specimens, are found several old Portuguese coins.

FRANCE.

THE French cultivated music at a very early period. Many of their early songs were written in Latin. Numerous instruments were employed on festive occasions, and the victories of their kings were celebrated in triumphal songs. The *Chansons* are of great antiquity and partly resemble the Teutonic ballads in their character, but have more of sprightliness about them.

The organ is generally believed to have been first introduced into France in 757, when a specimen was was presented to Pepin (father of Charlemagne) by the Emperor Constantine VI. The introduction of the Gregorian chant shortly followed. In Charlemagne's time, musical missionaries were sent from Rome to instruct the French in the service of the church. At this period secular music was largely popularized by the wandering minstrels and mimes. Their songs formed the principal part of the history of France and celebrated the heroic actions of her kings. The military songs of this time were long preserved, and one of them, in praise of Roland, the *Orlando inamorato a furioso,* was sung as late as the battle of Poictiers (1356), by the French warriors. Several musicians flourished in the country from the time of Charlemagne to that of Guido, among whom were Rabanus, Hayman, Remi, Odo, and Hubald. Both Remi and Hubald wrote treatises on music, and some of Odo's compositions are still preserved in the Romish church. The *Troubadours* appeared in Provence in the twelfth century. They were the founders of modern versification, and the poets of love and gallantry.

Wherever they travelled, they diffused a taste for poetry, music, and the fine arts generally. They sang their own songs to the melody of their own harps, and when they were not able to do so, minstrels, who accompanied them, recited the lays. Such minstrels were generally called *Jongleurs,* and were divided into *Violars,* or performers on the *vielle* and *viol*; *Juglars,* or flute-players; and *Musars,* or players on other instruments. The Provencal language and poetry were at their height of splendour about 1162. In the thirteenth century, after the time of Philip Augustus, songs in the French language became common. According to Dr. Burney, the notes then in use were square and written on four lines only, in the C clef, without any of the marks for time. It was not till towards the end of the reign of St. Louis or Louis IX (1215—1270) that the fifth line was added to the stave. The harp was the favorite instrument of this period. It was accompanied by the viol which, previous to the sixteenth century, was furnished with frets. It was subsequently reduced to four strings. The *vielle* mentioned above was not played with the bow, but its tones were produced by the friction of a wheel: This is said to be the same instrument as the old English *Rote,* and modern *Hurdy-gurdy.* According to Rousseau, the use of the *vielle* dates from the eleventh century.

In addition to the *harp, viol,* and *vielle,* the following instruments were used towards the close of the fourteenth century*:—Flutes, Hautboys, Bassoons, Trumpets, Kettle-drums, Cymbals, Tambourines, Hand-bells, Guitars, Bagpipes, Rebecs, and Regals, or portable

---

* Among the other ancient instruments of France are the *Archilute* (having 14 wire strings), the *Pochette,* (or dancing master's violin, so called because it was often carried in the pocket), and the *viole d' Amour* (having 3 strings of gut and 2 of silk covered with wire). The *Tambour* and *Tambourin a Cordes* are instruments characteristic of Provence. The *Flute Paliesy* is a small flageolet of china.

organs. In 1360, Guillaume Machault wrote a number of *Virelais*, ballads, and *Rondeaux*, chiefly in old French which he set for one and four voices. Prior to this time, music of more than two parts could not be found. The most ancient contrapuntist of the French school was Antonie Brumel, who flourished 1480—1520. Owing to the internecine wars which prevailed in the sixteenth century, music did not make much progress in France. To this century, however, belongs Clement Jaunequin, who made descriptive music his speciality. He composed *La Bataille* to commemorate the battle of Marignan (fought between the French and the Swiss in 1515), in which he gave imitations of the noise and din of war. He also wrote pieces in which he imitated the notes of birds, and the cries of the chase. These were the first rude attempts at musical imitation. It was in this century that Antony de Baif, private secretary to Charles IX., instituted the Academy of Music (1583). About the year 1580, the violin was introduced into France by Baltazarini (or Baltagerine), an Italian musician, and the best violinist of his day. He is said to have been also the first to introduce the Italian dances into Paris, and thus to have been the founder of the ballet, and, through the ballet, of the opera. About the close of this century, several theorists interested themselves in the question of the number of syllables used in solmization as left by Guido, some being for increasing that number and others for reducing it. It was ultimately decided that the syllable *si* should be adopted for the seventh of the key of C. To Le Maire, a singing-master of Paris, belongs the credit of adapting this new syllable to the sound it is meant to express. The reigns of Henry IV and Louis XIII. did little for music. It was during the reign of Louis XIV. that Jean Baptiste Lully (or Lulli), a Florentine musician, introduced Italian music into

France. He was born in 1633. He was the first violinist of his time, and effected great improvements in the lyrical drama and instrumental branch of music in France. While conducting a *Te Deum* (January 8, 1687) in honor of the King's recovery from a serious illness, he accidentally struck his foot with his baton; an abscess followed, in consequence of which he died on the 22nd March of that year. In 1669 the poet Perrin, and the musician Cambert, brought out the first French opera entitled *Pomona* at the Hotel de Nevers, and in 1677 in the Tennis Court at the Hotel de Guenegaud. This was the first French opera ever publicly performed in Paris. In 1672, Lully had obtained a Royal patent for the establishment of the *Academie de Musique*. His style was supplanted by Jean Phillippe Rameau who was born at Dijon, September 25, 1683. He was a composer as well as a theorist of eminence. In his great work *Demonstration du Principe de l' Harmonie* (which was published in 1750), he attempted to show that the whole system of harmony depends on one single and clear principle, *viz.*, the fundamental bass. It is stated by his admirers that he was the first to discover and make known to others the mutual dependance between melody and harmony. The *Iphigenie en Aulide* of Racine (1639—1699) was the first opera which Gluck composed for the French Theatre. At first the French musicians did not take kindly to the adaptation of a French work to foreign music, but, under the patronage of Marie Antoinette (who was his pupil in Germany), he succeeded in obtaining for this production as well as the subsequent ones an enthusiastic reception. The French were now in raptures with Gluck whom they began to consider as the only musician in Europe who knew how to express the real language of the passions. But a schism took place on Piccini's appearance in 1776. The young men were all for Piccini, and the old for Gluck;

and it is related that at one time the contest was conducted with so much zeal, that no door was opened to a stranger without the question being put to him, "Are you a Piccinist, or a Gluckist ?" The dispute was eventually settled by dividing the palm between the two One of the distinguished musicians of France of the nineteenth century was Daniel-Francois-Espirit Auber, who was born January 29, 1784, and died May 13, 1871. His master-piece is "La Muette de Portici," or "Masaniello" as it is commonly called after its hero, in which the form and character of the *Tarantella* have been faithfully exhibited. Another brilliant musician of the century was Charles Francois Goûnod, born June 17, 1818, and died October, 1893. His first opera was "Sapho," but his name and fame were firmly established by his "Faust" which was produced at the Theatre Lyrique March 19, 1859. The lyric element predominated in his musical compositions. The most distinguished musical writer of the century was Guilaume Andre Villoteau, born September 6, 1759, and died April 27, 1839. Though a Belgian by birth, the name of Fétis cannot be omitted in an account of France where he received his musical education. Francois Joseph Fétis was born March 25, 1784, at Mons, and died March 25, 1871, at Brussels. He was the most learned, laborious, and prolific musical litterateur of his time. He early learned to play the violin, piano, and organ, and completed his studies at the Paris conservatoire. In 1821 he became professor of counterpoint and fugue at the Paris conservatoire, and librarian of that institution in 1827. His fame rests not so much upon his compositions, as upon his writings on the theory, history, and literature of music, His works are all written in the French language. Charles Ambrose Thomas, the *doyen* of French composers, died February 12, 1896.

The French were celebrated for their *Chansons* which excelled, according to Rousseau, "not more in the turn and melody of their airs, than in the poignancy, grace, and delicacy of the words." The *Chanson* (from the Latin *cantio, cantionem*) is a little poem of which the stanzas or symmetrical divisions are called "couplets." As a rule, each couplet concludes with a repetition of one or two lines constituting the "refrain." All the modern songs are divided into four classes,—the Chanson historique ; the Chanson metier ; the Chanson d' amour ; and the Chanson bachique. Formerly, it was the custom with the French to sing these *Chansons* at table. About the middle of the reign of Louis XV. (when a taste for Italian music prevailed in France), Duni, Philidor, and Monsigny composed comic operas, after the *opera buffa* of Italy, whose popular airs passed from the theatre to the table and replaced the *Chansons*. The date and origin of the celebrated song Marlborough, or, as the French call it, "Chanson de Malbrouk," are not certain. It is said that the melody was brought to France by the Crusaders from the East ; but the more generally received opinion is that the Arabs originally adopted it from the French. The tune would probably have died out in France, had not Madame Poitrini used it as lullaby for the infant Dauphin in 1781. Marie Antoinette took a fancy to her baby's cradle song, and sang it herself, and it was soon spread over the whole country. Shortly after it became a favorite air for couplet in French Vaudevilles. The national hymn (if it may be so called), *Partant pour la Syrie,* is said to have been composed by Hortense, the mother of Napoleon III., with the help of her music master, the well-known Lesueur (January 15, 1763,—October 6, 1837). The 'Marseillaise' is a popular French hymn, the words and music of which are the compositions of Claude Joseph Rouget de

l'Isle (born May 10, 1760, and died June 27, 1836). He was a Captain of Engineers quartered at Strasburg when the volunteers of the Bas Rhin received orders to join Luckner's army. A regret having been expressed by the Mayor of Strasburg that the young soldiers had no patriotic song to sing as they marched out, Rouget de l'Isle returned to his lodgings, and in a fit of enthusiasm composed, during the night of April 24th, 1792, the words and music of the song which has immortalised his name. It was originally called "chant de guerre pour l'armee du Rhin," then "chanson" or "chant des Marseillais," and finally "La Marseillaise." It has been held in certain quarters that the words only of this song were composed by Rouget de l'Isle, and that one Holtzmann composed its music. It has been held in certain others that the tune belongs to an old German national song. But in a pamphlet published in Paris in 1865 by the nephew of Rouget de l'Isle, the claims of Rouget have been satisfactorily established by documentary evidence. The *Marseillaise* had such an effect in rousing the enthusiasm of the French soldiers that Kotzebue is reported to have exclaimed to the composer, "Monster! barbarian! How many thousands of my brethren hast those slain!" It is also related that, while the German poet Klopstock met Rouget de l'Isle in Hamburg, he addressed the composer with the words, "Sir, your hymn has mowed down 50,000 valiant Germans!"

The *Gavotte* is a French dance, the name of which is said to be derived from the Gavots, or people of the *pays de gap* in Dauphine. It is in common time, of moderately quick movement, and in two parts, each of which is, as usual with older dances, repeated. *Ballet* dancing dates from the foundation of the Academie Royale de Musique, or soon afterwards. In 1671, when the first French

opera "Pomona" was produced, "Psyche," a so-called tragedie-ballet by Moliere was brought out. Ballets, however, in the mixed style, were known much earlier. Louis XIV. took such a delight in ballets that he frequently appeared as a ballet-dancer, or rather as a figurant, himself. It is, indeed, recorded of him that in connection with "Les Amants magnifiques" (which he brought out jointly with Moliere), he played the part of author, ballet-master, dancer, mimic, singer, and instrumental performer. His Majesty was a player on the guitar, an instrument which he had studied under Franceso Corbetta. The music of Louis XIV.'s ballets was for the most part written by Lully who also composed the songs and symphonies for the dance-interludes of Moliere's comedies.

Music is not now cultivated in the provinces to the same extent as in the metropolitan cities. The conservatoire of music and the opera in Paris are great attractions. The music of modern France has partaken somewhat of the character of that of Germany and Italy, distinguished representatives of which are patronized and held in great favour in the capital.

ENGLAND

THE Britons, who were the aboriginal inhabitants of England, are known to have been passionately fond of music, vocal and instrumental, and their bards, who united in one person the characters of poet, and musician, were held in the highest regard. The bards played chiefly on the harp. After their conversion to Christianity, the Britons adopted the rites and ceremonies and, with them, the music of the Gallican church, as it existed prior to the introduction of the Gregorian chant. When the Saxons drove them into the fastnesses of the Welsh mountains, they took away with them their ancient Celtic music. In such honor was the harp held in Wales that a slave was not permitted to play upon it. The ancient laws of Hywel Dda mention three kinds of harps, *viz.*. the harp of the king, the harp of a Pencerdd (or master of music), and the harp of a nobleman. A professor of this instrument enjoyed rent-free lands, and had his person held sacred. In the battle between the Welsh and the Saxons which took place on the Rhuddlan Marsh, Flintshire, Caradoc, King of North Wales, and the leader of the Welsh, was defeated and slain. It is said that Caradoc's bard composed the plaintive melody "Morva Rhuddlan" (the plain of Rhuddlan), immediately after the battle (A. D. 795). Tradition says that the ancient melody "Davydd y garrig Wen" (David of the white rock) was composed, on his death-bed, by a bard of this name, who desired that it should be played at his funeral. Another pathetic and ancient song of the Welsh is "Torriad y Dydd" (the dawn of day). The Welsh are particularly rich in pastoral music which is

said to be graceful, melodious, and unaffected. It is chiefly written for the voice, the subject generally being Love and the beauties of Nature. Of dance music, the *Jig* appears to have been the most favorite with the Welsh. The *Penillion* singing is peculiar to the Welsh, and is believed to have dated from the Druids, who imparted their learning orally, through the medium of *Penillion*. The word *Penill* is derived from *Pen*, a head; and because these stanzas flowed *extempore* from, and were treasured in the head, without being committed to paper, they were called *Penillion*. Many of the Welsh have their memories stored with hundreds of them; some of which they have always ready in answer to almost any subject that can be proposed; or, like the *Improvisatore* of the Italians, they sing *extempore* verses; and a person conversant in this art readily produces a *Penill* apposite to the last that was sung. The singers continue to take up their *Penill* alternately with the harp without intermission, never repeating the same stanza (for that would forfeit the honor of being held first in the contest), and whichever metre the first singer starts with must be strictly adhered to by those who follow. From a Welsh manuscript, copied in the time of Charles I., it would appear that Gryffudd ab Cynan, King of North Wales, held a congress in the eleventh century for the purpose of reforming the order of the Welsh bards. The most important of the reforms effected was the separation of the professions of bard and minstrel, or, in other words, of poetry and music. The next was the revision of the rules for the composition and performance of music. The manuscript referred to embodies some of the most ancient pieces of music of the Britons which are supposed to have been handed down from the bards of old. The whole of the music is written for the *Crwth* (a favorite instrument of the Welsh, having a square

form, and a finger-board, and played with a bow), in a system of notation by the letters of the alphabet, with merely one line to divide bass and treble. The system of notation in the manuscript resembles that of Gregory in the sixth century, and may have been introduced into Britain when he sent Augustine to reform the abuses which had crept into the services of the western churches. Several Welsh airs have found their way into the compositions of musicians, indigenous or foreign, of a later day.

The Saxons brought their bards and their music with them to England. The character of their national airs, as well as of all the other Teutonic nations, is strongly contrasted with that of the Celts. The Saxons at that time were heathens. They were converted to Christianity by missionaries, sent over in 596 by Pope Gregory by whom the Gregorian service was introduced. Musical establishments were founded in connection with monasteries. The Venerable Bede, an English monk and ecclesiastical historian, who is supposed to have lived between 672 and 735 A. C., was a noted musician. Alfred the Great touched the harp with the hand of an artiste. He founded a musical professorship at Oxford. St. Dunstan, Archbishop of Canterbury, who lived 925—988, was a great musician. He furnished several churches with organs, and encouraged the study and practice of music. The monks of the time were musicians themselves, and it is to them that the suppression of the romantic and erotic songs of the Saxons is ascribed.

The Norman conquest, which took place in the eleventh century, did not interfere much with the progress of music in England. The army of William (the Conqueror) was accompanied by minstrels, one of whom,

by name Taillefer, is said to have advanced before the troops, singing the song of Roland, and, having rushed into the thickest of the fight, lost his life. After the Norman conquest, the professors of music became known by the general designation of *minstrels*, and by the specific ones of *rhymers, singers, strayregers, joculators* or *jugglers, testours* (or relators of heroic actions), *buffoons*, and *poets*. Richard I. (*Cœur de Lion*), (*b.* 1157—*d.* 1199) was not only the patron of poetry and music, but was himself a skilful player on the lyre. His imprisonment on his return from Palestine and the manner of the discovery of his prison by his minstrel Blondel are facts known to all students of English History. For a long period the minstrels were favored by the nobility and the fair sex and protected by royalty. It is stated by certain authorities that the degree of Doctor of Music was instituted by Henry II. (*b.* 1133—*d.* 1189). Others state, however, that the degree was not granted to graduates in any science in England till the reign of John, about 1207. Walter Odington, a monk of Evesham, who flourished in the thirteenth century, in the reign of Henry III., wrote a treatise on music from which it may be gathered that the notes were expressed by the first seven letters of the alphabet—great, small, and double; that solmization was practised according to Guido's method; that *longs* and *breves* were in common use in the chanting, or plain-song; and that five lines were used for the staves. He treated of the *Cantus Mensuralibus*, being the earliest writer on the subject of measured music, (except Franco of Cologne), and is said to have been the first to suggest a shorter note than the *semi-breve*. In the time of Chaucer (1328—1400), music was considered a general accomplishment. His "Squire" is described as always singing and playing on the flute; his monks, nuns, and friars are all vocalists; and he

mentions, among other instruments in use, the fiddle (Saxon for the French *vielle*), psaltery, harp, lute, citern (like a lute, played with a plectrun of quill), rote (half-fiddle, half lyre), and the organ. The most ancient English song met with, with the music, is one written and composed upon the battle of Agincourt in 1415. While practical music formed the diversion of the laity, the knowledge of the theory was confined almost exclusively to the clergy. It is not known for certain when the present system of musical notation was introduced into England. Thomas de Walsyngham, who flourished about 1400, mentions five characters as used in his day, *viz.*, the *large*, the *long*, the *breve*, the *semi-breve*, and the *minim.* He makes mention also of the *crotchet* as having been lately introduced, but thinks it an unnecessary subdivision of time. Musical characters were for the first time printed in England about 1495, but these had reference to church music only. Subsequent to this time, eight characters were used in secular compositions, *viz.*, *large*, *long*, *breve*, *semi-breve*, *minim*, *semi-minim*, *chroma*, and *semi-chroma*. These proceeded in regular gradations, the *large* being equal to two *longs*, four *breves*, eight *semi-breves*, &c. Any note written in red ink diminished its value by a fourth part; thus, a red *semi-breue* means three, and not four *semi-minims*. From these notes (which had their corresponding rests), the present system appears to have been derived. Turges was among the musicians of Henry VI. (*b.* 1421—*d.* 1471). Cornyshe who, according to Dr. Burney, was the first who had the courage to use the chord of the sharp seventh of a key, with a false fifth, was in Henry VII.'s chapel. Fayrfax, who was admitted to the degree of Doctor of Music at Cambridge in 1511, was a composer for the church. Music was well patronised by Henry VII. (*b.* 1456—*d.* 1509) and Henry VIII. (*b.* 1491

—*d.* 1547). The latter is said to have composed many pieces, secular and ecclesiastical, and to have possessed a good knowlege of counterpoint. A change took piece in the church music of England at the era of the Reformation. The Reformers took from the choral service the hymns to the Virgin, and those to the saints, but retained the *Te Deum,* the *Sanctus,* the *Gloria in Excelsis,* the *Gloria Patri, Magnificat,* and *Nunc Dimittis.* The Psalms of David were rendered into English and adapted to the ancient Gregorian chant. The antiphonal, or alternate manner of chanting, was also retained. The Romish ritual came into force during the reign of Mary (*b.* 1516—*d.* 1558). Upon the accession of Elizabeth (*b.* 1533—*d.* 1603), the Protestants, who had, during the persecution, been driven to the Continent, brought with them a predilection for congregational or metrical singing, which prevailed there. Among the founders of the present cathedral music of England were Doctor Tye, Marbeck, and Tallis. Among the vocal compositions of the Elizabethan period were the madrigal, the canon and the catch, or round, the canzone, the canzonet, the villanella (the lightest and least artificial kind of air known in music), the ballet, and the Freemen's songs, which were chiefly satirical or bacchanalian in their character. The principal instrumental compositions were the fantazia, for viols ; the pavan, a grave and majestic dance ; the passamezzo (meaning a step and a half) ; the galliard (a merry dance) ; the courant (from *courir* to run) ; the hornpipe (called after an obsolete instrument) ; and the Scotch jig. The lute and the virginal were the principal instruments for the drawing-room. The violin was not much known in the country ; but viols of various sizes, mounted with six strings, and fretted like the guitar, began to be used in drawing-room concerts. It is said

that when Elizabeth dined she was regaled "with twelve trumpets and two kettle-drums, which, together with fifes, cornets, and side-drums, made the hall ring for half an hour together." The church music of the period was particularly grand. On one occasion, when the French Ambassador accompanied Elizabeth to a service at Canterbury cathedral, he is said to have exclaimed, "O God! I think no prince in all Europe ever heard the like; no, not our Holy Father, the Pope himself!" The most eminent musician who flourished in the reign of Elizabeth was Dr. Bull, some of whose compositions find a place in the volume known as Queen Elizabeth's Virginal Book. John Bull was born in 1563, was made a Doctor of Music in 1592, and died in March, 1628. In the Music School of Oxford is preserved a portrait of his round the frame of which is written the following homely distich:—

"The bull by force in field doth raigne:
But Bull by skill good will doth gayne."

Music seems to have accompanied the drama in England at a very early period. It was used in the Mysteries and Moralities, in the Pageants, and in the Masques. In Gorboduc, the first regular tragedy extant, which was written in 1561, the following directions appear concerning the music:—"Order for dumb show before each act. First, the music of violins to play. Second act, the music of cornets. Third act, the music of flutes. Fourth act, the music of hautboys. Fifth act, drums and flutes." In many of the old plays, songs are sung. The dramas of Shakespeare (1564—1616) abound in songs or in allusions made to music. The Masques, which were so much in vogue in the reigns of Elizabeth and James I. (*b.* 1516—*d.* 1625), preceded the musical drama. Ben Jonson (1574—1637), Beaumont (1586—1616), Fletcher (1576—1625), Sir William Davenant (1605—

1668), and Milton (1608—1674), wrote a number of Masques. The incidental songs in these Masques, with the overtures, and act-tunes in the plays, included the whole of the theatrical music in the reign of James I. and in that his son. The rebellion in the reign of Charles I. (*b.* 1600—assasinated 1649) put a stop to the progress of music. In 1643, the performance of cathedral music was prohibited, and the theatres were soon after closed. The restoration of the monarch was followed by the restoration of music. Charles II. (*b.* 1630—*d.* 1685), whose musical taste had been formed in France, caused a different and lighter style of music to be introduced into the church. In this reign, the violin came into general use in England. John Banister (1630—1679) was the first noted violinist of the day, and the first who established anything like public concerts in England. Another musician of distinction of the period was Mathew Lock, the celebrated composer of the music in Macbeth. He died in 1677. But the most distinguished composer of the seventeenth century was Henry Purcell who was born in 1658. His compositions for the church, chamber, and the theatre are numerous, and are spoken of in the highest terms of praise. He died in 1695. A tablet erected to his memory bore the following inscription, said to have been written by Dryden :—" Here lyes Henry Purcell, Esq. ; who left this life, and is gone to that blessed place where only his harmony can be exceeded."

It was Purcell who converted the Masques into the shape of the Opera and created a taste for this kind of music. The first Italian opera, which was called *Almahide* and performed throughout by Italian singers, was represented in England in 1710. Towards the close of that year, Handel arrived in England, and composed

and produced the piece *Rinaldo* from Tasso's "Jerusalem." In 1722, the Royal Academy of Music was established and a fund raised to establish permanently the Italian opera. Handel was engaged as composer. Bononcini, who was invited from Bologna, was also engaged as composer. They differed, and the dissensions continued till the departure of the latter in 1727. Gluck's music was first introduced into England in 1746, when his opera of *La Caducta de Gigante* was performed. The comic operas were represented here in 1748 by a company of buffa singers. In the piece *Orione*, in 1763, clarionets were first introduced into the orchestra. In 1773, Miss Cecilia Davies, the first Englishwoman who was considered worthy of being the prima donna at the principal Italian theatres, appeared in *Lucio Vero*. On the 18th June, 1789, the Opera House was destroyed by fire, and the new Opera House was opened on the 26th January, 1793, under the management of Mr. Taylor Mozart's music was first introduced into England in 1806, in which year Angelina Catalini (1779—1849) was engaged as prima donna. In 1817, Rossini's music became known in the country. In 1824 Madame Rossini, wife of the composer, made her *debut* at the Opera House in *Zelmira*. In 1825, Giovanni Battista Velluti (1781—1861) first appeared in London at a private concert. On the 23rd of July of that year, he introduced Meyerbeer's opera *Il Crociato in Egitto*, for the first time into England. On the 19th April 1828, Countess Rossi Henriette Sontag (1805—1854) appeared for the first time in England and continued to be the rage for some years. Of the modern artistes of foreign countries who have secured deserved popularity in England, the sisters Patti and Nilsson are worthy of prominent notice. Adelina Patti (born February 19, 1843) made her *debut* in

England May 14, 1861, at the Royal Italian Opera as *Amina,* with wonderful success, and from that time became famous. She married Henri Marquis de Caux, Equerry to Napoleon III., July 29, 1868. Her elder sister, Carlota Patti, born in 1840, appeared for the first time in England, April 16, 1863, at a concert at Covent Garden Theatre. On September 3, 1879, she married Ernst de Munck of Weimar, a violoncellist of note. Christine Nilsson, a Swedish lady, born in 1843, first appeared in England, June 8, 1867. Jenny Lind, another Swedish singer of note, who appeared in London in 1847, was born in 1820 and died in 1887.

The first indigenous *Opera* of England, the *Beggar's Opera,* was written by John Gay in 1727, and brought out at Lincoln's Inn Fields Theatre, January 29, 1728. The music for it was arranged by John Christopher Pepusch, Mus. Doc., (1667—1752), and consisted of the loveliest English and Scottish melodies that could be collected either from the inexhaustible treasury of national song, or the most popular ballad-music of the day. The success of this venture was unprecedented and resulted in the sequel of this piece being made ready for performance in 1729, though not presented to the public until 1777, when it was played, for the first time, under the name of *Polly.* In 1733, Thomas Augustine Arne, Mus. Doc., (1710—1778), produced a piece called "Tom Thumb, the opera of operas," in which his little brother, Master Arne, sang the part of the hero with great success. A large number of what are called "Ballad" operas were written on the model of the *Beggar's Opera,* and produced from time to time. Among the eminent musicians of England who devoted their

talents to the composition of the English opera were Charles Dibdin (1745—1814); John Braham (1774—1856); Sir Henry Rowley Bishop (1786—1855); Michael Kelly (of Ireland, 1764—1826); Michael William Balfe (also of Ireland, 1808—1870); and Sir William Bennett, Mus. Doc., (1816—1875). Among the celebrated operatic composers of the present day are Sir Julius Benedict, a foreign musician who has settled in England, born November 27, 1804; George Alexander Macfarren, Mus. Doc., born March 2, 1813, Principal of the Royal Academy of Music; and Sir Arthur Sullivan, born May 13, 1842, and knighted by the Queen on May 15, 1883.

It would be invidious to particularise the distinguished musicians who flourished in the latter part of the eighteenth or the beginning of the present century, and enriched the musical literature of the world by the results of their learned researches. Among these, however, may be mentioned Dr. Burney, Sir John Hawkins, Dr. Crotch, Mr. Nathan, and Sir Gore Ouseley. Charles Burney was born April 7, 1726, and made Doctor of Music by the University of Oxford, June 23, 1769. His famous work, the "General History of Music," the first volume of which appeared in 1776, is the result of extensive travels in the Continent of Europe. Most of the musical articles that appeared in Rees' *Cyclopædia* were the contributions of Dr. Burney.. He died on April 12, 1814. John Hawkins was born March 30, 1719. In 1776 he gave to the world the work on which his fame rests—his "General history of the science and practice of music," on which he had been engaged for 16 years, and the first volume of which appeared in 1776, about the same time when Dr. Burney's first volume was brought out. Contemporary judgment was divided on the merits of the two

productions, and party feeling was so strong at one time as to give rise to the following lines :—

"Sir John Hawkins !
Burn his history !
How d'ye like him ?
Burn his history !
Burney's history pleases me !"

Hawkins died from the effects of paralysis on May 14, 1789. William Crotch, Mus. Doc., was born July 5, 1775. It is said that while yet a child, scarcely five years old, he gave a public performance on the organ. At the age of 14, he composed an oratorio, "The Captivity of Judah," which was performed at Trinity Hall, Cambridge, June 4, 1789. He is the author of "Specimens of various styles of Music, referred to in a course of Lectures on Music read at Oxford and London." He died while seated at dinner, December 29, 1847. Isaac Nathan was born of Hebrew parents in 1792. His "Essay on the History and Theory of Music" is an important production. Latterly he emigrated to Sydney, where he was accidentally killed, being run over by a tramway car, June 15, 1864. The Rev. Sir Frederick Gore Ouseley, Bart., an eminent orientalist and a practical and theoretical musician of great renown, was born August 12th, 1825, and died April 6, 1889. Though a Hanoverian by birth, Carl Engel spent a great portion of his life in England, and wrote his works in English, and on that account it would perhaps not be deemed inappropriate if his name were mentioned in connection with those of the eminent musicians of this country. He was born July 6, 1818. The first fruits of his archæological studies were shown in the publication of "The Music of the Most Ancient Nations" in 1864, which was followed by "An Introduction to the Study of National Music," in 1866. He died in England, November 17, 1882. His favourite Harpsichord, Clavichord, and Lute are now in

the possession of Mr. Herbert Bowman, and Mr. A. J. Hipkins. Alexander John Ellis, F. R. S., who was born in 1814, and died lately, devoted much of his talents towards the scientific aspects of music, and in enquiries into the history of musical pitch.

Her Majesty the Queen, and Their Royal Highnesses the Prince and Princess of Wales, are noted for their substantial encouragement of music and their unstinted patronage of musical talent irrespective of the nationality of the persons representing it. His Royal Highness the Duke of Edinburgh is a practical musician himself, being a skilful player on the violin. Among the prominent musicians of the present day are William George Cusins, born October 14, 1833, and appointed Master of Music to the Queen in 1870; Sir Michael Costa, belonging to a Spanish family, born in 1810, and made in 1871 "Director of the Music, composer and conductor" at Her Majesty's Opera; Dr. John Hullah, born June 27, 1812, and the author of "History of Modern Music;" John Sims Reeves, born October 21, 1822, one of the greatest vocalists of the day; Sir John Stainer, born June 6, 1840, eminent composer and player; and Sir George Grove, D. C. L., Director of the Royal College of Music, London, and author of a comprehensive "Dictionary of Music and Musicians."

As already mentioned, the Royal Academy of Music was established in 1722. In April 19, 1738, the Royal Society of Musicians of Great Britain was founded, with which the Royal Society of Female Musicians (established in 1839) has been amalgamated since 1866. The Academy of Ancient Music which was formed about 1710 continued its work up to 1792. The Musical Antiquarian Society, "for the publication of scarce and valuable works by the early English composers," which

was opened in 1840, closed its labors after seven years useful existence. The Musical Association was founded in 1874. The National Training School for Music, the idea of which emanated from the late Prince Consort, but which was not founded till 1873, has for its chairman H. R. H. the Duke of Edinburgh. The Handel Festival was organised in 1857, and has since been periodically held. The Sacred Harmonic Society was established in 1832. Its library has now become the largest collection of music and musical literature ever gathered by a musical body in England. The Society also possesses some interesting portraits, statuary, and autograph letters. The Society, of British Musicians was, founded in 1834, with the object of advancing indigenous talent in composition and performance. The Musical Artists' Society was founded in 1874, "to encourage living musicians by giving performances of their compositions." The Madrigal Society, founded in 1741, enjoys the distinction of being the oldest musical association in Europe. The Philharmonic Society was founded in 1813 for the encouragement of orchestral and instrumental music. The Wandering Minstrels, an amateur orchestral Society, was started in 1860. The first "smoking concerts" in London were instituted by this Society.

Musical journalism began in England in 1818 with the *Quarterly Musical Magazine and Review*, which existed for a period of 10 years only. The *Harmonicon* began in 1823, and also existed for a period of ten years. Of the present periodicals, the *Musical World* was started in 1836 ; the *Musical Times* on June 1, 1844 ; the *Musical Standard*, on August 2, 1862; the *Monthly Musical Record*, in 1871 ; the *London and Provincial Music Trades Review*, in November, 1877 ; the *Lute*, in 1883 ; the *Quarterly*

Musical Review in February, 1885; the *Musical Society*, in March 1886; and the *British Bandsman and Orchestral Times*, in September 1887.

The music of "Rule, Britannia!"—the noble "ode in honor of Great Britain," which, according to Southey, "will be the political hymn of this country as long as she maintains her political power," was composed by Dr. Arne for his Masque of *Alfred*, and first performed at Cliefden House, Maidenhead, August 1, 1740. Cliefden was then the residence of Frederick, Prince of Wales, and the occasion was to commemorate the accession of George I., and the birth-day of Princess Augusta. The Masque was afterwards altered by Arne into an Opera, and it was so performed at Drury Lane Theatre, on March 20, 1745, for the benefit of Mrs. Arne. The score of "Rule, Britannia!" was printed by Arne at the end of "The Judgment of Paris," which had been produced also at Cliefden, in 1740. The air was adopted by Jacobites as well as Hanoverians. Beethoven composed five variations (in D) upon the air, and other composers have done the like. The words of the song have been ascribed to Thomson (1700—1748).

The first performance of the "National Anthem" of England is stated to have been at a dinner in 1740 to celebrate the taking of Portobello by Admiral Vernon (November 20, 1739), when it is said to have been sung by Henry Carey (1696—1743) as his own composition, both words and music. In 1745 it became publicly known by being sung at the theatres as "a loyal song or Anthem," during the Scottish Rebellion. The Pretender was proclaimed at Edinburgh, September 16, and the first appearance of "God Save the King" was at Drury Lane, September 28. For a month or so it was much sung at both Covent Garden and Drury Lane. Dr. Burney harmonised it for the former,

and Dr. Arne for the latter. There are several tunes in existence older than the "National Anthem", which are said to have furnished the music of it. Among those are a Scotch Carol, "Remember, O thou man," 1611; a ballad, "Franklin is fled away" (first printed in 1669); and a piece in a collection of lessons on the Harpsichord or Spinet, composed by Purcell, 1696. The tune of the Anthem was a great favorite with Beethoven and Weber, both of whom have introduced it in some of their compositions. In 1882, a movement, headed by the Revd. Frederick K. Harford (Minor Canon, Westminster), Sir Henry Rawlinson, Sir George Birdwood, and several other notabilities, was set on foot in England with a view to popularize a revised version of the hymn, throughout the East, by means of translating it in 15 languages, the version being meant to be sent "as a friendly offering from Her Majesty's subjects in Great Britain to Her Majesty's subjects in Hindusthan." The hymn was, accordingly, translated into Sanskrit by Professor Max Muller, into Persian by Mirza Mahammud Bakir Khan, and into Bengali by the writer of the present work. These translations have been accepted and adopted by the "National Anthem for India" Committee, at whose further request, the writer of the present work has set the revised version to twelve varieties of Indian melody. This version has been arranged by the Revd. Mr. Harford, for the use of churches, with an additional stanza composed by him "acknowledging the Almighty's Protection in the Past and Present." The following is the full text of the revised version:—

God save our Gracious Queen;
Long live our Noble Queen;
God save the Queen.
Send Her Victorious,
Happy and Glorious;
Long to reign over us;
God save the Queen.

II.

[For Her Majesty's Armies in times of Peace or War.]

O Lord, our God! arise;
Scatter Her enemies,
And make them fall.
Bless Thou the brave that fight—
Sworn to defend Her Right,
Bending we own Thy Might,
God save us all.

[Or this against Sedition.]

O Lord, our God! arise;
Scatter Her enemies,
And make them fall.
Break Thou Rebellion's wings;
Smite when dark Treason springs,
Almighty King of Kings,
Ruler of all.

[Or this in time of Pestilence.]

O Lord, our God! arise;
Help, while destruction flies
Swift o'er us all!
Stay Thine afflicting Hand:
Heal Thou our stricken land,
Father! in grief we stand,
On Thee we call.

II or III.

Thy choicest gifts in store,
Still on Victoria pour—
Health, Peace, and Fame.
Young faces year by year
Rising Her heart to cheer,
Glad voices, far and near,
Blessing Her Name.

III or IV.*

Saved from each traitor's arm,—
Thou Lord, Her Shield from harm
  Ever hast been.
Angels around Her way
Watch, while by night and day
Millions with fervour pray,—
  "God save the Queen."

* This is the additional stanza.

SCOTLAND

THERE is a belief that the earliest Scottish music was constructed on a series of sounds which has been styled Pentatonic, not, however, peculiar to Scotland, for tunes of a similar character have been found so wide apart as China and the West Coast of Africa. Many are of opinion that the style was brought here by its earliest known inhabitants—the little dark men of the Iberian race. Others attribute its introduction to the Celts, whose love of music is generally admitted, and whose origin as well as language may also be traced to the East. In his "Historical Essay on Scottish song," Joseph Ritson (a celebrated English antiquarian and critic who wrote towards the close of the eighteenth century) treats of the poetry of the songs, beginning with mere rhymes on the subject of the death of Alexander III. (1285), the seige of Berwick (1296), Bannockburn (1314), and so on to the times of James I (*b.* 1393—*d.* 1437), whose thorough English education resulted in his being both a poet and a musician. James I. composed several anthems, introduced the organ into the cathedral and abbeys, and established a full choir of singers in the church service. Accounts are on record as to what value was placed on the services of musicians who, at various times, visited the courts of James III. (*b.* 1443—*d.* 1483) who "delighted more in singing and playing on instruments than he did in the defence of the borders," and James IV. (*b.* 1472—*d.* 1513). James V. (*b.* 1512—*d.* 1542) is believed to have written two songs

on the subject of certain adventures which befel him while wandering through the country in disguise; these are "The gaberlunzie man," and "The beggar's meal-pokes" (mealbags). Of the reign of Mary (*b.* 1542—*d.* 1587), there are two curious works into which a number of songs are embodied; the first "The Complaynte of Scotland" (1549) gives some ballads and part-songs; the second "The Gude and Godly Ballates" (ballads) (1578) furnishes a collection of metrical versions of psalms, hymns, and what have been described as "sacred parodies of secular songs." The music of the church in Scotland before the Reformation was identical with that of Rome. Among the musicians of the pre-Reformation period were Andrew Blackhall, David Peblis, and Sir John Futhy. It was in 1629 that Charles I. granted an annual pension of £2,000 to the musicians of the Chapel Royal in Stirling, and made preparations for the celebration of religious service according to the forms of the church of England, and it was in his reign that the first certain glimpse of early Scottish folk music was obtained. Two manuscripts of this reign have lately been discovered, called the Straloch and Skene MSS. The first was written by Robert Gordon of Straloch, Aberdeenshire, in 1627-29, and presented to Dr. Burney in 1781, but its present whereabouts are not known. The second was formed by or for John Skene of Hallyards, Midlothian, and includes the ancient original melody of "The flowers of the forest." In the collection of airs, made by the Revd. Patrick McDonald and his brother between 1760 and 1780, are a number of beautiful airs. The specimens given in it of the most ancient music show the kind of recitative to which old poems were chanted, and among these are, "Ossian's soliloquy on the death of all his contemporary heroes." The old melodies are said to wander about without any

attempt at rhythm, or making one part answer to another. In contrast to these are the *Liuneags*, short snatches of melody, sung by the women not only at their diversions, but also during almost their every day work. The men too have *iorrums* or songs for rowing, to which they keep time with their oars. The word *jorram* (pronounced *yirram*) means not only a boat-song, but also a lament. It acquired this double meaning from the *jorram* being often chanted in the boats that carried the remains of chiefs and nobles over the Western Seas to *Iona*. The Gaels or Highlanders occupy themselves chiefly with the sentiment and expression of the music, and with this view they dwell upon the long and pathetic notes, while they slur over the inferior and connecting notes. Sir Walter Scott (1771—1832) and Robert Burns (1759—1796) wrote several songs which have attained great popularity in the country.

The bagpipe appears to have come into general favour in Scotland at the close of the fifteenth century. But it is an instrument, in one or other of its forms, of very great antiquity. It was called by the Romans *Tibia utricularis*. It appears on a coin of Nero, who is said to have been himself a performer upon it. It is mentioned by Procopius as the instrument of war of the Roman infantry. In Louis XIV.'s time the bagpipe formed one of the instruments included in the band of the "Grande Ecurie" and was played at court concerts. The essential characteristics of this instrument have always been, first, a combination of fixed notes or "drones," with a melody or "chaunter;" secondly, the presence of a wind-chest or bag. Although it has no doubt been reinvented in various times and places, it seems to be connected with the Celtic race. The presence of this instrument in some form or other has been noticed in the

oriental countries. At the present time there are four principal forms of the instrument used in Scotland,—the Highland, the Lowland, the Irish, and the Northumbrian. The Highland pipe is blown from the chest, the others from bellows. The music of the bagpipe exercises a great influence over the Scotch people. The following instances of this are mentioned by "An Amateur" in his "Preceptor for the Highland Bagpipe," Edinburgh, 1818:—

"At the battle of Quebec, in 1760, while the British troops were retreating in great disorder, the General complained to a field officer in Fraser's regiment of the bad behaviour of his corps. 'Sir,' said the officer with some warmth, 'You did very wrong in forbidding the pipers to play this morning: nothing encourages the Highlanders so much in the day of battle; and even now they would be of some use.' 'Let them blow like the devil, then,' replied the General, 'if it will bring back the men.' The pipers were then ordered to play a favorite martial air; and the Highlanders, the moment they heard the music, returned and formed with alacrity in the rear." "When the brave 92nd Highlanders took the French by surprise in the late Peninsular war, the pipers very appropriately struck up 'Hey Johnny Cope, are ye wauking yet,' which completely intimidated the enemy, while it inspired our gallant heroes with fresh courage to the charge which, as usual, was crowned with the fruits of victory."

The Jew's-harp (which is possibly a corruption of Jaw's-harp) is much used in the Highlands, under the name of *Tromp.* This simple instrument consists of an elastic steel tongue, rivetted at one end to a frame of brass or iron, similar in form to certain pocket cork-screws, of which the screw turns up on a hinge. The free

end of the tongue is bent outwards, at a right angle, so as to allow the finger to strike it when the instrument is placed to the mouth, and firmly supported by the pressure of the frame against the teeth.

The *Pibroch* (Gaelic *Piobaireachd*, a pipe tune) is a series of variations for the bagpipe, founded on a theme called the *urlar*. The *Pibrochs* are the highest form of bagpipe music, and are often very difficult to execute properly. The variations, generally three or four in number, increase in difficulty and speed, until the composition concludes with a *creanluidh*, or quick movement. Like all bagpipe music, *pibrochs* are not written in any proper scale, and it is impossible to note them down correctly for any other instrument, owing to the peculiarly imperfect tuning of the bagpipe. *Pibrochs* are generally of a warlike character, including marches and dirges; they often bear the names of various historical and legendary events.

The dance music of Scotland consists mainly of Reels and Strathspeys. A number of foreign dances have been introduced, but these are confined to the upper classes. The peasantry keep to their national dances, which have since become fashionable in the highest circles, alike in England and Scotland. The Revd. Patrick Macdonald says that the St. Kildeans, being great lovers of music, met together at the close of the fishing season and sung and danced to the Jew's-harp, their only musical instrument. Some of the notes of the Reel seem to be imitations of the cries of the sea-fowl which visit the outer Hebrides as certain seasons of the year. At one time the music of these Reels and Strathspeys over all Scotland was played by the bagpipe, but at a later period Neil Gow (1727—1807) and his sons did much in

promoting the use of the violin in playing the dance music. The violin has at the present day been superseded to a great extent by the piano. The nature of the Scotch dances tends to induce the players and dancers to accelerate the speed as the dancing proceeds: this tendency has been graphically described by Burns in his "Tam O' Shanter." The word *Strathspeys* is derived from the strath or valley of the Speys, in the north of Scotland, where it appears to have been first danced. The music of the Reel is composed of a series of passages of equal quavers, while the Strathspeys consists of dotted notes and semi-quavers. The latter frequently precede the long note, and this peculiarity has received the name of the Scottish "Snap." The use of the piano in Scotland is said to have interfered with the old style of singing songs in their original and native simplicity. A Scottish song properly rendered is now to be heard only in the rural districts. Among the public musicians of Scotland of the present century may be named John Wilson (1801—1849) and John Templeton (born July 30, 1802), who was "tenor" to Maria Malibran (the distinguished French songstress), from 1833 till her death in 1836. Several eminent foreign composers arranged and wrote accompaniments to many Scottish airs, but their efforts are not known to have been very successful in keeping up the character of the original melodies.

In 1881 the Scottish Musical Society was started by an influential Committee. Its object is to promote music in Scotland by maintaining professional orchestras, conferring scholarships, organising concerts, and aiding poor musicians and their families. General John Reid, who died in 1807, left funds for endowing a chair of music in the University of Edinburgh and founding a concert to be given annually on his birth-day, February

13th, in which a march and a minuet of his composition were to be included "to show the taste for music about the middle of the last century, and to keep his name in remembrance." The Professorship was founded in 1839 The Edinburgh University Society of Music was started in 1867, and has for its object the encouragement and promotion, among, the students, of the practical study of choral music. H. R. H. the Duke of Edinburgh is the Patron of this Society. The Euing Library in Glasgow and the Library belonging to the chair of music in the University of Edinburgh contain a large collection of valuable compositions. The latter possesses among other rarities an autograph Ms. of the great B minor Prelude and Fugue for organ by Sebastian Bach. Sir Herbert Stanley Oakeley, Kt., Mus. Doc., born at Ealing, July 22, 1830, was elected Professor of Music in the University of Edinburgh in 1865, and knighted in 1876.

IRELAND.

ANTIQUARIAN researches have established the fact that Ireland was in early times the seat of Christianised learning and a remarkable artistic civilization. The harp-playing in this country has been favorably commented on in the writings of Brompton, Giraldus Cambrensis, and John of Salisbury. The latter considered the skill of the Irish in instrumental music to be superior beyond comparison to that of any nation he had seen. Fuller remarked that in the Crusade conducted by Godfrey of Boulogne, all the concert of Christendom would have made no music, if the Irish harp had been wanting. Fordun (thirteenth century), Clynn (fourteenth century), Polidore Virgil and Major (fifteenth century), Vincenzo Galilei, Bacon, Spenser, Stanihurst, and Camden (sixteenth century) speak with equal warmth. Chappell, in his "Popular Music of the Olden Time," reproduces three Irish airs from Queen Elizabeth's Virginal Book: these are (1) "The Ho-hoane" (Ochone), (2) an "Irish Dumpe," and (3) "Callino Casturame." To the last-mentioned air, there is a reference in Shakespeare's Henry V. (Act 4, scene 4), where Pistol addresses a French soldier thus:—"Quality! Calen O custure me!". This is evidently an attempt to spell as pronounced the Irish phrase, "Colleen, oge astore!"—young girl, my treasure! The earliest published collections of Irish music are by Burke Thumoth (1720);

JJ

by Neill of Christ Church Yard, Dublin, a few years later; and by the son of Carolan in 1747. This music was for the flute or violin.

The harp, which, in the earlier times, was a high favorite with the Irish nation, bore a great resemblance to the Oriental harp, and is said to have been derived from it. In describing some ancient representations of Irish musical instruments, Michael Conran, in his "National Music of Ireland," Dublin, 1846, mentions a harp which forms an ornamental compartment of a sculptured cross near the antique church of Ullard, in the county of Kilkenny, which, from the style of its architecture, and workmanship, is supposed to have been erected prior to 830. "In this ornament", says he, "the figure is represented as playing upon a harp which rests on his knee; and it cannot fail to be regarded with interest, as being the first specimen of a harp without a fore pillar that has been hitherto discovered out of Egypt." The Irish harp was mounted with many strings of brass or some other metal. The specimen preserved in the Trinity College, Dublin, has 30 strings; that of Robin Adair (an Irish chieftain), preserved at Hallybrooke in county Wicklow, has 37 strings; and the Dallway Harp (1621) has 52 strings. The instrument was held in so much favor that it appeared on the coinage of Henry VIII., and had also been appended to some State papers, 1567. Among the famous harpers of the 16th and 17th centuries were Rory Dall O'Cahan; Gerald O'Daly (the composer) of *Aileen-a-Roon*); Denis Hempson (who, in 1745, when 50 years old, went to Scotland and played before Charles Edward); and and James Duncan, who having adopted the profession of a harper in order to obtain funds to carry on a law-suit in defence of his patrimony, was successful, and

died in 1800, in the enjoyment of a handsome competerce. Among the attempts that have been made to arrest the decay of the Irish Harp School may be cited the "Contentions of Bards" held at Bruree (county of Limerick), 1730—50; a meeting of harpers at Granard, (county of Longford), in 1781; and the assemblage of harpers at Belfast, 1792, when the promoters engaged Edward Bunting (1773—1842) to write down the music as performed. From this arose Bunting's famous collection of Irish music, the first volume of which appeared in 1796, the second in 1809, and the third and last in 1840. Ten performers from different parts of Ireland attended the meeting of 1792, and their instruments, tuning, and use of musical terms agreed in a remarkable manner. The harpers of old played with their nails, and not with the fleshy tip of the fingers. The harp is now almost extinct, it having been, to a great extent, superseded by the violin and the flute. The ancient bagpipe of Ireland, like that of Scotland, was an instrument of shrill and warlike tone, by which the natives were aminated as other people are by trumpets. The Irish bagpipe is distinguished from the Scottish one by being blown with bellows instead of the mouth; on account of this as well as from the delicacy of its reeds, the tone is softer. The scale is said to be more accurate than the Scotch. The following are among the ancient wind instruments of Ireland:—(1) The *Ben-Buabhill* (pronounced Ben-Buffal), a real horn, generally that of a wild ox, or buffalo; (2) the *Buinne*, a metal trumpet; (3) the *Corn*, a large curved tube; (4) the *Stoc* and (5) the *Sturgan*, (varieties of the trumpet); (6) the *Musical Branch*, adorned with numerous bells, something like the "Jingling Johnny," once used in the British army. There were single bells called *Clothra*. The *Tympan* was not a drum, as was erroneously supposed,

but a stringed instrument played with a bow. The players on the horn and trumpet were assigned regular places in the famous banquetting hall of Tara.

Among the dances of Ireland are (1) the *Planxty*, or *Pleraca*, 6—8 time, with strains of unequal number of bars ; (2) The *Jig*, of which there are 4 varieties, *viz.*, the Single Jig, the Double Jig, the Hop-Jig, and the *Moneen*, or Green-sod Jig ; (3) The *Reel* ; (4) The *Hornpipe* ; (5) *Set dances* chiefly by one dancer ; and (6) the *Country dance*. In his "Irish Sketch-Book," London, 1857, Thackeray thus describes a performance of the Jig that he witnessed in Ireland :—"Round each set of dancers the people formed a ring in which the figurantes and coryphees went through their operations. The toes went in and the toes went out ; then there came certain mystic figures of hands across, and so forth. I never saw less grace or seemingly less enjoyment, no, not even in a quadrille. The people, however, took a great interest, and it was 'Well done, Tim,' 'Step out, Miss Brady!' and so forth during the dance."

Every domestic occupation in Ireland had its specific music : thus, the milking the cows, spinning, and ploughing had each its tune. The *certan* was some sort of chirping sound by female singers ; the *dordfiansa*, a warlike song accompanied by the clashing of spears after the Greek manner. The *cronan* was softly sung by a chorus, while the principal voice sustained the solo. Thomas Moore (1779—1852), the celebrated lyric poet, composer, and singer, of Ireland, has furnished the words for several of the vocal compositions of his country. His "Lalla Rookh" was made into an opera by C. E. Horn (1786—1849), and produced in Dublin in or about 1820. The resemblance between some Irish and Scottish airs has led some authorities to suppose that the former were

derived from the latter. According to a writer in a Dublin periodical, *The Examiner*, August, 1816, the Irish melodies " are formed of 4 strains of equal length: the first soft, pathetic, and subdued; the second, ascending in the scale, becomes more bold, energetic, and impassioned; the third, a repetition of the second, is sometimes a little varied and more florid, and leads, generally, by a graceful or melancholy passage, to the fourth, which is always a repetition of the first." *Gramachree* in Moore's lines "The Harp that once through Tara's hall" is cited as an illustration, as also the marching tune, " Byrne of Ballymanus." Of late years, brass and reed bands have become popular in Ireland, and play through the streets of the towns. Choral classes are not popular throughout the country: they meet with little favor among the peasantry of the South and West. Oratorios are fairly supported by the middle class in the Northern town of Belfast. Much of the ancient music of Ireland is supposed to have perished with the population during the terrible famine of 1847, which was followed by fever and emigration on a large scale that laid whole districts waste. The advent of foreign musicians and the introduction by them of the music of other countries soon after the Hanoverian succession was settled, had the effect of leading the nobility and the gentry to adopt English models, and, to a great extent, of putting the Irish melodies out of fashion.

Among the distinguished musicians of Ireland who flourished in the 18th century was John Clegg, who was born in 1714. He appears to have been a pupil of Dubourg at Dublin, and afterwards of Bononcini. He was a celebrated violinist of his time and a composer for his instrument. In 1742, owing probably to excessive practice, he became insane and was confined in Bedlam

Hospital, where, as Dr. Burney states, "it was long a fashionable, though inhuman amusement to visit him there, among other lunatics, in hopes of being entertained by his fiddle or his folly." As regards the musicians of the present century, Catharine Hayes, the celebrated soprano, was born in Ireland in 1825 or 1826. On her departure for abroad Thackeray wished her farewell in his Irish Sketch-Book. She made a professional tour of Europe, America, India, Australia, and Polynesia and returned home with a fortune in 1857. She died August 11, 1861. Michael Kelly, another distinguished musician of Ireland, was born in Dublin about 1764. In 1789 he made his first appearance as a composer by the production of the music to two pieces called "False Appearances" and "Fashionable Friends," and from that date till 1820 furnished the music for 62 dramatic pieces, besides writing a large number of English, Italian, and French single songs, &c. On September 5, 1811, at Dublin, he made his last appearance on the stage. He died October 9, 1826.

The Royal Irish Academy of Music, has, among its collections, the library of the long defunct "Antient concerts." The Library of Christ Church Cathedral contains valuable MS. copies of anthems and services by Purcell, Child, and others, which are said to differ greatly from those printed in England during the last fifty years.

ICELAND.

THERE are some works extant on the poetry and melodies of Iceland, these works being chiefly in the languages of the Continent of Europe. The Rev. Frederick Metcalfe, who travelled in Iceland, has in his "Oxonian in Ireland," London, 1861, written down a lullaby which he heard sung by the women in that country. It is said to be very old, and is addressed to an infant which has lost its mother. The lullaby runs thus in its modernised form :—

Take me, bear me, shining moon,
Bear me up to the skies ;
Mother mine, she's sitting there
Carding wool so fine.

AMERICA.

GENERAL REMARKS

THE aboriginal inhabitants of America have been generally considered as a department of human family widely distinct from the people of the Old World. The peculiar position of the Continent, and the fact that it was so long unknown, are among the circumstances which have contributed to produce this impression. Some historians and ethnologists are of opinion that the American Indians originally migrated to America from Asia. In his "Researches concerning the Institutions and Monuments of the Ancient Inhabitants of America", (translated by H. M. Williams, London, 1814), Alexander von Humboldt thus remarks:—"A long struggle between two religious sects—the Brahmans and Buddhists—terminated by the emigration of the Chamans to Thibet, Mongolia, China, and Japan. If tribes of the Tartar race have passed over to the North-West coast of America, and thence to the South and the East, towards the banks of the Gila and those of the Missouri, as etymological researches seem to indicate, we should be less surprised at finding among the semi-barbarous nations of the new continent idols and monuments of architecture, a hieroglyphical writing, an exact knowledge of the duration of the year, and traditions respecting the first state of the world, recalling to our minds the sciences, the arts, and the religious opinions of the Asiatic nations." Referring to the languages of some of the American nations, Humboldt says that the idioms "have resemblances of internal mechanism similar to those which are found in the Sanskrit, the Persian, the

Greek, and the German languages." It would appear from several authorities, that the Americans at one time were possessed of various civilised arts and acquirements. Latterly, they have fallen off from their elevated position. They are now not all hunters; there are many fishing tribes among them. Some are nomadic, while others cultivate the earth, and live in settled habitations; and of these a part were agriculturists before the arrival of the Europeans. As regards the music of these nations, there are undisputable proofs that the pentatonic arrangement of intervals was observed by the Mexicans and Peruvian Indians, long before the discovery of the New World. Musical instruments have been found in tombs, dating from the time of the Aztecs, and of the Peruvians under the Incas, which emit no other than the pentatonic intervals. Among these instruments, which have been deposited in museums of antiquities, are Pandean pipes made of reed, in which each note must have been purposely chosen to attain this end. As has already been said in the earlier portion of this work, the North American Indians sometimes employ signs written upon birch bark to assist them in remembering their songs: examples of these are given in George Catlin's "Letters and Notes on the Manners, Customs, and Condition of the North American Indians," London, 1841, and in "Kitchi-Gami; wanderings round Lake Superior," by J. G. Kohl, London 1860. America was discovered by Columbus in 1492, and the Spaniards were the first with whom the aboriginal tribes came in contact. Other nations followed, and like the Spaniards, introduced the music of their mother countries into their respective settlements. Thus the Spaniards have introduced into Mexico and other parts of America their *Bolero* and similar songs and dances of their original home, and the

Portuguese, the *Modinha,* (their characteristic national song), into Brazil. The Indians in several parts of America still retain, with their ancient customs, the music of their own inherited from their ancestors. This music is generally in the same state of rude simplicity in which the earliest discoverers found it, and, with one or two exceptions, it is this music only that will be shortly noticed in the following pages.

NORTH AMERICA.

SPEAKING of the North American Indians, Dr. Schoolcraft observes that "there is no feast and no religious ceremony among them, which is not attended with dancing and songs," and these are invariably accompanied by the drum and the rattle. The most striking feature of the Indian songs is the prominence of the rhythmic element. The dance is practised both in religious ceremonies and secular amusements. The prophet or the medicine man is an important figure in matters musical. He is not only the repository of the sacred songs and chants, but also of the traditions and general lore of the tribes, and he is generally the composer of songs and leader of the dance and ceremonies. "The songs of the Indian", observe Mary E. Brown and William Adams Brown, in their admirably got up joint production, "Musical instruments and their homes," New York, 1888, "are the natural expression of his feelings. Every event in life is celebrated with its appropriate songs. The medicine man sings, or rather chants, as he performs his mysterious rites; the chief incites his followers to battle with a song; the warriors sing as they rush into the fray; the hunters console themselves by singing for ill success in the chase; the mother sings as she rocks her infant to sleep; the youth expresses the depth of his affection by a song."

GREENLAND.

Greenland, otherwise called the Danish America, was first discovered by a Norwegian in 981, and soon after colonised from Iceland. Davis re-discovered the region in 1587, and in the seventeenth century, the Danes re-established a communication with the lost Colony. The natives, or Esquimaux (literally, "eaters of raw fish"), are employed, chiefly in fishing and seal-hunting. In his "Journal of a Second Voyage for the Discovery of a North-West Passage from the Atlantic to the Pacific," published in London in 1824, Captain W. E. Parry describes a song of the Esquimaux, which was repeatedly heard by him and carefully noted down. This song is founded upon the diatonic scale, with the introduction of a chromatic interval twice in the last two bars. He remarks that "the termination, which is abrupt and fanciful, is usually accompanied by a peculiar motion of the head, and an expression of archness in the countenance which cannot be described by words." The Esquimaux celebrate annually the return of the sun in dances and songs like the following :—

> The welcome Sun returns again,
> Amna ajah, ajah, ah-hu !
> And brings us weather fine and fair,
> Amna ajah, ajah, ah-hu !

This festival takes place at the hyemal solstice in December, and the words, "Amna ajah, ajah, ah-hu," are sung in chorus by all the people who take part in the ceremony as a response to the first and third stanza, which are sung *solo* by the conductor who accompanies himself upon a kind of tambourine called the "Keeloun." The tune of this song seems to be a general favorite with the Esquimaux. The *Keeloun* is formed of a very

thin deer skin, or the envelope of the whale's liver, stretched over one side of a wooden hoop, to which a handle is attached, and upon which the instrument is struck and not upon the membrane. The dances of the Esquimaux are noted for their simplicity, the dancer having the option of inventing his own steps. There is a dance in which a number of women stand in a ring, with their hands under the front flaps of their jackets, and sing, with half closed eyes, the favorite "Amna ajah" song. The dancers are represented by one man, who stands in the middle of the ring, moves about his head and arms, utters sharp yells from time to time, and occasionally flings his leg as high as he can. There is a special dance in vogue among the women which consists in kneeling on the ground and leaping to their feet as fast as is possible. The following touching "Lamentation of a Greenlander on the death of his son" appeared in the "History of Greenland," by David Crantz, London, 1767 :—

Woe is me, that I see thy wonted seat, but see it empty !

Vain are thy mother's toils of love to dry thy garments.

Lo ! my joy is gone into darkness ; it is crept into the caverns of the mountains.

Once, when the even came, I went out and was glad :

I stretched out my eager eye, and waited thy return.

Behold, thou camest ! Thou camest manfully rowing on, vying with young and old.

Never didst thou return empty from the sea; thy kajak brought its never-failing load of seals or sea-fowl.

Thy mother, she kindled the fire and boiled ; she boiled what thy hand acquired.

Thy mother, she spread thy booty before many invited guests, and I took my portion among them.

Thou espiedst the shallop's scarlet streamer from far, and joyfully shoutedst: "Behold, Lars *cometh!"

Thou skippedst over the strand with haste, and thy hand took hold of the gunnel of the shallop.

Then were they seals produced, and thy mother separated the blubber; for this thou receivedst shirts of linen, and iron barbs for thy spears and arrows.

But now, alas, 'tis over! when I think on thee, my bowels are moved within me.

O, could I weep like others! for then might I alleviate my pain.

What shall I wish for more on earth? Death is now become the most desirable thing.

But then, who shall provide for my wife, and the rest of my tender children!

I will still live a little while; but my joy shall consist henceforth in denying myself all that is desirable to man.

* The factor.

THE UNITED STATES.

A great part of what are now called the "United States" belonged to Britain till the year 1775, when the colonists rebelled against the Government, and finally succeeded in throwing off the British yoke. Their independence was acknowledged in 1783, when the first Congress assembled in Philadelphia. In 1789, the constitution was adopted and Washington was elected President. Literary institutions are numerous and the Republic can boast of not a few distinguished names in science and letters. Music is much cultivated in this country both publicly and in private families. The Philharmonic Society of New York, founded April, 1842, has for its object the cultivation and performance of instrumental music. Its first concert was given at the Apollo Rooms, December 7, 1842. The Chinese Rooms, Niblo's Garden, Irving Hall, and the Academy of Music, have been successively used for the concerts and public rehearsals. The Philharmonic Society, Brooklyn, New York, which was incorporated in 1857, has for its object the "advancement of music in the city of Brooklyn, by procuring the public performance of the best works in this department of art." Under the auspices of this Society, important works have been produced for the first time in America, including several by native composers. Philadelphia is remarkable among the cities of the United States for its musical life. No less than 65 Musical Societies exist within its precincts. The Musical Fund Society, which is the oldest of all, was established February, 1820. Among the other institutions are the Beethoven Society organised in 1869; the Orpheus Club (a choral society for men's voices), organised August, 1872; and the Cecilian Society, organised May 25, 1875. The University of Pennsylvania, located

in Philadelphia, has established a faculty of music and confers musical degrees. Among the other musical organizations of the United States may be specified the College of Music (established 1872) attached to the Boston University, Massachusetts; the Peabody Institute, Baltimore, Maryland, founded by George Peabody in 1857; and the College of Music, Cincinnati, Ohio, which was incorporated in 1878. A feature peculiar to the United States is the "Normal Musical Institutes," held in the summer, at some sea-side or mountain watering-place, by leading professors, with the object of giving higher lessons to would-be teachers. Another feature is the holding of a meeting of teachers from all parts of the Union, once a year, also in the summer. The meeting, the place of which is previously fixed, is called "The National Music Teachers' Association," and hereat matters of interest to the profession are discussed and lectures delivered. Out of this has started, since 1884, the American College of Musicians, the object of which is to examine candidates for employment as teachers, and to grant graded certificates of ability. The principle of what is known as the American organ was first discovered about 1835 by a workman in the factory of M. Alexandre, the most celebrated harmonium-maker of Paris. M. Alexandre constructed a few instruments on this plan, but as they wanted in expressive power, he soon gave up the plan. The workman subsequently went to America carrying his invention with him. The instruments first made in America were known as "Melodeons" or "Melodiums," and the American organ, under its present name, and with various improvements suggested by experience, was first introduced by Messrs. Mason and Hamlin of Boston, about 1860. Since then it has become a general favorite, both in America and Europe.

The work called "Slave Songs of the United States," published in New York in 1871, contains a very large collection of the words and tunes of Negro songs. Prior to their emancipation in 1865, the Negroes danced or sung to traditional tunes, some of which were held to have come from Africa, their original home. Most of their present tunes show traces of Catholic or Methodist teachings. The Negroes pay a great deal of attention to rhythm. A Jig is invariably accompanied with bones (played like castanets), or tambourines, and when neither is available, with the alternate slapping of their hands together and on their knees. The Banjo is also an instrument in use among them. They sing while engaged in loading or unloading ships, or in pumping a fire-engine, or in any other work where they have to move in company. One of them gives a line or two, while the rest form the chorus by singing the refrain. Sometimes, when the words are not remembered, improvisation is resorted to. The Negro Minstrel show, a specimen of which is known as the "Christy's Minstrels," had its origin in "Jim Crow,"—the name both of the song and of the Negro whose performance of it was so much admired in Louisville, Kentucky, in 1830.

ALASKA.*

The drum and the rattle are the native instruments of the Indians of Alaska (along the north coast of which the Eskimos live). The size of the former varies greatly, from 3 feet to 7 inches in diameter, as would appear from collections of specimens contained in the American Museum of Natural History. The stick of the

* Alaska is not situated within the geographical limits of the United States. The country is treated of here, because it belongs to the United States.

former is made of a thin piece of wood bent back at the end so as to form a loop, and decorated with eagle's feathers. The use of the rattle dates from a very remote period. It is said that in days of yore an old man and his nephew lived in the Nass River country. Being provoked by the conduct of the latter, who was an idle and worthless fellow, the former put an axe into his hand and sent him to the forest to cut down a tree for fire-wood. In the centre of a large tree which the nephew felled and commenced to split up, he found a rattle, waist cloth, and other dancing gear. These he took with him to his uncle who put them into use at once, and from these all others were copied by visitors. This is all that is known in the country regarding the origin and use of the rattle. The variety of this instrument, used by the chiefs in their dances, is generally in the form of a crow, the under-half carved to represent an owl, and on the back a dead man with protruding tongue, and other figures such as the frog, land otter, kingfisher, &c. The rattle is also an important article in the functions of the Shaman, the Alaskan prophet or medicine man. It is used both in his exhibition dances and in the treatment of the sick. The Shaman's rattle, which is usually ornamented with the skin of the ermine, is sometimes carved to represent the crow, or the oyster-catcher, and on the outside the land otter, mountain-goat, mink, devil-fish, and the witches and spirits. Some of these rattles represent *kush-tar-kar,* or "spirit of the drowned", a creature half-way between man and otter, who cannot sing, but only whistle, and is supposed to be constantly playing tricks on mortals. In the collection of the late Mr. John Crossby Brown of New York, there is a curious rattle from Rasbonisky, which consists of a long stick ornamented with feathers, to which is attached, by a

cord of sinews, a small wooden box filled with pebbles. In this collection is also to be found a rude stringed instrument from Yac-a-tat. The body of this is made of thin pieces of wood, neatly fastened together, and painted or stained with a variety of rude figures in red and blue. It is mounted with two strings. Although this specimen was obtained from a tribe of Indians who come rarely in contact with white people, it is surmised that it is only a rude imitation of some instrument of the violin kind which the tribe might have come across by some chance or other. In addition to the drum and the rattle which the Shaman uses in his ceremonies, there are a number of wooden sticks which are distributed to various members of his family, and are beaten by them upon the floor of the house where he is to practise, as a sort of accompaniment to the drum and the chant which he sings.

DAKOTA.

The musical instruments of the Sioux, the natives of Dakota, are the drum, rattle, tapper, whistle, flute, and flageolet. The drums are of three kinds, *viz.*, (1) the war drum, which consists of a frame of wood with a single head of skin (which is moistened in order to secure the required sound), is usually painted black, and is beaten with a stick similar to that used by the Shamans of Alaska; (2) the conjuror's or medicine man's drum, which has its two heads profusely smeared with vermillion, is never moistened, and is beaten with a wooden stick with a head of hollow rawhide; and (3) the common or lay man's drum, which is usually not much decorated, and is considered very sedative in its effects. The rattle of the Sioux is made of all sorts of materials, such as wood, bits of copper and tin, bells, pieces of horn, elk tusks, deer toes, bones, quills, turtle

shells, and even the rattles of the rattle snake. The bracelet rattle which consists of a piece of rawhide, to which are attached bits of tin and bone, is used in orchestra playing. The conjuror's rattle is made by the conjuror himself with mysterious ceremonies, and each is prepared for the occasion it is required, having somewhere about it the image or images of the special spirit who is supposed to preside over the ceremony at which it is to be used. The "tapper" plays an important part in the orchestral performances of the Dakotas. It is a smooth, hard rod about 12 or 18 inches in length, held lightly with the fingers of the right hand, and tapped briskly upon some sonorous object such as the blade of a tomahawk or a buffalo rib. The whistle of the Sioux is made of a hollow bone, or quill, or a wooden cylinder, and is used sometimes singly, and sometimes in pairs or three, but never exceeding the last number. The war-whistle, which is used exclusively by the chiefs, is made of a piece of bone and yields two distinct tones, according as it is blown through one end or the other. The *He-ha-kha-zo-zo*, or the long flute or Moose-Call, is one of the peculiar wind instruments of the Sioux. The instrument is 3 to 4 feet long and its compass an octave, the scale being produced by the force of the breath. The notes of this flute are supposed to resemble "the whistling tones of the love-sick elk." The *Cho-tonka*, or the love flute, which is made generally of a single piece of wood and furnished with six finger-holes, is a kind of flageolet without a reed, and produces upon it melodies which are said to resemble in character many Scotch and Irish airs. This flute is indispensable to the Dakotas for the purpose of courting their lady-loves, The scalp dance and the dog dance are two of the chief terpsichorean exercises of the Sioux. The

former is performed in the night by the light of their torches, just before going to bed. When a victorious party return from war, bringing home with them the scalps of their enemies, a number of young women are selected to stand in the centre of a circle, holding up these scalps, while the warriors dance, or rather jump, round them, brandishing their weapons and giving forth a frantic yell. This dance is performed for fifteen nights in succession, and is supposed to be propitiatory of the spirits of the slain. The dog dance is a very repulsive performance. In this, the hearts and livers of two or more slain dogs are cut into strips, and, in a raw state, hung as high as a man's head, upon two crotches. The dancers then proclaim their own exploits, and at the same time proceed two at a time to the stake and bite off a piece of the hearts or livers and swallow it. Care is taken that the step is not lost nor the harmony of their voices interrupted, during the devouring process. The meaning of the dance is that none can join in it who cannot boast that he has killed his foe and swallowed a piece of his heart.

ARIZONA.

The Apaches of Arizona have drums, rattles, and wind instruments similar in character to those of the Sioux. Mr. J. Crossby Brown collected a small flute consisting of a reed with four finger-holes. The specimen, however, is an extremely rare one. The Apaches also have a small violin which is mounted with a single string made of a number of horse-hairs. The bow is furnished with a coarse string of horse hair. The Pueblos of Arizona possess rattles of different kinds as their principal instruments. The common variety of the rattle is a gourd filled with small stones. Another variety is made of the shell of a turtle to which are attached, by strips of

rawhide, bits of bone, horn, &c. It is fastened above the knee of the dancer by a cord of rawhide, and makes a sound in time with the movements of his body.

NEW MEXICO.

The Moquis of New Mexico use several varieties of the gourd rattle. One of their rattles is represented by a notched stick, which is played by moving a wand of willow across the notches. This is used to keep time in their dances. The people of New Mexico have a sheep bell, which is a rude bell made out of the horn of the sheep of the Rocky Mountains which traverse the country. The clapper consists of a small stone fastened to the end of a strip of rawhide. Dr. Schoolcraft makes mention of a curious dance of the Moquis of New Mexico in which twenty men and as many women, dressed in a fantastic fashion, took part. The gourd rattle kept time with the performance. The dancers "furnished their own music, and a most strange sound it was, resembling very much the noise, on a large scale, of a swarm of blue-bottle flies in an empty hogshead. Each one was rolling out *aw aw aw*, in a deep bass tone; and the sound coming through a hollow visor produced the effect described."

BRITISH AMERICA.

CANADA.

Canada was discovered in 1497 by John and Sebastian Cabot. It was taken possession of by the French in 1525. In 1608, Quebec, the first settlement, was founded; and for many years the French were engaged in conflicts with the aboriginal tribes of Indians. In 1759, Quebec was taken by the British under General Wolfe, and in 1763, the whole territory of Canada was ceded to the British by the treaty of Paris. Lieutenant Back

who accompanied Captain Franklin in his expedition for exploring the country from Hudson's Bay to the mouth of the Copper Mine river, collected a number of airs as he heard them sung by the "Voageurs" or Canadian boatmen; and these airs, with symphonies and accompaniments, but without the words, were published by Edward Knight in 1823. Lieutenant Back says: "They were gathered in a three years' intercourse with the Canadians; by whom they are sung, as they paddle down the rivers, *sotto voce*, and in a subdued tone, as they near the Rapids; but with a burst of exultation, when the peril is over." They are pretty and melodious, but cannot be accepted as genuine specimens of Indian national melodies as they are a composite of European music and the simple notes of the natives. The Vaudevilles of France and the ballads of England seem to have entered largely into the composition of these airs.

BRITISH COLUMBIA.

The Haida Indians of British Columbia use dance-rattles almost similar to those in use among the Thlinkets of Alaska. They have also a number of wooden pipes and other wind instruments, varying in length and shape. Besides these, the Haidas possess also a small instrument with two tubes on the syrinx principle, and a well-constructed flute with four finger-holes. The Emmons collection is said to contain a very curious instrument, in which the wind, instead of being furnished by the breath of the performer, is supplied by the action of a small bellows of wood and skin.

VANCOUVER ISLAND.

The Ahts of Vancouver Island are remarkable for the accuracy of their ear. They are able to reproduce exactly both the notes and the expression of European

songs, after they have heard them for a few times. At their dances, the spectators sing, and beat time on their wooden dishes and bearskin drums. In some cases the dancers join in the song. The performances of the sorcerers among the Ahts are also accompanied by the beating of bearskin drums and are characterised by a frightful howling.

MEXICO.

Mexico, which was wrested from the natives by the Spaniards under Cortez in 1521, continued in the possession of Spain till 1821, when it became an independent federal republic. In 1864, Maxmilian, son of Archduke Charles of Austria, was elected Emperor of Mexico. By Imperial decree, 1865, all Negroes on Mexican soil were made free, subject to surveillance for five years. In June 1867, Mexico ceased to be an empire by the abdication of Maxmilian, who was taken prisoner by the republican forces and shot by sentence of a military tribunal, and again became a federal republic. The capital of the country, Mexico, has several theatres and an academy of arts.

The Aztecas were supposed to have entered Mexico about 640 after the Christian era. There are records in existence showing the advancement which the Aztecas made in the pursuits of the arts and sciences. It is said that the natives of Mexico erected stupendous edifices which rivalled those of Egypt ; that they had calendars carrying back the notion of time and marking the different passages of their history ; and that they had historical paintings of which the traditional explanation was repeated orally by the Mexicans to some of their conquerors, and Spanish and Italian ecclesiastics. The little flageolets and whistles of the ancient

American Indians, of which many have been found in tombs, especially in Mexico and in Central America, are of pottery formed to represent animals, and bear, in many other respects, a close resemblance to the Babylonian pipe. Carl Engel gives the scale of one of these flageolets with four finger-holes, which seems to be one of the pentatonic order, the notes represented being A, B, C Sharp, E and F sharp. He also mentions a long wooden trumpet in present use in Mexico called *Acocotle*, or *Clarin*, which derives its designation from the dry stalk of a plant (known among the Indians by the name of Acocotl) of which the tube is made. The peculiarity of the instrument lies in the fact that the performer does not blow into it, but inhales the air through it ; in other words, he produces the sound by sucking the mouth-piece. There is a kind of rattle in use in Mexico which is represented by a notched stick and played by passing a thin wand of wood over the notches. Among the instruments introduced into the country by the European invaders and in present use are the Guitar (strung with ten strings of gut) ; the *Bandolon* (strung with 6 sets of 3 wire strings and played with a small plectrum); and the Harp (mounted with 32 gut and 5 wire strings and having its head carved, as in some specimens, to represent a serpent). With regard to the form and character of the musical instruments of the early Mexicans, Mr. Rowbotham in his "History of Music," 1885, makes the following observations :—"They made their whistles in the shape of birds, frogs, men's heads ; their teponaztlis, even the ordinary ones, were covered with carvings, but the teponaztlis used in war—the war drums, as we should call them—were cut in the figure of a man crouching on his knees ; his back was the drum, and he had eyes of bone and beautifully

braided hair, ear-rings, necklaces, and boat-shaped shoes on his feet, all carved in a mulberry-colored wood, and highly burnished. And while other nations have been content to make their tambourines of a round frame covered with a piece of skin, the Mexicans made theirs in the form of a snake biting a tortoise's head. The snake was coiled up in three coils on the tortoise's back, and the arch of its neck served as a handle, and the belly of the tortoise served as the tambourine, being made of a fat slice of tortoise shell (the rest of the tortoise was of wood) and struck by the right hand, while the instrument itself was held by the left. And here was a peculiar thing about these snakes and tortoise tambourines: there were holes in the tortoise's back which served as stops, and were covered by the fingers. So delicate an ear had the Mexicans for all the shades of percussional sounds, that they could appreciate the variation caused by the stopping and unstopping of a hole in the body of a tambourine no bigger than the hole of an ordinary flute-stop. And they had rattles in the shape of a snake crushing a toad in its coils; and things very much like the Chinese egg-instruments, that were really flageolets with two mouth-pieces, that could play a bass and a treble at the same time; and pipes and rattles combined in the form of three human heads, supporting a pedestal—the pedestal was the pipe, and the heads, which were filled with stones, were the rattles."

NORFOLK SOUND.

Captain Dixon, in his "Voyage Round the World," London, 1789, states that the Indians of Norfolk Sound, North-Western America, have a great variety of tunes, but the method of performing them is universally the same. He thus describes their musical performances:—

"The Chief (who always conducts the vocal concert) puts on a large coat, made of the elk skin tanned, round the lower part of which is one, or sometimes two rows of dried berries, or the beaks of birds, which make a rattling noise whenever he moves. In his hand he has a rattle, or more commonly a contrivance to answer the same end, which is of a circular form, about nine inches in diameter, and made of three small sticks bent round at different distances from each other. Great numbers of bird's beaks and dried berries are tied to this curious instrument, which is shaken by the chief with great glee, and in his opinion makes no small addition to the concert. Their songs generally consist of several stanzas, to each of which is added a chorus. The beginning of each stanza is given out by the chief alone, after which both men and women join and sing in octaves, beating time regularly with their hands or paddles. Meanwhile the chief shakes his rattles and makes a thousand ridiculous gesticulations, singing at intervals in different notes from the rest; and this mirth generally continues near half-an-hour without intermission." Captain Dixon has transcribed one of these songs in which the chief sings out the words "Al-la coosch" followed by an interminable series of the syllable "hoh" "hoh" "hoh," and the women and the men sing the words "Haigh al-la coosch al-la coosch al-la" "heig-ha haigh haigh haigh"—followed by repetitions of the latter phrases.

PORT DES FRANCAIS.

La Perouse, author of "Voyage de La Perouse autour de monde," relates, with reference to the people of Port des Francais (who belong to the same nation as the people of Norfolk Sound), that he frequently heard them singing. When the chief of a tribe came to visit

him on board the ship, he usually approached singing and crossing his arms as a sign of friendship. Having come on board with his followers, they used to perform some pantomime relating to a combat, a surprise, or a death. The song which preceded this pantomimic dance is described as pleasantly melodious, and to some extent, it was also possessed of harmony. Some of the women sang the melody an octave higher than the men, except in the two bars where it descends rather low: here they would frequently pause. Some of the women sang an accompaniment exactly a third above the melody.

NOOTKA SOUND.

The various hordes who inhabit Nootka Sound and the lower tracts of the Columbia River are included in the southern tribes termed Nootka Columbians. They differ from the northern tribes in being fatter and more muscular, in having their cheek-bones more prominent, and in their complexion having more of the copper hue. The practice of flattening the head (the operation being performed on the heads of new-born infants) is universal among the Nootka Columbians. These people are distinguished from the native Americans in general on account of their remarkable fondness for music. Captain Cook speaks highly of the skill which they display in the composition of their songs. "Their music," he observes, "is not of that confined sort found among many rude nations; for the variations are very numerous and expressive, and the cadence and melody powerfully soothing."

LAKE SUPERIOR.

The Ojibbeways, otherwise called Chippeways, who are now situated around Lake Superior, extending north-west towards Lake Winnipeg, and west to

Red River, are reckoned a tribe of the northern branch of the great Algonquin-Lenápe family. The following two specimens of their songs appeared in Kohl's "Kitchi-Gami" :—

SONG OF AN OJIBBEWAY INDIAN GIRL.

Dear friend, worthy friend, look up, look up !
Our Ninimoshin * has promised that in three months he will be here again.
The time has nearly expired, and the end is quickly approaching.
To-morrow, perhaps, we shall see his red canoe in the white foam of the cataracts ;
To-morrow, perhaps, see him sitting in his red canoe, our sunburnt friend !

SONG OF AN OJIBBEWAY INDIAN YOUTH.

[This song was made by a young Indian warrior, to console his three sisters who were mourning for him at home.]

Weep not, ye three sisters, for your brother !
For your brother is a brave !
Weep not, ye three sisters, for your brother !
For your brother is a man !
Weep not, ye three sisters, for your brother !
For he is returning as a victor !

* Cousin, or friend.

THE WEST INDIES.

CUBA.

CUBA, which is the largest of the West India Islands, was discovered by Columbus in his first voyage in 1493. In 1511, the first settlement was made by the Spaniards, and soon after the aboriginal inhabitants were almost wholly extirpated. The Negroes of Cuba have the rattles and drums as their principal instruments. There are several varieties of the former in use. The *Cacha*, a kind of *Maraca* (or rattle), is made of Castilla cane, with hard seeds resembling marbles inside. It is used by the Creoles as an accompaniment to the Guitar. The *Maruga* is a tin rattle, with shot inside. The *Guiro* is a long thin gourd, with notches cut on the back, along which a thin stick is scraped. The *Guiro* is sometimes made of tin. The *Tohona* is a rude drum made of a wooden keg, and having its two heads covered with hide.

JAMAICA.

Jamaica was discovered by Columbus in 1494, colonized by the Spaniards in 1510, and taken by the English in 1655. In 1807, the slave trade was abolished, and on the abolition of slavery in the British possessions in 1833, a very large sum was paid by the Government as compensation to the slave-owners. The following little song refers to a harrowing incident which took place, shortly before the abolition of slavery in Jamaica, on an estate called "Spring Garden," "the owner of

which," says Mr. Mathew Gregory Lewis, in his "Journal of a Residence among the Negroes in the West Indies," London, 1845, "is quoted as the cruelest proprietor that ever disgraced Jamaica." The incident is described by Mr. Lewis as follows :—"It was his constant practice, whenever a sick Negro was pronounced incurable, to order the poor wretch to be carried to a solitary vale upon his estate, called the Gulley, where he was thrown down and abandoned to his fate—which fate was generally to be half devoured by the John-crows before death had put an end to his sufferings. By this proceeding the avaricious owner avoided the expense of maintaining the slave during his last illness ; and in order that he might be as little a loser as possible, he always enjoined the Negro bearers of the dying man to strip him naked before leaving the Gulley, and not to forget to bring back his frock and the board on which he had been carried down. One poor creature, while in the act of being removed, screamed out most piteously that he was not dead yet, and implored not to be left to perish in the Gulley in a manner so horrible. His cries had no effect upon his master, but operated so forcibly on the less marble hearts of his fellow slaves, that in the night some of them removed him back to the Negro village privately, and nursed him there with so much care that he recovered, and left the estate unquestioned and undiscovered. Unluckily, one day the master was passing through Kingston, when, on turning the corner of a street suddenly, he found himself face to face with the Negro whom he had supposed long ago to have been picked to the bones in the Gulley. He immediately seized him, claimed him as his slave, and ordered his attendants to convey him to his house ; but the fellow's cry attracted a crowd round them before he could be dragged away : he related his melancholy

story, and the singular manner in which he had recovered his life and liberty; and the public indignation was so forcibly excited by the shocking tale, that Mr. B. ..was glad to save himself from being torn to pieces, by a precipitate retreat from Kingston, and never ventured to advanced his claim to the Negro a second time."

SONG OF THE NEGRO SLAVES IN JAMAICA.

Take him to the Gulley! Take him to the Gulley!
But bringee back the frock and board.

"O! massa, massa! me no deadee yet!"
Take him to the Gulley! Take him to the Gulley!
Carry him along!

CENTRAL AMERICA.

THE musical instruments of the aboriginal tribes of Central America consist chiefly of drums, rattles, whistles, and flutes. The Indians of the South-eastern Costa Rica use a rattle which is represented by a gourd filled with pebbles. The handle is made of a small bone and is held in place by a cord of sinews. The *Marimba* (which has been already described as an instrument peculiar to Africa) is in great favor with the Negroes of Guatemala, who are said to have introduced its use from Africa. It has, in some of the specimens, twenty-two wooden keys, beneath which are placed hollow pieces of wood for the purposes of resonance. It is played with rubber-tipped hammers, and sometimes three persons play on one instrument at the same time.

SOUTH AMERICA.

As in the other parts of the New World, the principal instruments in use in South America are drums, rattles, flutes, whistles, trumpets, and Pandean pipes. The *Botuto,* which is a sacred trumpet made of wood, now diminishing in number, is used by a number of tribes in the vicinity of Orinoco, and held in great veneration. It is said that one must be of pure morals and have lived single before he could be initiated into the mysteries of the *Botuto.* The *Ture* is in general use among several Indian tribes on the river Amazon who employ it chiefly in war. It is like an Oboe or a Clarionet and produces a harsh and loud sound. It may be mentioned here in passing that the Aryans of India had a war trumpet which was called *Turi.* The fact that many of the South America tribes use the conch as a trumpet is an additional confirmation of the supposition that America was in the olden days colonized by the people of India.

GUIANA

Guiana was discovered in 1504. The Dutch formed the first settlement in 1558, on the Pomeroon; the British in 1590, near Berbice and Surinam. In 1667, the British settlements were given up to the Dutch, but again re-occupied by the English; and in 1814 the settlements between the Corentyn and Marony rivers were restored to the Dutch. In the Journal of the Ethnological Society of London, Vol I, Sir R. Schomburgk says, with reference to a song, which consisted only of three notes, that the Macusi—one of the Indian tribes of Guiana—"amuse themselves for hours singing this monotonous song, the words of which, *hai-a, hai-a,* have no further signification." Refer ring to the *Pehi,* a rattle of the Indians of Guiana, mentioned under the heading of "The Savage Nations" in the present work, the missionaries say that the natives "would not dare to shake it except on special occasions. They would rattle it all night over a person who was ill, and at the same time sing their wild songs." The maquarri dance is the most curious of all the Guianan dances. It is called after the maquarri, or whip, which forms its principal element. The object of the dance is giving and receiving cuts with the whip, and though the hurt given in the contest is sometimes severe, the utmost good humour prevails during the performance. One of the dances of the Arawaks is described as rather picturesque in its character. Twelve young men arrange themselves in parallel rows, but instead of carrying maquarri whips, they bear slender rods, the ends of which they strike against the ground, keeping time with the measure, while they dance backward and forward. These rods are tipped with small gourds having stones inside. From time to time the women run up to the dancers, seize their arms, and

dance with them, but when the men clash the rattling ornaments of beetle's wing cases with which their wrists and legs are decorated, the women give up their hold, and fly back to their companions like so many frightened deer. One of the dances of the Warau tribes consists of steps, accompanied with stamping, while the dancers throw their right arms over their right-hand neighbour's shoulders, and their left arms round their left-hand neighbour's waist, swaying their bodies to and fro. Sometimes the women would insert themselves between the men and join in the performance. This dance is intended to represent the antics of a herd of kairounies, or bush hogs, and the chant, which is sung in unison, is a succession of mocking or jeering expressions. Mr. H. Bernau collected from Guiana a rather elegantly formed rattle. The small hollow gourd which forms part of this rattle is suspended from a series of three hoops which are strung with beetle wings. The slightest movement of the string by which the instrument is held sets all the wings clattering against each other, and the noise produced thereby is described as wonderful in its effect. The natives of Guiana make flutes of the bamboo, and sometimes of the leg bone of the jaguar. A modern specimen of a Pandean pipe collected from Guiana is described as consisting of fourteen reed pipes, arranged in sets of two, and varying in length from 4 feet 2 inches to 5 feet 10 inches. These are set in a hollowed and rounded piece of wood, one end of which is furnished with a hole for the breath. The hands of the performer rest against the sides of this, while the fingers cover a series of small holes in the pipes, just above the wooden handle. The instrument is held and played like the Chinese *Cheng*, and is almost identical in form to the *Phan* which is met with in the northern part of Siam and in the Laos state.

COLOMBIA.

One of the representative instruments of the United States of Colombia is the *Tambeau* which is a drum made by the Indians near Carthagena, the capital of Bolivia. The body is made of a single piece of cork wood, hollowed and covered with a head of skin which is kept in place by a rope made of the bark of the same tree. As in the case of the *Mridanga* of India, a number of wooden wedges are inserted between the rope and the body of the drum, and by pushing these up or down the tension of the skin may be increased or decreased. The *El Pito* is a rude fife also made by the Indians near Carthagena. A rattle box is in use in the remote valleys of the Andes. This consists of a round wooden box, in the interior of which a number of wooden pins are crossed at right angles in such a way as to obstruct the free motion of the seed with which the box is filled. This rattle is used to accompany singing and dancing.

PERU.

Among the Peruvian nations, the dominant race were the Quichuas, or Incas, distinguished by their language, which is the Quichuan. Peru was conquered from the dynasty of the Incas by the troops of Pizarro in 1532, from which time it remained one of the most important possessions of Spain, until its independence in 1821. When it was first visited by the Spaniards, Peru was, with the exception of Mexico, the most civilized country in the New World. It is stated that the old Incas calculated with accuracy the duration of the solar year; had acquired the art of sculpture; recorded the events of history by symbols and by quipus, or knotted cords; worked the precious metals; had a code of laws; practised oratory, poetry and music; and

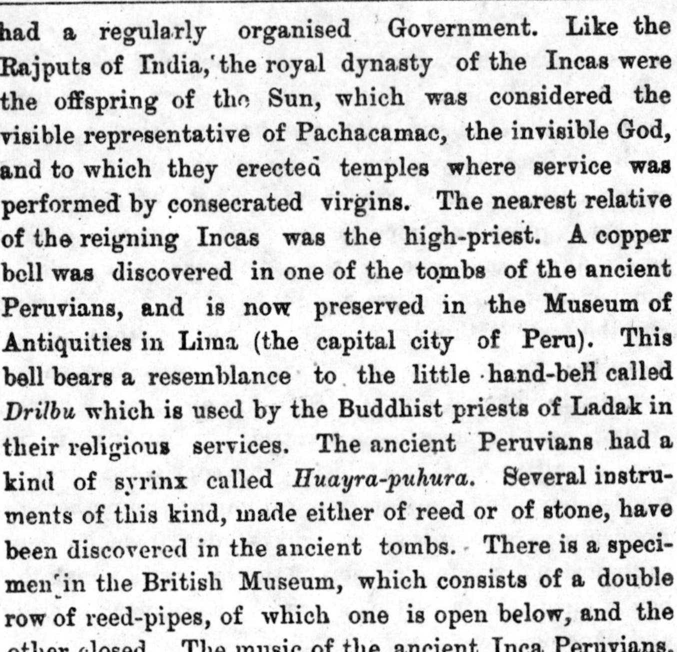

had a regularly organised Government. Like the Rajputs of India, the royal dynasty of the Incas were the offspring of the Sun, which was considered the visible representative of Pachacamac, the invisible God, and to which they erected temples where service was performed by consecrated virgins. The nearest relative of the reigning Incas was the high-priest. A copper bell was discovered in one of the tombs of the ancient Peruvians, and is now preserved in the Museum of Antiquities in Lima (the capital city of Peru). This bell bears a resemblance to the little hand-bell called *Drilbu* which is used by the Buddhist priests of Ladak in their religious services. The ancient Peruvians had a kind of syrinx called *Huayra-puhura*. Several instruments of this kind, made either of reed or of stone, have been discovered in the ancient tombs. There is a specimen in the British Museum, which consists of a double row of reed-pipes, of which one is open below, and the other closed. The music of the ancient Inca Peruvians, as also of the Aztecs in Mexico, was founded on the pentatonic scale. In specimens of the old Peruvian songs, called *Haravi,* no indications of the use of this scale are traceable; and the reason given for this is that these specimens are tainted by the influence which Spanish music exercised over them.

CHILI.

Chili was invaded and taken possession of by the Spaniards after the conquest of Peru, and a settlement formed at Santiago in 1541. The colonists threw off the yoke of Spain 1818, when the country became an independent Republic. The aborigines (Araucanians) inhabit almost exclusively the country south of the Biobio River. The Araucanians form a branch of the Andian family of South America. They are a celebrat-

ed war-like race who defended long the mountains of Chili against the Spaniards. The following "Extempore Song of Araucanian Indian Women, engaged in grinding corn," appeared in "The Araucanians: or, Notes of a Tour among the Indian Tribes of Southern Chili;" by E. R. Smith, London, 1855 :—

> We are grinding wheat for the stranger
> Who has come from a long way off.
> May the flour be white to his eye,
> And pleasant to his taste:
> For he has brought us beads;
> He has given us bells to deck our hair.

The watchmen in the town of Valparaiso carry a loud and shrill whistle, the sounds of which are varied as occasion requires, and by it a Police force can be collected in a few moments. When they cry the hour, which, it is said, they do in a pleasing manner, they all sing the same tune, but the pitch is ranged according to the scope of the voice. The words sung are—"Viva Chili! Viva Chili! Lasdiez anda, y serena!" In the morning a prayer is added—"Ave Maria purissima, las cinco y media." The music is the same as that of the night-song, a few notes being added for the additional words.

BRAZIL.

Brazil was discovered by the Portuguese in the year 1500, and begun to be colonized by them in 1531. In 1808, John VI. of Portugal took up his residence in Brazil; and in 1815 constituted it a kingdom. In 1822 it declared itself an independent state, and the Government was vested in hereditary Emperor (sprung from the Royal family of Portugal), a senate elected for life by the Emperor, and a representative chamber chosen by the people. In 1891, a disturbance took place,

resulting in Dom Pedro, the last Emperor, abdicating the throne, and in Brazil being declared a republic. The Eastern Guarani are the Tupi, or native inhabitants of Brazil. The general language of Brazil is called Tupi from the name of the first Indians who were converted to Christianity. The aboriginal inhabitants are said to employ harmony in their songs. In his "Narrative of the United States Expedition," Captain Wilkes says of the Negro slaves in Rio de Janeiro (the capital city of Brazil) :—"The coffee-carriers go along in large gangs of twenty or thirty, singing. One half take the air, with one or two keeping up a kind of hum on the *Common Chord,* and the reminder finish the bar", the "bar" here being evidently meant for a musical phrase or sentence. Dr. von Spix and Dr. von Martius (Munich, 1823), have published a number of songs and dance tunes of the Indian tribes in Brazil. Some of these melodies conclude with a chord to be sung in full chorus. The *Maraca* of the Brazilian Indians has already bee mentioned under the heading of "The Savage Nations ;" when shaken it produces a loud and hollow sound.

BOLIVIA.

Bolivia, under the name of Upper Peru, was formerly a part of the Spanish Viceroyalty of Buenos Ayres. It acquired its independence in 1825, and the present name was assumed in honor of Bolivar, the great champion of South American independence, who, in 1826, drew up its first constitution. The Indians form about one-eighth of the population of Bolivia, and these are principally the Moxos and the Chiquitos. The former were, before the conquest, fishermen, hunters, and cultivators of the land. The chase was only used by them as a recreation, but fishing was a necessary employment,

while agriculture procured them provisions and the materials necessary for a favorite liquor which, as among the Chiquitians, was made in a common house where strangers were received and where, on certain days, the inhabitants met to drink, sing, and dance. The Jesuits who founded missions in the provinces of the Moxos and Chiquitos, have been partly successful in uniting all the tribes under a uniform language (Chiquito), which is said to be sweet and melodious, and presents no harsh sounds or redundance of consonants. Alcide d'Orbigny, in his "Voyage dans l'Amerique Meridionale," has published an account of the music of several Indian tribes in Bolivia, with tunes. The melodies collected by him show unmistakeable traces of harmony. There is no reason to suppose that the musical taste of the Chiquitos, as represented in these songs, has been to any great extent modified by that of the European inhabitants of Bolivia.

OCEANIA.

THE people of Oceania are divided into three groups—the Malayan, Pelagian Negroes (often called the Papuans), and the Alforas. The Malayan stock is, again, subdivided into three branches—(1) Indo-Malayans, comprehending the Malays proper of Malacca, and the islanders of the Indian Archipelago, as the inhabitants of Sumatra, Java, Celebes, the Moluccas, and the Philippines; (2) Polynesians, comprehending the Tonga Islanders, the New Zealanders, the Tahitians, and the Hawaii; and (3) the Madecasses, or the people of Madagascar (very recently made a French colony).

MALAYSIA.

THE Malays inhabit the southern portion of the Peninsula of Malacca, possess a considerable part of the Island of Sumatra, and have formed settlements in most parts of the Indo-Chinese Seas. They are the Phœnicians of the Eastern Seas. They are people of one dialect, and nearly of the same manners and cultivation. Mr. John Crawfurd thus describes the dances of the Malays in his "History of the Indian Archipelago":— "All orders executed in the presence of a Javanese monarch on public occasions are accompanied by a dance. When a message is to be conveyed to the royal ear, the messenger advances with a solemn dance, and retreats in the same way. The ambassadors from one native prince in Java to another follow the same course when coming into and retiring from the presence of the sovereign to whom they are deputed. When the persons, whose business it is to let the tiger loose from his cage into the hollow square of spearmen, have performed their duty, and received the royal nod to retire, an occasion, one would think, when dancing might be spared, they do so in a slow dance and solemn strut, with some risk of being devoured by the tiger in the midst of their performance. Previous to the introduction of the Mahomedan religion, it appears to have been the custom of all oriental islanders, for the men of rank, at their public festivities, when heated with wine, to dance. Upon such occasions, the exhibi-

tion appears to have been a kind of war dance. The dancer drew his kris, and went through all the evolutions of a mock fight. At present the practice is most common among the Javanese, with every chief of whom dancing, far from being considered scandalous, as among the people of Western India, is held to be a necessary accomplishment." Mr. Crawfurd remarks that among the Malays "whatever be the occasion in which dancing is exhibited, it is always grave, stately, and slow, never gay nor animated. As in all Asiatic dancing, it is not the legs but the body, and specially the arms, down to the very fingers, that are employed." The descendants of the Portuguese settlers in Malacca, who are a mixed race of Portuguese and aborigines, are described as great musicians. At the close of the day the married men are said to sit in the verandahs, playing on the violin some melancholy dirge for the amusement of their wives and families who are gathered round them. The influence of Spanish music is reported by travellers to have made itself felt in the musical performances of the people in the Philippine Islands, and other places where the Spaniards at any time established a footing.

The following is a specimen of a Malay song, which has a misanthropic ring in it :—

The painful feeling of my love will only cease
When the wicked of the world,
The knaves, the thieves, and the liars,
The scandalous and those who steal,
And the banditti, are all held in contempt ;
When the robbers and plunderers are all destroyed,
And cock-fighters are in despair ;
When gamblers are cast out,
Then, perhaps, the sadness of my heart may cease ;
Then may I be restored to peace and happiness.

JAVA.

It is stated that the Hindus, at an early period, settled in the Island of Java, and held sway over it until 1478, when it was conquered by the Arabs, and since when its possession has been chiefly Mahomedan. Java contains the ruins of several considerable cities and temples showing unmistakeable traces of Hindu civilization, the principal being Mojopahit and Boro-Budor. The prevailing religion of Java is Mahomedanism with an admixture of Buddhism. The Javanese are of the Malay family and speak three dialects of the Malay language. They have an ancient sacred language which contains a number of Sanskrit words. They have also a national literature, and translations from the Arabic and Sanskrit. The Portuguese formed a settlement on the Island in 1511, and the Dutch in 1575. The British held it from 1811 to 1816. It is now under the Government of the Netherlands, and forms the principal of the Dutch East India islands.

Some Javanese tunes are given in Sir Stamford Raffle's "History of Java," from which it would appear that the Javanese people make extensive use of the pentatonic scale. The melodies published in Mr. John Crawfurd's "History of the Indian Archipelago" are constructed on a similar scale. In this book is found a letter from Dr. Crotch in which it is mentioned that the Javanese instruments brought to England by Sir Stamford Raffles "are all in the same kind of scale as that produced by the black keys of the pianoforte." This statement is borne out by authorities who had an opportunity of inspecting the instruments in the British Museum. They state that the instruments are tuned in the pentatonic scale which is, in fact, the order of

intervals represented by the black keys on the piano-forte.

Of the wind instruments of the Javanese, the widest and earliest is the *Angklung,* which is confined to the mountaineers. The *Suling* and *Serdum* are flutes or fifes used by the Malay tribes, and played alone. Of the stringed instruments, the principle ones are the *Chalempung* (mounted with from 10 to 15 wires) ; the *Trawangsa* (the same sort of lute which among the Malays goes under the name of *Kachapi*) ; and the *Rabab* (which is borrowed from the Persians, but is mounted with two strings and played with a bow). The Javanese have drums of a large variety including those borrowed from the Arabs and Europeans. The *Gong* (or *Gung,* as the word is correctly written in all the dialects of the Archipelago) is another instrument used in many of its varieties in Java. A series of gongs, arranged in a double row upon a wooden frame, go under the name of *Kromo* and *Bonang.* The *Gambang,* or staccado, presents a large variety and is extensively used throughout the Archipelago. The wooden staccado is called *Gambang Kayu.* A modification of the metallic variety is known by the name of *Gander.* The simplest and most ancient band (called *Gamalan* in the Javanese language) is styled the *Manggang.* The *Gamalan Kodok Ngorek* means the band resembling the "croaking of frogs." The *Salendro, Miring,* and *Pelag* are bands specially used to accompany the different kinds of dramatic exhibitions. The *Gamalan Choro Bali* is the band according to the fashion of the neighbouring Island of Bali. The *Sakaten* is the band played only before the monarch, and on religious and other solemn festivals. The *Srunen* is the martial music of the country. The dance of Java has already been described under the general heading of "Malaysia."

"Bandi Lori" and "Surung Dayung" are known to be two of the most popular airs of Java. The following translation of a Javanese song is taken from Raffle's "History of Java", Vol. I, London, 1817 :—

> My handsome girl ! in bringing a purchase from the market,
>
> When you have paid the price, cast not your eyes behind,
>
> But move quickly
>
> Lest men may seize upon you.

BORNEO.

Borneo (native name *Bulo-Kalamantin*) was discovered by the Portuguese in 1521. The most important event in the recent history of the Island is the enterprise of the late Sir James Brooke, who first visited Borneo in 1839, and took an active part in the suppression of piracy, the administration of justice, and in the promotion of arts and commerce. The population of Borneo consists of Malays, about one-fourth ; Dyaks, two-thirds ; and the remainder Chinese and Europeans. The sword dance of the Dyaks is accompanied by the music of the gongs and tom-toms, which instruments they have borrowed from the Malays. These gongs, like the Javanese, are thick with a broad rim and very different from the Chinese instruments of the same class. Like the Malays, the Dyaks use the gongs and tom-toms in war and also as signals at night. Sometimes the sword dance is performed with the shield as well as the sword. In connection with these dances, sometimes a chief would step forward with a whip, somewhat like a cat-o'-nine-tails, while another would produce a human head, and both begin to chase each other. The chief with

the head would then stop, and with one foot in the air begin to pirouette slowly, swinging the head to and fro, while the chief with the whip would lash vigorously at the spectators and laugh derisively at each cut. When these performers retired to refresh themselves, their place would be taken by four or five others carrying rhinoceros horn-bills. Then suddenly a number of gongs would be beaten and over the mass of human beings would arise swords, heads, rhinoceros horn-bills and whips in profusion, the Dyaks being, for the time, almost mad with excitement, but maintaining the strictest discipline and decorum.

AUSTRALASIA.

AUSTRALIA.

THE Portuguese, in the year 1540, were the earliest European discoverers of Australia, though little was known of it until Dampier, Wallis, and Cook explored its coasts. The name of New Holland, given by the Dutch to the north-west coasts, which were first discovered by them, and subsequently extended to the whole of the mainland, has now been superceded by the term Australia. The aborigines are a race distinct from the Pelagian tribes of any class, and come exclusively under the designation of Alforian. The dialects are numerous and are not understood by tribes even near each other. Many of the tribes go naked, practising cannibalism and having scarcely any notion of a Deity or of social arts or order. The British settlement of New South Wales was made in 1788. In his "Musical curiosities," London 1811, Mr. Edward Jones says, with reference to a song of the natives of New South Wales, that its air "was written down from the singing of Benelong and Yamroweny, the two chiefs who were brought to England, some years ago, from Botany Bay by Governor Phillips. The subject of their song is in praise of their lovers; and when they sang, it seemed indispensable to them to have two sticks, one in each hand, to beat time with the tune; one end of the left-hand stick rested on the ground, while the other in the right hand was used to beat against it, according to the time of the notes." Captain Wilkes states that the natives of New South Wales usually

finish their songs, especially those to which they dance, "with a loud *whoo* or screech an octave above the key-note." With regard to the *Corroborie* or *Palti*, which they dance, around a large fire, in numbers of about twenty, all painted with broad white lines almost all over the body, he says:—"The skeletons, as I may term them, for they truly resemble them, suddenly seem to vanish and reappear. This disappearance is effected by merely turning round, for the figures are painted only in front, and their dusky forms are lost by mingling with the dark background. The trees, illuminated by the fire, were brought out with some of the figures in bold relief, while others were indistinct and ghost-like. All concurred to give an air of wildness to the strange scene." The *Kangaroo* dance is performed by the men only, while the women are singing and beating time by striking two pieces of wood together. The dancers imitate the grunting of the kangaroo, whereby they furnish a kind of bass to the singing of the women. In the Frog-dance, the performers, who paint themselves in a grotesque fashion, as they do in all their dances, take their *wirris* (club) in their hands, beat them together, and then squat down and jump after each other in circles, imitating the movements of the frog. In the Emu-dance, the gestures consist of the imitation of emu hunting, the man who represents the bird imitating its voice. The Canoe dance obtains in some parts of Australia. The men and women, who take part in this dance, paint their bodies with white and red ochre, and are each furnished with a stick which stands for the paddle. They commence dancing by placing themselves in two lines, but with the stick across their backs and held by the arms, while they make steps with their feet alternately to the tune of the accompanying song. At a given signal, they all bring the sticks to the front, and

hold them as they do paddles, swaying themselves in regular time as if they were engaged in paddling in one of their light canoes. Another dance, called the *Peduku*, is a great favorite with the Moorundi natives. This consists in stamping simultaneously with the left foot, and shaking the fingers of the extended arms. In this both men and women join, the former standing in a line and the latter being collected in group and beating time together. There is a rather curious dance with which the performance of the evening is often concluded. The performers sit cross-legged round their fire, beating time with their spears and *wirris*. Suddenly they all stretch out their arms as if pointing to some distant object, rolling their eyes fearfully as they do so, and finish by leaping on their feet with a simultaneous yell that echoes for miles through the forest. The Parnkalla tribes have a curious dance in which both men and women take part. The men all sit down, while a women takes her place in the centre. One of the men then dances up to her, from side to side, and swaying his arms in harmony with his movements. The woman commences to jump as her partner approaches, and then they dance back again, making room for a fresh couple. On account of its being usually held on clear moonlight evenings, this dance has been supposed by some to be a religious ceremony. Sometimes, however, it is performed during the day-time. The *Kuri* dance, which is in vogue among the natives of the Adelaide district, seems to have one point in common with the cotillon of Europe, *viz.*, that it can be varied, shortened, or lengthened, according to the fancy of the players; so that one witnessing this dance performed six or seven times will never see the movements repeated in the same order. The "Corroborie," or as it is also called the "Palti,"

which has been described above, is the commonest dance of the Australians. Once in a year, the natives of some of the districts in the interior have a very grand dance styled the "Cobongo Corroborie," or great mystery dance. An account of this dance appeared in the *Illustrated London News* of October 3, 1863. The time selected for this dance is every twelfth moon, and during her declination. At the appointed time, *i. e.*, when the moon rises—the fact being announced by one of the old "wammaroogo," (medicine men)—the women beat the fire-sticks together, keeping time to a peculiar monotonous air, and repeating the words, the burden of which when translated may be

> "The Kangaroo is swift, but swifter is Ngoyulloman;
>
> The snake is cunning, but more cunning is Ngoyulloman," &c.,

each woman using the name of her husband or favorite in the tribe. The men spring to their feet with a piercing shriek, and brandishing their spears, boomerangs, &c., begin their dance, flinging themselves into all sorts of attitudes, howling, laughing, grinning, and singing; and this they continue till compelled to desist by sheer exhaustion. This is called the mystery dance, because, previous to commencing it, their medicine men light a fire round which they walk and into which, while muttering sentences, they throw portions of old charms which they have worn round their necks for the past twelve months. The mystery "Corroborie" combines several of the peculiar movements which are to be found in the various dances of the Australians.

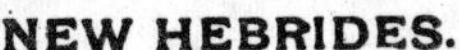

NEW HEBRIDES.

The New Hebrides are peopled by a race having a general resemblance to the New Caledonians who have their hair crisp and much curled. Captain Cook, in describing the customs of the natives of Tanna Island, one of the New Hebrides, says that at day break he heard a noise in the woods, on the east side of the harbour, which appeared to him not unlike the singing of psalms. He was told that similar sounds had been heard every morning at the same time. He was further told that at the east point of the harbour was something sacred to religion, as people who had attempted to go towards it were prevented by the natives.

NEW ZEALAND.

The territory was discovered in 1642 by Tasman, who examined the western coast, and by Cook on the east side in 1769. The country was first formally taken possession of as a British colony in 1840. In 1853 a free constitution was proclaimed, and is now in force. The aborigines, who are said to be derived from the Polynesian stock, are rapidly on the decline. It is rather curious that drums, while they resound in all the islands of the Pacific, should be utterly unknown to the New Zealander. The only really musical instrument which he possesses is a sort of fife made out of human bone, generally the thigh-bone of a slain enemy. There are, besides the fife, two noise-making instruments in use in the country, which might be called the war bell and the war trumpet. The former goes by the name of *Pahu*, and consists of a block of hard wood with a deep groove in the centre, which is slowly and regularly struck with a stick made of heavy wood. The *Pahu* is never sounded by day, the object being to tell the people inside the village that the sentinel is awake, and to

tell any approaching enemy that it would be useless for him to attempt an attack by surprise. The *Putara-putara*, by which name the war trumpet is called, is hollowed out of a piece of hard wood. It is used only on occasions of alarm. A smaller trumpet is used in times of war, in some places. The body of this instrument is always made of a large shell, generally that of a triton, and the mode of blowing it differs according to the locality. Regarding the general character of the songs of the New Zealanders, Dr. Van Dieffenbach, in his "Travels in New Zealand," writes as follows :—Some songs are lyric, and are sung to a low, plaintive, uniform, but not at all disagreeable tune. . . . . E'Waiata is a song of a joyful nature ; E'Haka one accompanied by gestures of mimicry ; E'Karakia is a prayer or incantation used on certain occasions. In saying this prayer there is no modulation of the voice, but syllables are lengthened and shortened, and it produces the same effect as reading the Talmud in synagogues. Most of these songs live in the memory of all, but with numerous variations . . . . To adapt words to a certain tune, and thus to commemorate a passing event, is common in New Zealand." The New Zealanders, or, as they are also called, the Maories are said to possess a remarkably fine ear for distinguishing quarter-tones. Mr. James A. Davis thinks that the succession of intervals employed by them closely resembles the *Enharmonic genus* of the ancient Greeks, which consisted of a succession of a quarter-one, another quarter-tone, and a major third. He has noted down two of their airs, the "Whakarongo," and "He Walata Aroha" or "Bride's Complaint," showing the intervals used. George Forster, in his "Voyage Round the World," London 1777, has published a New Zealand tune in two-part harmony. "Of this tune," he says, "they

continue to sing the first two bars till the words of their song are at an end, and then they close with the last. Sometimes they also sing an under-part which is the third lower, except the last two notes, which are unisons." Mr. Forster has also published a dirge from New Zealand which relates to the death of a chief whose name was Tupaya. The words are "Aghee, matte awhay Tupaya!" (Departed, dead, alas! Tupaya!). Forster who frequently heard this dirge sung remarks: "There is an extreme simplicity in the words, though they seem to be metrically arranged in such a manner as to express the feeling of the mourners by their slow movement." In his "Manners and Customs of the New Zealanders," London, 1840, Mr. J. S. Polack says that the Maories are so very fond of singing that they will often spend the whole night in its gratification. They prosecute all laborious work, such as hauling heavy logs of wood or canoes overland, with the aid of the song. Mr. Edward Shortland has published some of these chants, in his "Traditions and Superstitions of the New Zealanders," London, 1856. The following is a specimen taken from it:—

Solo.—Pull, Tainui, pull the Arawa,
To launch them on the ocean.
Surely glanced the bolt of
Thunder, falling hitherward,
On my sacred day.
The Kiwi cries.

Chorus.—Kiwi.
Solo.—The Moho cries.
Chorus.—Moho.
Solo.—The Tieke cries.
Chorus.—Tieke.
Solo.—A belly only.
Chorus.—Fork it out, fork it out!
Solo.—Keep in the path.
Chorus.—Fork it out!
Solo.—'Tis the second year to-day.

Chorus.—Cheerily, men!
Solo.—'Tis the man-catcher.
Chorus.—Cheerily, men!
Solo.—Give this way, and carry it.
Chorus.—Cheerily, men!
Solo.—But whither carry it?
Chorus.—Cheerily, men!
Solo.—Ah! to the root.
Chorus.—Root of Tu.
Solo.—O wind.
Chorus.—Pull away!
Solo.—Pull onwards the root.
Chorus.—Root of Tu.

The *Solo* part is sung by the leader, and the chorus by the laborers who respond, and haul the boat at the same instant all together. The *Kiwi, Moho,* and *Tieke* are names of birds.

The Maories have a tradition that their ancestor, a chief named Turi, having first landed in the country with his men, built a *pah* or fortress and cultivated the soil; and the chant which they sung, "to encourage themselves and to keep time as they dug," was, according to the tradition, as follows:—

Break up our goddess mother,
Break up the ancient goddess earth;
We speak of you, oh, earth! but do not you disturb
The plants we have brought hither from Hawaiki the noble;
It was Maui who scraped the earth in heaps round the sides in Kuratan.

According to Maori tradition, the ancestors of the present race came, about 500 years ago, from a distant island named Hawaiki, lying in a northerly or north-easterly direction from New Zealand.

In describing the dances of the New Zealanders Mr. Polack says:—"But few songs and choruses are chanted unaccompanied by action; thus, in describing a

voyage, the cantator represents with his body the uneasy motion of the waves; and if the horrors of war are the theme, the several passages in it are represented with fidelity, and the arm is bared to indicate the closing scene of cannibalism, the actor pretending to gnaw the limb with marks of the most intense gratification."

Before engaging in war, the Maoris feel bound to join in the war-dance which is described as being guided by strict discipline and characterised by a wonderful precision. When they assemble for the dance, they excite their naturally passionate disposition to the highest pitch by contorting their faces and thrusting out their tongues as an act of defiance, interspersing these gestures with shouts, yells, and challenges to the enemy. The dance itself begins with stamping the feet in perfect time with each other. The vigor of the stamp keeps increasing, when suddenly, with a yell, the whole body of men leap side-ways into the air, as if actuated by one spirit, and, as they touch the ground, come down on it with a mighty stamp that makes the earth tremble. Even when war is not impending, the magic influence of the dance affects the performers as strongly as if they were close to a *pah* or fort of the enemy, ready for battle, and they become so furiously excited that they are quite dangerous until they have had time to cool.

The following "Complaint of a Maori Girl" appeared in Shortland's work cited before :—

My regret is not
To be expressed ! Like a spring,
The tears
Gush from my eyes.

I wonder whatever Te Kaiuku * is doing ;
He who deserted me. Now
I climb upon
The ridge of mount Parahaki:
From whence is clear the view
Of the Island Tuhua.
I see with regret
The lofty Taumo, †
Where dwells Tangiteruru. ‡
Let me hang in my ear
The shark's tooth.
How fine, how pretty I'll look !—
But see, whose ship is that
Tacking in the distance ?
Is it yours ? O Hu ! §
You husband of Pohiwa,
Sailing away
On the tide to Europe.
O Toru ! pray give me
Some of your fine things ;
For beautiful are
The clothes of the sea-god. ||
Enough of this.
I must return to my rags,
And to my nothing-at-all.

The following "Lament of the Maori Chiefs on the Death of the Prince Consort" was sent from New Zealand to Her Majesty the Queen Victoria, with an address of sympathy and condolence, signed by twenty Maori Chiefs. The piece appeared in *The Times*, November 15, 1862 :—

Great is the pain which preys on me for the loss of my beloved.

Ah, you will now be buried among the other departed kings !

* Name of her lover.

† The name of a high hill at Tuhua, where there is a village.

‡ The name of the Chief of Tuhua.

§ Hu, or Pohiwa, a Maori woman, was the wife of a European and having plenty of fine clothes, she was the admiration of her country women.

|| Tipua, the sea-god ; a fabulous monster, supposed to inhabit the ocean or the lakes. It is here used for the white man.

They will leave you with the other departed heroes of the land ;

With the dead of the tribes of the multitude of Ti Mani.

Go fearless then, O Pango, my beloved, in the path of death , for no evil slanders can follow you.

Oh my very heart ! Thou didst shelter me from the sorrows and ills of life.

Oh my pet bird, whose sweet voice welcomed my glad guests !

Oh my noble pet bird, caught in the forests of Rapaura !

Let, then, the body of my beloved be covered with royal purple robes ;

Let it be covered with all rare robes !

The great Rewa, my beloved, shall himself bind these round thee.

And my ear-ring of precious jasper shall be hung in thy ear.

For, oh ! my most precious jewel, thou art now lost to me.

Yes, thou, the pillar that didst support my palace, hast been borne to the skies.

Oh, my beloved ! you used to stand in the very prow of the war-canoe, inciting all others to noble deeds.

Yes, in thy life-time, thou wast great.

And now thou hast departed to the place where even all the mighty must at last go.

Where, oh physicians, was the power of your remedies ?

What, oh priests, availed your prayers ?

For I have lost my love ; no more can he revisit this world.

NEW CALEDONIA.

New Caledonia was discovered by Captain Cook in 1774. It was taken possession of by the French, with its dependency, the Isle of Pines, as a French colony, September 20, 1853. The population are of the Papuan Negro race. The natives make a sort of mask, very ingeniously cut out of wood, having the mouth opened and the eyes closed. The wearer looks, not through the eyes, but through some apertures made in the upper part of the mask. Mr. J. G. Wood, author of "The Uncivilized Races of Men", conjectures that this mask, which is said to be used in war with a view to enable the combatants to disguise themselves from their enemies, is nothing more than an ornament employed in the native dances. It is the "momo" described by recent travellers. When complete, the "momo" is decorated with plumes of feathers, long tufts of hair, and a thick, coarse network, which does duty for a beard, and descends as far as the knees of the wearer.

NEW GUINEA.

New Guinea or Papua is inhabited partly by Malays, and partly by a Negro race, termed the Papuan Negro, and some such as the Mafors, who have Caucasian affinities. The Papuans are fond of singing and dancing, and are said to be in the habit of composing extempore songs. Their musical instruments consist chiefly of the cylindrical drum, a trumpet made of a triton shell, and a sort of Pandean pipe, composed of six or seven reeds of different lengths firmly lashed together. There is also a wind instrument, which is nothing more than a bamboo tube some two feet in length. The cylindrical drum is called "Baiatu," and is made of palm wood, about two feet in length and four inches in diametre.

One end is covered with lizard-skin, and along the side there run longitudinal slits. Mr. J. Crossby Brown of New York collected a drum, called *Arpa*, from the Gulf of Papua, New Guinea. This instrument is shaped in imitation of the head and jaws of the crocodile, is two and a half feet long, and is held by a wooden handle in the centre. The head is covered with snake skin. To the accompaniment of these instruments the Papuans perform their dances. One of these dances consists of advancing and retreating together by sudden jerks, and chanting a song, the cadence rising and falling according to the action. In the war dance, the performer holds in one hand a large wooden shield, and in the other a portion of the snout of the sword-fish. Placing himself in a crouching attitude, with one hand covered by the shield, and holding his weapon (the snout) in a position to strike, he advances rapidly in a succession of short bounds, striking the inner side of his shield with his left knee at each jerk, causing the large *cowries* hung round his waist and ankles to rattle violently. At the same time, he loudly chants a song of defiance. The rest of the pantomine is expressive of attack and defence, and exultation after victory. There is another dance which is performed by a number of people, each carrying a blazing torch in his hand. At one time they extend rapidly into line, at another close, dividing into two parties, advancing and retreating, crossing and recrossing, and mixing up with each other.

POLYNESIA.

MANY of the Polynesian Islands seem to have been raised from the ocean by the labors of the coral insect; others show traces of volcanic origin. In 1767, Wallis, and subsequently Cook, explored and described the leading islands. Soon after this, Christian missionaries began to settle in the region and proselytize the natives. The earliest missionaries found among the aborigines an institution which has been called the Areoi Society, the members of which consisted of strolling players who travelled from one island to another and gave public exhibitions of their music and dances. These representations are said to have partaken somewhat of the histrionic character. Public events were alluded to, and the priests and others fearlessly ridiculed in these performances. Originally, the Areoi constituted a religious sect considering itself as the special favorite of the god *Oro*, and the public pastimes were devotional exercises.

MARQUESAS ISLANDS.

Four of these Islands were discovered by Mendana in 1596, the others by Captain Cook in 1774. The natives of Nukahiva (the principal island of the Marquesas Archipelago) are said to distinctly intone quarter-tones in their vocal performances. Councillor Tilesius who visited them at the beginning of the present century heard them sing a song with the rythmical accompaniment of drums and clapping of hands. The performance was, in fact, a kind of dramatic representation of their exploits,

and referred to the strife they had with the inhabitants of the neighbouring island of St. Christina. It commenced with the return of the warriors from battle. It was night. One of the savages saw in the distance a fire rising and asked where it was. The chorus answered that it was upon Tauhuata Montanioh (St. Christina) with their enemies who were roasting their slain brethren. This incited them to revenge, and the subsequent part of the song contained detailed accounts of the preparation for a feast upon some unhappy captive taken in battle, the horridness of which was relieved by expressions indicating the sympathetic cries of the victim's parents or sisters. It should be noted here that this representation took place at a period when cannibalism was in vogue in the Islands. Tilesius adds that the performance of that song, in a slow movement, by several hundred savage warriors with their wives and children, singing in unison and octaves, dancing around a large fire, or lying on the ground and gnawing human bones, almost drove him to desperation, and made him feel as if he heard his own funeral dirge. In every village there is a sort of amphitheatre or *Pahooa*, as it is called, where dancing and other amusements are conducted. For this purpose the Marquesans select a covered and level spot, surrounded on all sides with rising banks. The middle of the amphitheatre is carefully smoothed and covered with mats, and the rising banks serve as seats for the spectators. When a dance is to be performed, the mats are laid afresh, and a large amount of food is prepared. The spectators take the food with them and, seated on the banks, remain there throughout the greater part of the day. The dances consist chiefly of jumping without moving from the same spot. Various ornaments are used by the dancers, the most curious of which are the finger-rings, which are made of plaited fibre, adorned

with the long tail-feathers of the tropic bird. When women dance, they are not allowed to wear clothing of any kind, and this for a curious reason. None dance except those whose husbands or brothers have been killed in war or taken prisoners, and the absence of clothing indicates mourning on their part, and vengeance on that of the spectators.

THE SOCIETY ISLANDS.

The natives of the Society Islands, including Tahiti, or Otaheite, are, according to Cook, of the largest size of Europeans. The men are tall, strong, well-limbed, and finely shaped. The women of the superior rank are also in general above the middle stature. Their complexion is a kind of olive, or *brunette*. In features and color they resemble the people of the Marquesas Island. Most of them have been converted to Christianity and taught the arts of civilized life. Since 1843, the Society Islands have been under the protection of France. Mr. Georger Forster who witnessed a dance of the natives of one of the Society Islands has described it in his "Voyage Round the World," London, 1717. In this dance, three men performed a sort of pantomime, which represented travellers asleep and thieves skilfully making away with their goods, round which the former had placed themselves.

The Tahitans are fond of singing, and are possessed of good voices and accurate ears. Some of them have become apt pupils in European music. As a rule, they prefer singing the air, the elaborate movements of concerted music being not to their taste. Their native mode of singing is of a monotonous character, nasal in tone, and marked by frequent transitions from the highest to the lowest notes. The subjects of their national song are chiefly love and war. Patriotic songs

and pieces in praise of their national scenery and fertile soil are sometimes sung. The women are the principal singers. The singing and dancing are accompanied by the drum which is gently tapped with the fingers. The Tahitans hold the Jews' harp in high favor. The chief native instrument that is capable of producing different notes is a sort of flageolet or "hoe" which emits a low, deep tone, something like the "drone" or the bagpipe. Surrounding the mouth-piece (which is split longitudinally) is a ring of soft wood, and by driving this forward or backward, the performer can tune his instrument with some nicety, the former movement producing a sharp, and the latter a graver tone. The "hoe" is generally used as an accompaniment to the dances. In both singing and dancing the Tahitans keep admirable time.

FIJI ISLANDS.

The Fiji, sometimes called the Viti Islands, were discovered by Tasman in 1643, and formed into a British colony in 1875. The inhabitants are called Kai Viti (or people of Viti) by themselves. The root *kai* means "to eat," or "to live," and it seems Fiji is the corruption of the name *Viti* in the Tonga language. The Fijians are possessed of greater physical and mental energy than any of the fair Polynesians. They have a mythological history and tradition of their own, differing from those of the Tongans, Samoans, and Tahitians.

The musical instruments of the Fijians consist of drums (wooden cylinders), trumpets (conch shells blown through a hole in the side), and pipes, of which last there are two kinds, *viz.*, a kind of Pandean pipe, and the flute. The flute is played by placing the aperture close to one nostril and breathing through it, while the other is stopped with the thumb of the left hand. It is called

the *Mbita ni Tangi*. It is made of bamboo, ornamented with charred lines, and has five holes in front at considerable intervals, and one on each side opposite the middle hole. The nose-flute is found in several of the neighbouring islands, and its use is said to have been introduced there from India. Mr. Rowbotham believes that the flute was first played through the nose. The reason for this practice may be found in the fact that in India a man of a higher caste cannot touch with his lips any thing which may have been similarly touched by one of a lower caste, and the practice of blowing with the nose obviates the difficulty. Music and dancing are extensively cultivated by the Fijians, and are always used at the celebration of a marriage. Any one who has learnt a new dance can make a good deal by teaching it. The dances, in which sometimes several hundred men are engaged, while the musicians number 20 or 30, are carefully got up, and partake more of the character of military movements than that of any thing else. Sometimes, with a view to enliven the performance, a professional buffoon is introduced, who goes through a number of grotesque movements and secures the applause of the spectators.

The national airs of the Fijians are constructed of an extraordinarily small number of intervals. Captain Wilkes has published a melody which contains all the diatonic intervals in the compass of a *fifth*. The translation of the words of the song is as follows:—

I was sleeping in the Tambu-tangane;
A red cock crowed near the house,
I woke up suddenly and cried;
I was going to get some Kundravi flowers
For a wreath in the harmonious dance.

Here is another song of the Fiji Islanders :—

In Rewa a fine southerly wind was blowing ;
The wind was blowing from the point of Rewa,
And it shakes down the flowers of the Sinu tree;
So that the women may make garlands.
String the Sinu and cover it with Lemba flowers ;
When put together I will hang it on my neck ;
But the queen begs it and I take it off,—
Queen ! take our garland of Lemba ;
I throw it on the little couch.
Take ye the garland that I have been making,
That the ladies may make a great noise in coming.
Let us go to the thungiawa.*
The mother of Thangi-lemba was vexed ;
Why did you give away our dance ?
The basket of dance-fees is empty,
This world is a world of trouble ;
They will not succeed in learning to dance,
The sun goes down too soon in Muthuata.

SANDWICH ISLANDS.

When Cook discovered the group, each island had a separate ruler ; but afterwards the whole of the islands were consolidated under one government, and idolatory was abolished. Missionaries commenced their labors in 1820, and the natives are now almost all Christians. A treaty of friendship, navigation, and commerce between Her Majesty the Queen of England and the King of the Sandwich Islands was signed at Honolulu (the capital of the group), July 10, 1861. Hawaii or Owyhee is the largest and southern-most of the Sandwich Islands. Through an uuhappy misunderstanding with the natives of Hawaii, Captain Cook was murdered in Kutakokooa Bay, on the west coast, February 14, 1779. The Sandwich Islanders are a branch of the Polynesian stock, standing next to the Tahitians, to whose language theirs is closely allied. While employed in the preparation of their favorite drink, called

* A house.

ava or *kava*, the Sandwich Islanders invariably sang sacred hymns. When Captain Cook was received by the natives, one of their priests approached him singing a chant to which his companions made regular responses. This song was more one of adoration than of welcome. The priest having approached the Captain with gestures of high reverence, threw over Cook's shoulders a piece of red cloth, and then, stepping back a few paces, made him an offering of a small pig. Captain Cook observes that the ceremonies performed with regard to him were very nearly those usually practised by the priests before their idols. Mr. William Ellis, who resided for nearly eight years in the Society and Sandwich Islands, describes the *Vivo*, or the variety of the nose-flute which is in use in the latter place. "The sound," observes he, "was soft and not unpleasant, though the notes were few; it was generally played in a plaintive strain, though frequently used as an accompaniment to their *pehes*, or songs." He gives the following account of the conch-trumpets that are found among the Sandwich Islanders: "The largest shells were usually selected for this purpose, and were sometimes above a foot in length, and seven or eight inches in diameter at the mouth. In order to facilitate the blowing of this trumpet, they made a perforation about an inch in diameter, near the apex of the shell. Into this they inserted a bamboo cane about three feet in length, which was secured by binding it to the shell with fine braid; the aperture was rendered air-tight by cementing the outsides of it with a resinous gum from the bread-fruit tree. These shells were blown when a procession walked to the temple, or their warriors marched to battle, at the inauguration of the king, during the worship of the temple, or when a tabu or restriction was imposed in the name of the gods."

The music of the Hawaiians is described as weird and sentimental. They sing from the full chest and exercise the whole gaunt of their voice. Kalakua I., the last King of Hawaii, was an enlightened monarch and a liberal patron of music. His Majesty kept in his establishment a large number of singers, musicians, and dancers, who regaled the guests with songs and music at dinner time. Serenades are often given to high class people. Herr Bandmann, the dramatic player, gives in his "Tour" an account of a native dance called *hulakui* which was performed in his presence by His Majesty's dancers, at the conclusion of a banquet in which King Kalakua I. was present:—"It was formerly danced by men and women in their natural state; but now they cover their bodies, from the loins to their ankles, with a sort of petty coat made of long weeds. The dancers go through a most varied programme, in which there are very wonderful contortions of the body and gymnastic feats; while the singers desci'bing the performance act somewhat after the manner of a Greek chorus. There is certainly a great amount of agility necessary to its execution, and the wild numor of the dance is fully understood and appreciated by those who are familiar with the native language and history." *Hawaii Ponoi* is the name of the Hawaiian national anthem which was struck up by the royal band whenever His Majesty the King appeared in public, and also on ceremonial occasions.

SAMOAN OR NAVIGATOR'S ISLANDS.

It is said that the Samoan or Navigator's Islands were first seen in 1722 by Admiral Roggewein and that they are the group named by him Isles of Baumann, after the captain of the ship. The discovery, however, is commonly attributed to Bougainville, the first navigator,

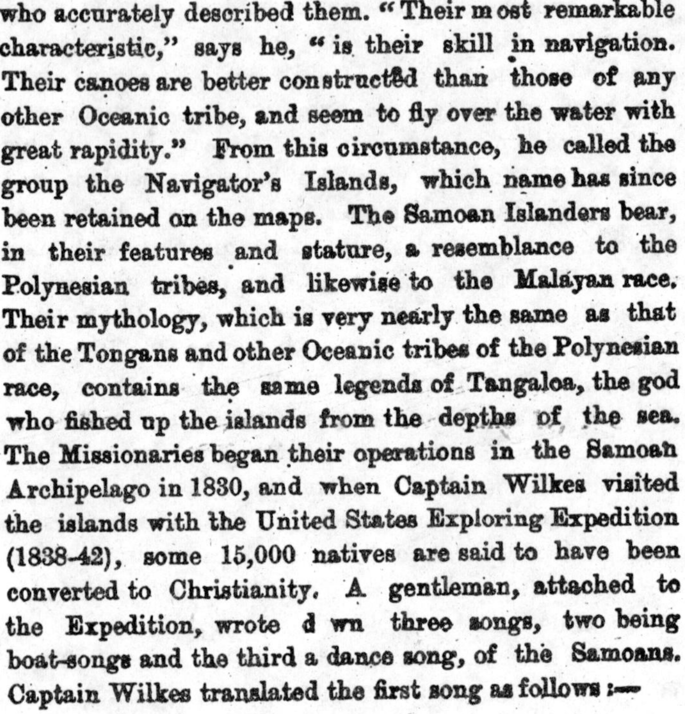

who accurately described them. "Their most remarkable characteristic," says he, "is their skill in navigation. Their canoes are better constructed than those of any other Oceanic tribe, and seem to fly over the water with great rapidity." From this circumstance, he called the group the Navigator's Islands, which name has since been retained on the maps. The Samoan Islanders bear, in their features and stature, a resemblance to the Polynesian tribes, and likewise to the Malayan race. Their mythology, which is very nearly the same as that of the Tongans and other Oceanic tribes of the Polynesian race, contains the same legends of Tangaloa, the god who fished up the islands from the depths of the sea. The Missionaries began their operations in the Samoan Archipelago in 1830, and when Captain Wilkes visited the islands with the United States Exploring Expedition (1838-42), some 15,000 natives are said to have been converted to Christianity. A gentleman, attached to the Expedition, wrote d wn three songs, two being boat-songs and the third a dance song, of the Samoans. Captain Wilkes translated the first song as follows :—

Cook tells you pull away ;
I will do so, and so must you.

The Captain adds that the natives had some knowledge of Cook derived from their communication with the Friendly Islands. Captain Wilkes further mentions that in their pleasure trips, called *Malanga*, taken from town to town, the Samoans were frequently to be met with singing their boat-songs. The words of the dance song "are comprised in short sentences, each of which finishes suddenly with a staccato note and a violent gesture." The following song of the Samoan Islanders appeared in the Narrative of the Expedition mentioned before :-

The Papalangi has come to Samoa;
The Papalangi has come to Vaiusu.
Let us all go down to the spring.
The Papalangi is fond of the siva.*
Where is the pig? Where is the fattened fowl?
The Papalangi cannot join in the siva.
Kindle up a light blaze! Where are the virgins?
I am going to get some cocoa-nuts.
Look at this Samoan, how finely he dances!

The marriage dance of the Samoans differs somewhat from the dances which are usually seen among the Polynesians. On the day of marriage, the bride is taken to an open space in the centre of the village, accompanied by the two duennas who have had charge of her, and who chant her praises and extol her virtues before the public assembly. The object of this assembly is to prove whether the girl is worthy to be the wife of a chief. If the verdict be against her (which is rarely the case), all the male members of her family, including her father and brothers, rush on her with their clubs and kill her on the spot, to wipe out the disgrace she has brought on her house. Should the verdict be in her favor, she is presented to the people as the chief's wife. After she has been led away to the house, a grand dance takes place. The spectators being seated in a circle and keeping up a monotonous chant, the men first enter the circle led by a young chief, who then goes through a number and variety of steps, his movements being imitated by his followers. After the men have danced and retired, a number of girls enter and go through a number of similar evolutions, and afterwards both men and women dance together.

TONGA OR FRIENDLY ISLANDS.

The Tonga Islands were discovered in 1643 by Tasman, and subsequently visited by Cook, who, on account of the disposition of the natives, gave them the

* A dance.

collective name of "Friendly Islands." The Tongans are a tribe of people nearly resembling the New Zealanders, especially as regards their language. They are divided into several distinct hereditary castes, to whom different offices are assigned by fixed institutions.

Among the musical instruments used by the inhabitants is the Syrinx. One of these was brought by Captain Fourneaux from Tongataboo, (formerly called the Isle of Amsterdam), and described in Vol. 65 of the "Philosophical Transactions of the Royal Society." Out of two others, deposited in the British Museum, one consisted of nine and the other of ten pipes. The arrangement in the succession of the notes on these instruments is supposed to have been suggested by the notes of some birds. Mr. William Mariner, who, according to Stafford's "History of Music" (1830), was in 1805 made captive by, and lived for several years among, the natives of the Tonga Islands, mentions several kinds of their songs, some of which, he says, are of the character of the recitative, specially those according to the *Neuha* mode—*Neuha* being the name of one of the Navigator's Islands. Mr. George Forster heard the natives of the Tonga Islands on some occasions singing in harmony. A gentleman, connected with the United States Exploring Expedition, wrote down an air with the bass and harmony, as he heard it sung by the inhabitants of Tongataboo, when they were advancing in a boat with their chief. This music, it is said, bore a great resemblance to that of the Samoan group, and it was the custom in both to sing it while at work. It is rather remarkable that harmony should have been known to people who had never had foreign music taught them, as the missionaries, who were among them, did not sing, and declared that "they were not able to distinguish 'Old Hundred' from 'God

Save the King', if the same words were adopted to both."

The following song appeared in "An Account of the Natives of the Tonga Islands, compiled from the communications of W. Mariner," by John Martin, London, 1817. This song, Mariner observes, "is very often sung by the Tonga Islanders, or, to speak perhaps more correctly, is given in a sort of recitative by either sex, and the Tonga language has neither rhymes, nor regular measure, although some of their songs have both".

> Whilst we were talking of *Vavaoo tooa Lico*, the women said to us: Let us repair to the back of the island to contemplate the setting sun;
>
> There let us listen to the warbling of the birds and the cooing of the wood-pigeon.
>
> We will gather flowers from the burying-place of Matawto, and partake of refreshments prepared for us at Lico O'ne.
>
> We will then bathe in the sea, and rinse ourselves in the Vaoo A'ca.
>
> We will anoint our skins in the sun with sweet-scented oil, and will plait in wreaths the flowers gathered at Matawto.
>
> And now, as we stand motionless on the eminence over Anoo Manoo, the whistling of the wind among the branches of the lofty *toa* shall fill us with a pleasing melancholy.
>
> Or, our minds shall be seized with astonishment as we behold the roaring surf below, endeavouring but in vain to tear away the firm rocks.
>
> O! how much happier shall we be thus employed, than when engaged in troublesome and insipid affairs of life!
>
> Now, as night comes on, we must return to the Mooa.
>
> But hark! hear you not the sound of the mats?—They are practising a *bo-oola** to be performed to-night in the *marly* at Tanea.

* A kind of dance performed by torch-light.

Let us also go there. How will that scene of rejoicing call to our minds the many festivals held there before *Vavaoo* was torn to pieces by war!

Alas! how destructive is war! Behold! how it has rendered the land productive of weeds, and opened untimely graves for departed heroes!

Our chiefs can now no longer enjoy the sweet pleasure of wandering alone by moonlight in search of their mistresses.

But let us banish sorrow from our hearts, since we are at war we must think and act like the natives of Fejee, who first taught us this destructive art.

Let us, therefore, enjoy the present time, for to-morrow, perhaps, or the next day, we may die.

We will dress ourselves with the *chi eoola*, and put bands of white *tappa* round our waists.

We will plait thick wreaths of *jiale* for our heads, and prepare strings of *hooni* for our necks, that their whiteness may show off the colour of our skins.

Mark how the uncultivated spectators are profuse of their applause!

But now the dance is over. Let us remain here to-night, and feast and be cheerful; and to-morrow we will depart for the Mooa.

How troublesome are the young men, begging for our wreaths of flowers, while they say in their flattery: "See how charming these young girls look coming from Licoo!

How beautiful are their skins, diffusing around a fragrance like the flowery precipice of Mataloco."

Let us also visit Licoo.—We will depart to-morrow.

APPENDIX.

A FEW FACTS CONCERNING HINDU MUSIC.

THE THREE GRAMAS.

In page 8 of this book, it has been stated that there are three gramas in Hindu music, *viz.*, the *Sa* grama, the *Ga* grama, and the *Ma* grama. The reason why the three notes *Sa*, *Ga*, and *Ma*, and no others, have been selected to represent the three gramas is that it is the scales of these three notes which between them furnish, to use the language of the Pianoforte, the seven "white" keys and the five "black" keys of the diapason. Thus:

When *Sa* (*C*) is made the key-note, the seven "white" keys are obtained, *viz.*, Sa (C),* Ri (D), Ga (E), Ma (F), Pa (G), Dha (A), Ni (B). When Ga (E) is made the key-note, four of the "black" keys are obtained, *viz.*, Ma (F) Sharp, Dha (A) Flat, Ri (D) Flat, Ga (E) Flat, which respectively represent the D, E, A, and B of that scale.

When Ma (F) is made the key-note, the fifth "black" key is obtained, *viz.*, Ni (B) Flat, which represents the F of that scale.

It should be noted, however, that the above represent the popular version of the functions of the three gramas. For what constitutes the three gramas, strictly according to the system of Hindu music, as laid down in the Sanskrit treatises of old, the curious may be referred to the "Musical Scales of the Hindus", and "Six Principal Rágas of the Hindus", by the author of the present work.

---

* It must not be supposed that the intervals of the Hindu scale are exactly the same as those of the European scale. They correspond very nearly to each other.

The table given below shows at a glance how the notes C, E, and F form the twelve keys.

	1	2	3	4	5	6	7	8	9	10	11	12						
The twelve keys are	C,	D Flat,	D,	E Flat,	E,	F,	F Sharp,	G,	A Flat,	A,	B Flat,	B,	(C,	D Flat,	D,	E Flat,	E	F)
C as key-note	C		D		E	F		G		A		B	(C).					
E as key-note					C		D		E	F		G		A		B	(C)	
F as key-note						C		D		E	F		G		A		B	(C)

THE SIX RAGAS.

The number of original *Rágas* (melody-types) was fixed at six, probably because the first six notes of the heptachord, respectively, stand as their *Vádí* (the note which, by the frequency of its application and by the length of its duration, shows to the best advantage the character and peculiarity of a *Rága*). Thus:

The	*Rága*	Nata Náráyana	has	C	for	its	*Vádí*.
„	„	Megha	„	D	„	„	„
„	„	Srí	„	E	„	„	„
„	„	Panchama	„	F	„	„	„
„	„	Bhairaví	„	G	„	„	„
„	„	Vasanta	„	A	„	„	„

The fact of the seventh note, *B*, being kept out of count is partly corroborative of the remark generally made that the pentatonic scale was in common use in Asia at a very early period. "Children," says Carl Engel, "in their first attempts to repeat the diatonic scale after it has been sung to them are apt to omit the *fourth* and *seventh*." The seventh note, it is true, occurs in all the six original *Rágas*, but it is not used in a very prominent manner. Another fact to be noted in this connection is that, out of the innumerable *Ráginís* that have been evolved from the original six *Rágas*, there are few, if any, that have the seventh for their *Vádí*.

THE EIGHT RASAS.

The number of *Rasas* (affections of the mind), as employed in music, is eight, namely, (1) Sringára (love), (2) Hásya (mirth), (3) Karuná (tenderness), (4) Raudra (anger), (5) Víra (heroism), (6) Bhayánaka (terror), (7) Vibhatsa (disgust), and (8) Adbhuta (surprise). Each of these affections has a *Rágini* or a number of *Ráginís* capable of giving it expression, the arrangements of their intervals and time-durations being so made as to produce in the hearer the

effect desired. The first of the *Rasas* is also called *Adi*, (which means primary), as this is the *lowest* and the *first* passion of all sentient beings. In poetical compositions, a ninth *Rasa* is admitted, namely, *Sánti*, or quiescence, which is the highest development of human feeling, leading man to the contemplation of, or pleasurable communion with, the deity. In music, however, this *Rasa* is merged in that of tenderness.

THE SEAT OF MUSIC IN THE HUMAN BODY.

For mystical, astrological, or chiromantic purposes, the human body has been divided into six *chakras* (depressions, rings, or circles). These are (1) Muládhára, the part about the pubis, above that (2) Svádhisthána, or umbilical region, and above that (3) Manipura, or pit of the stomach or epigastrium; (4) Anáhata, the root of the nose; (5) Visuddhi, the hollow between the frontal sinuses; and (6) Ajná, the fontenelle or union of the coronal and sagittal sutures. Various faculties or divinities are supposed to be present at these circles.

Visuddhi is the abode of Sarasvatí, the goddess of music. From the sixteen folded petals of which the Visuddhi consists, the following are respectively produced;—(1) Pranava (the mystic syllable *Om*), (2) Udgítha, (a portion of the Sáma Veda), (3) Humphat (mystical syllable used in incantations), (4) Vaushat Vashat, (5) Svadhá, and (6) Sváhá, (exclamations used in offering oblations to the deity or manes), (7) Namas (the term used in connection with the name of a deity to signify veneration), (8) Amrita (ambrosia), the seven musical notes, namely, (9) Sharja, (10) Rishabha, (11) Gándhára, (12) Madhyama, (13) Panchama, (14) Dhaivata, and (15) Nisháda, * and (16) Bisha (poison).

When the vital spirit of a man resides in the first, eighth, eleventh, or twelfth fold of the Anáhata circle, that man becomes qualified to cultivate his musical faculties. When

* Ordinarily called after their respective initials, Sa, Ri, Ga, Ma, Pa, Dha, and Ni.

the vital spirit resides on the fourth, sixth, or the tenth fold of the same circle, his musical faculties are destroyed. When the vital spirit resides in any of the folds of the Visuddhi circle beginning with the eighth and ending with the fifteenth, the musical efforts of the man are crowned with success; when it resides in the sixteenth fold, they meet with failure. The presence of the vital spirit in the tenth or eleventh fold of the Lalaná circle (which has its seat in the forehead) is favorable to the cultivation of music, while its presence in the first, fourth, or fifth fold of the same circle is unfavorable. When the vital spirit resides in the Sudhádhara circle (which is located in the *Brahma randhra**), and regales itself by bathing in the ambrosia trickling from it, the man becomes proficient in musical knowledge. The presence of the vital spirit in circles other than those, and the particular folds of them, that are favorable to the development of musical powers, has the effect of rendering the man altogether indifferent to the cultivation of the musical art.

THE ORIGIN OF SOUND.

WHENEVER the vital spirit wishes to speak or utter a sound, it sets the mind in motion. The mind, in its turn, moves the *audarya* fire which pervades the body and which, on being so moved, sends up the vital air, which, in its upward course, strikes against the navel, the heart, the throat, the head, and the mouth, and produces sound. These five organs produce, respectively, the very minute, the minute, the developed, the undeveloped, and the artificial sound. The very minute sound is audible only to *Yogis* contemplating *Brahma*. The minute sound also is not audible to the generality of men; it may sometimes, but rarely, be heard by closing one's ears. When the vital air, stirred by the fire, enters into the twenty two arteries that are arranged

* The aperture in the crown of the head through which the soul is said to escape on its leaving the body.

tortuously and attached to the *Sushumná*,* they produce twenty two different sounds, each higher than the last in pitch. These sounds are each known by the name of *Sruti*, and these twenty two *Srutis* generate the seven musical notes.

MURCHCHHANA.

The ascension and descension of the notes of the heptachord in succession is called *Murchchhaná*. As there are seven notes in each grama, there are in all 21. *Murchchhanás* in the three gramás. No notice of the *Murchchhanas* of the Gándhára gráma will be taken here, as the use of that *grámá* is confined to the celestial regions. The 14 *Murchchhanas* belonging to the other two gramas only will be dealt with. Though it is possible for *Murchchhanas* to begin with any note of any of the three heptachords in use in Hindu Music, namely, the *Mandra* (lower), the *Madhya* (middle), and the *Tára* (higher), the practice is to commence the first *Murchchhana* of the Sharja grama from the *sa* of the middle, and that of the Madhyama grama from the *ma* of the same heptachord. The 14 *Murchchhanas* are formed thus :—

Sharja Grama.

1st Murchchhaná		...	sa,	ri,	ga,	ma,	pa,	dha,	ni,
2nd	do.	...	ni,	sa,	ri,	ga,	ma,	pa,	dha,
3rd	do.	...	dha,	ni,	sa,	ri,	ga,	ma,	pa,
4th	do.	...	pa,	dha,	ni,	sa,	ri,	ga,	ma,
5th	do.	...	ma,	pa,	dha,	ni,	sa,	ri,	ga,
6th	do.	...	ga,	ma,	pa,	dha,	ni,	sa,	ri,
7th	do.	...	ri,	ga,	ma,	pa,	dha,	ni,	sa.

* One of the three canals (the other two being named *Ira* and *Pingalá*) which, according to the anatomy of the *Yoga* School of Philosophy, run from the os-coccygis to the head, and are the chief passages of breath and air.

Madhyama Grama.

1st Murchchhaná	...	ma, pa, dha, ni, sa, ri, ga,
2nd do.	...	ga, ma, pa, dha, ni, sa, ri,
3rd do.	...	ri, ga, ma, pa, dha, ni, sa,
4th do	...	sa, ri, ga, ma, pa, dha, ni,
5th do.	...	ni, sa, ri, ga, ma, pa, dha,
6th do.	...	dha, ni, sa, ri, ga, ma, pa,
7th do.	...	pa, dha, ni, sa, ri, ga, ma.

Each of the above 14 *Murchchhanas* is classed under four heads, *viz.*, (1) Suddha (pure), (2) Kakali Sahita (with Kakali), (3) Antara Sahita (with Antara), and (4) Kakalyantara Sahita (with Kakali and Antara). There are, therefore, 56 kinds of *Murchchhanas* in the two gramas, 14 × 4 giving that number. When *ni* takes the first and the second Srutis of *sa* and becomes thus a note of 4 Srutis, it is termed *Kakali ni*; when *ga* takes the first and the second Srutis of *ma* and becomes thus a note of 4 Srutis, it is called *Antara ga*.

The *Murchchhanas* of the *sa* and *ma* gramas, respectively, take their serial numbers from the position of *sa* and *ma* in the Murchchhanás. Thus the *Murchchhana* sa, ri, ga, ma, pa, dha, ni is called the *first Murchchhana* of the *sa* grama, because *sa* is the *first* note in that *Murchchhana*; the *Murchchhana* ni, sa, ri, ga, ma, pa, dha, is called the *second Murchchhana* of the same grama, because *sa* is the *second* note; and so on to the seventh. In the *ma* grama, the *first Murchchhana* is ma, pa, dha, ni, sa, ri, ga, because *ma* is the *first* note of that *Murchchhana*; the *second* is, ga, ma, pa, dha, ni, sa, ri, because *ma* is the *second* note; and so on to the seventh. Each of the 56 Murchchhanas mentioned before is divided into 7 kinds, from the fact of their beginning with the first, second, third, fourth, fifth, sixth, or seventh note of the

serial and ending in a succession of seven. Thus (to take the Sudha *sa* grama);

The first	...	sa,	ri,	ga,	ma,	pa,	dha,	ni,
The second	...	ri,	ga,	ma,	pa,	dha,	ni,	sa,*
The third	...	ga,	ma,	pa,	dha,	ni,	sa,	ri,
The fourth	...	ma,	pa,	dha,	ni,	sa.	ri,	ga,
The fifth	...	pa,	dha,	ni,	sa,	ri,	ga,	ma,
The sixth	...	dha,	ni,	sa,	ri,	ga,	ma,	pa,
The seventh	...	ni,	sa,	ri,	ga,	ma,	pa,	dha.

The total number of *Murchchhanas* is, therefore, (56 × 7) or 392.

SUDDHA TANA.

WHEN the *Suddha Murchchhanas* are comprised respectively of six notes (*sharava*) and five notes (*aurava*), they go so longer by the name of *Murchchhanas*, but are called *Suddha Tanas*. In the *sa* grama, each of the seven *Murchchhanas* becomes *sharava*, by being, one at a time, deprived of the notes, sa, ri, pa, and ni. Consequently, there are, in the total seven *Murchchhanas* seven without sa, seven without ri, seven without pa, and seven without ni, or a total exclusion of 28 notes. In the *ma* grama, each of the seven *Murchchhanas* becomes *sharava*, by being, one at a time, deprived of the notes, sa, ri, and ga. Consequently, there are, in the total seven *Murchchhanas*, seven without sa, seven without ri, and seven without ga, or a total exclusion of 21 notes. The total number of *sharava tanas* in the two gramas is therefore (28 + 21) or 49. In the *sa* grama, the *Murchchhanas* become *aurava*, by each of them being deprived, one at a time, of the pair of notes, sa and pa, ga and ni, and ri and pa. The number of *aurava tanas* thus becomes 21. In the *ma* grama, the *Murchchhanas* become

* In this and the two preceding tables, the notes with a dot below them represent the lower, and those with a dot above them, the higher heptachord. All others belong to the middle heptachord.

aurava, each of them being deprived, one at a time, of the pair of notes, ri and dha, and ga and ni. The number of *aurava tanas* thus becomes 14. The total number of *aurava tanas* is, therefore, (21 + 14) or 35.

KUTA TANA.

When the *Murchchhanas*, whether they are complete (*Purna*) or not, are rendered without reference to their order of succession, they are called *Kuta Tanas*. Each complete *Murchchhana* rendered with and without reference to its order of succession becomes 5,040 in variety, for 1 × 2 × 3 × 4 × 5 × 6 × 7=5,040. The 56 *Murchchhanas*, therefore, give 2,82,240 complete *Kuta Tanas*. The incomplete (*Apurna*) *Kuta Tanas* are described below :—

If from the *Purna Kuta Tana*, the last note of the series is taken out, one after the other, there will be six varieties of *Kuta Tanas*, namely, the six-noted, the five-noted, the four-noted, the three-noted, the two-noted, and the one-noted kind. The permutation of the six-noted vari ety is 1 × 2 × 3 × 4 × 5 × 6=720 ; that of the five-noted one is 1 × 2 × 3 × 4 × 5 = 120; that of the four-noted one, 1 × 2 × 3 × 4 = 24 ; that of the three-noted one, 1 × 2 × 3=6 ; that of the two-noted one, 1 × 2=2 ; and that of the one-noted one, 1. These varieties are respectively named, Sharava, Auruva, Svarantara, Samika, Gathika and Archika. When the *Sharava Kuta Tana* includes in its range the notes *ni* and *ga*, it is divided into four classes, *viz.*, Suddha, Kakali Sahita, Antara Sahita and Kakalyantara Sahita. The absence of *ni* brings it under the classes Suddha, and Antara Sahita, and the absence of *ga* brings it under those of Suddha and Kakali Sahita.

From the table of the 14 *Murchchhanas* given before, it would be seen that there are in either grama a succession beginning with *sa* and one beginning with *ma*. As *ni* is excluded in the *sharava* succession beginning with *sa*, that succession is subdivided into Suddha and Antara Sahita;

and as *ga* is excluded in the *sharava* succession beginning with *ma*, that succession is subdivided into Suddha and Kakali Sahita. There being thus a multiplication of the four kinds by two, the total comes to 8. The two successions beginning with *sa* and the two beginning with *ma* being thus disposed of, each of the remaining 10 *Murchchhanas*, having *ni* and *ga* in its range, is subdivided into 4 varieties, namely, Suddha, Kakali Sahita, Antara Sahita, and Kakalyantara Sahita; or a total of 40 is arrived at. 8 and 40 make 48 ; and as it has already been shown that the number of *sharava* (six-noted) permutations is 720 in each case, the total number of *sharava Kuta Tanas* is (720 × 48) or 34,560.

The *aurava Kuta Tana* is arrived at by depriving each of the 14 *Murchchhanas* that compose the two gramas by its last two notes. Each of the two series beginning with *ga*, of the two beginning with *dha*, and of the two beginning with *ni*, having both *ni* and *ga* in it, it is classed as Suddha, Kakali Sahita, Antara Sahita, and Kakalyantara Sahita. The varieties, therefore, come to (6 × 4) or 24. The remaining eight *Murchchhanas* being without either *ni* or *ga*, they are each classed as either Suddha and Antara Sahita, or Suddha and Kakali Sahita, as the case may be. The varieties, therefore, come to (8 × 2) or 16. The total of the two varieties is 24 + 16 or 40 ; and as the number of the *aurava* (five-noted) permutations has already been shown to be 120, the total number of *aurava Kuta Tanas* is 120 × 40 or 4,800.

When the last three notes are eliminated from each of the 14 *Murchchhanas*, the two series beginning with *ni*, which have both *ni* and *ga* in them, are each divided into four (namely, Suddha, Kakali Sahita, Antara Sahita, and Kakalyantara Sahita). 4 × 2=8. The remaining twelve series being without either *ni* or *ga*, they are each divided into two (*i.e.*, either Suddha and Antara Sahita, or Suddha and Kakali Sahita.) These twelve series make up the number (12 × 2) or 24. The total of the two varieties is 8 + 24 or 32. This multiplied by the number of the four-noted permutations (which

has been shown to be 24), gives a product of 768 which is the number of the *four-noted Kuta Tanas.*

When the last four notes are eliminated from each of the *Murchchhanás,* the two series beginning with *ma* admit of no subdivision as there is no *ni* or *ga* in either of them. They stand, therefore, at 2. The remaining 12 series admitting either *ga* or *ni,* they are each subdivided into two, and produce a total of (12 × 2) or 24, which added to the 2, mentioned above, make up a grand total of 26. This being multiplied by the number of the three-noted permutations (6), gives a product of 156 which is the number of the *three-noted Kuta Tanas.*

Whe the last five notes are eliminated from each of the 14 *Murchchhanás,* the two series beginning with *ri,* the two beginning with *ga,* the two with *dha,* and the two with *ni,* being each subdivided into two (owing to the fact of its including *ni* or *ga* in its succession) give a total of 16. The remaining six admitting of no variety, (there being no *ni* or *ga* in them), they stand at 6. The total of the two is (16 + 6) or 22, which multiplied by 2 (the number of two-noted permutations), gives a product of 44 which is the number of the *two-noted Kuta Tánas.*

There being no variety possible in the *Ekasvara* or *one-noted Kuta Tanas,* their number is 14, *i.e.,* the same as the number of *Murchchhanas* in the two gramas.

The number of nett *Kuta Tanas,* as arrived at by excluding one set of the two that are common to both the *sa* and *ma* gramas, is shown as under.

It will be observed from a glance at the two tables referred to, that the 1st *Murchchhana* of the *sa* grama is the same as the 4th *Murchchhana* of the *ma* grama. The difference lies only in the value of *pa,* which, in the case of the former, consists of four Srutis, and in that of the latter, of three. It follows, therefore, that the *Murchchhanas* of the two, down to *ma* next preceding the *pa,* are the same. Now as the group of the first four notes preceding the *pa* includes

ga, it is divided into two classes (Suddha and Antara Sahita), and as the number of the four-noted permutations is 24, the number of *redundant four-noted Kuta Tánas* is (24 × 2) or 48. The group of the first three notes contains *ga* in it; hence it is divided into two (Suddha and Antara Sahita). The number of the three-noted permutations being 6, the number of *redundant three-noted Kuta Tanas* is (6 × 2) or 12. There being no *ni* or *ga* in the group of the first two notes, it is classed as Suddha only. The number of the two-noted permutations being 2, the number of *redundant two-noted Kuta Tánas* is (2 × 1) or 2. A single note can give only one variety. The total number of *redundant Kuta Tanas beginning with sa*, is, therefore, 48 + 12 + 2 + 1 or 63.

A reference to the two tables will further show that the 2nd *Murchchhana* of the *sa* grama is the same as the 5th *Murchchhana* of the *ma* grama, the difference beginning with *pa* and continuing in the succeeding notes. The *Kuta Tanas* of the five notes from *ni* to *ma*, are, therefore, the same in both the gramas. As the group beginning with *ni* and ending in *ma*, has *ga* and *ni* in it, it is divided into 4 (Suddha, Antara Sahita, Kakali Sahita, and Kakalyantara Sahita). As the number of five-noted permutations is 120, the total number of *redundant five-noted Kuta Tanas* is 120 × 4 or 480. The group of four notes beginning with *ni* and ending in *ga*, including both *ni* and *ga*, it is divided into 4 classes. The number of *redundant four-noted Kuta Tanas* is, therefore, 24 × 4 or 96. The group of three notes (*ni* to *ri*) including *ni* only, it is divided into two (Suddha and Kakali Sahita). The number of *redundant three-noted Kuta Tanas* is, therefore, 6 × 2 or 12. The group of two notes (*ni* and *sa*) including *ni* only, it is also divided into two. Hence, the number of *redundant two-noted Kuta Tanas* is 2 × 2 or 4. A single note can give only one variety. The total number of *redundant Kuta Tanas beginning with ni* is, therefore, 480 + 96 + 12 + 4 + 1, or 593.

The two tables will also show that the 3rd *Murchchhana* of the *sa* grama is the same as the 6th *Murchchhana* of the *ma* grama. The difference begins, as has been explained, with the

note *pa*, and continues in those succeeding. The *Kuta Tana* of the six notes (*dha* to *ma*) is, therefore, the same in both the gramas. As the group (*dha* to *ma*) includes both *ga* and *ni*, it is divided into 4 classes, and as the number of the six-noted permutations is 720, the *redundant six-noted Kuta Tanas* number 720 × 4 or 2,880. The group of five notes (*dha* to *ga*) includes both *ni* and *ga*, and is, therefore, also divided into 4 classes, and as the number of five-noted permutations is 120, the number of *redundant five-noted Kuta Tanas* is 120 × 4 or 480. The group of four notes (*dha* to *ri*) including only *ni*, it is divided into 2 classes; and as the number of four-noted permutations is 24, the number of *redundant four-noted Kuta Tanas* is 24 × 2 or 48. The group of three notes (*dha* to *sa*) also includes *ni*, and is, therefore, divided into 2 classes (Suddha and Kakali Sahita). The number of three-noted permutations being 6, the number of *redundant three-noted Kuta Tanas* is 6 × 2 or 12. The group of two notes (*dha* and *ni*) also including *ni*, it is also divided into 2 classes, and two being the number of two-noted permutations, the number of *redundant two-noted Kuta Tanas* is 2 × 2 or 4. The single note *dha* gives only one variety. The sum of 2,880 + 480 + 48 + 12 + 4 + 1 is 3,425, which represents the number of *redundant Kuta Tanas beginning with dha*. Grand total of the *redundant Kuta Tanas beginning with sa, ni*, and *dha*: 63 + 593 + 3,425 = 4,081.

It has been shown above that the number of the *Purna suddha tana* is 392, that of the *sharava suddha tana* is 48, that of the *aurava suddha tana* is 40, that of the *svarantara suddha tana*, 32, that of the *samika suddha tana*, 26, that of the *gathika suddha tana*, 22, and that of the *archika suddha tana*, 14. This last has, however, to be diminished by 3 on account of the redundant *tanas* of the 3 groups beginning with *sa, ni*, and *dha*. Hence the total of the *suddha tanas* is 392 + 48 + 40 + 32 + 26 + 22 + 11, or 571.

The total of *Kuta Tanas* is Purna 2,82,240 + sharava 34,560 + aurava 4,800 + svarantara 768 + samika 156 + gathika 44 + archika 14, or 3,22,582.

The sum of *redundant Kuta Tanas* and *suddha Tanas* is 4,081 + 571 or 4,652. Deducting this sum from the total of *Kuta Tanas*, the remainder is (3,22,582—4,652) or 3,17,930, which is the number of nett *Kuta Tanas.**

MUSIC AS A MEANS TO SALVATION.

THE intelligent man can by utilizing the body in specified ways secure happiness and salvation. The worship of *Saguna Brahma*† leads to the enjoyment of the pleasures of the earth and the celestial regions; that of *Nirguna Brahma*, ‡ to final beatitude. The worship of the latter entails perfect concentration of the mind which is difficult of attainment by average humanity. Hence, the sages seek salvation by adopting the method of worship called *Anaha a Nada* § *Upasana*. But as even this proves impracticable to the ordinary man, he tries the *Ahata Nada Upasana* ‖ method, which possesses the quality of giving pleasure to mankind. As music comes within the purview of *Ahata Nada*, the utilizing of the art of music for the purpose of the worship of the deity by man is held to bring him salvation.

THE END.

* It should be mentioned here that the accounts given under this and the two preceding headings have been summarised from Sanskrit treatises on Music, simply with the object of showing the numerous variations of the notes that were used in Indian music of the ancient period. The theories have little application in the music as it is practised in the modern days, except in Southern India, where the rules given in the above are observed to a certain extent.

† The Supreme Being endowed with all qualities.

‡ The Supreme Being devoid of all qualities.

§ Also called *Akása Sambhava Náda*, *i.e.*, the Náda (sound) produced in the *Akása* (the ethereal element which pervades the universe). It is evident that there is in the *Akása* an aptitude to produce *Náda*, as well as a capacity in the ear to receive it. There is a saying in Sanskrit —" Náda Brahma," which means Sound is the Supreme Being.

‖ *Ahata Náda* is the sound produced by the concussion of two bodies.

ADDENDA

DANCING.

In page 2 of this publication occurs the following sentence :—" Time plays an important part in music, and like music itself is born in nature." The art of dancing has its foundation also in nature. It might be said that the graceful movements of the turkey and the peacock have furnished mankind with the idea of dancing.

The various styles of dance mentioned in the Sanskrit works have been described in the treatise, called *Nrityankura*, brought out by the writer of the present publication.

THE THREE GRAMAS.

It has been stated in page 8, notes, of the work, that " the idea of these gramas seems to be connected with that of the three primitive vowels, *a* (अ), *i* (इ), and *u* (उ), from which, according to philologists, all the various vowel sounds in the Aryan languages have been developed." To illustrate ; अ and अ make आ; इ and इ make ई; उ and उ make ऊ ; अ and इ make ए; अ and ए make ऐ; अ and उ make ओ ; and अ and ओ make औ. The vowels known as ऋ ॠ and ऌ ॡ are evidently produced by the combination of vowels and consonants. Thus, र् and इ make ऋ; ऋ and ई make ॠ; ल् and इ make ऌ, and ऌ and ई make ॡ. None of the consonants can be produced without the aid of vowels ; thus क् and अ make क ; क् and आ make का, and so on.* In short, no letters of the alphabet could

* According to the *Kalapa* Grammar,

व्यञ्जनमस्वरं परं वर्णं नयेत्

i e, the consonant without the vowel sound unites with the next letter, as the consonants have no power of expressing themselves without the help of vowels. The vowel does not unite with the next letter as it can express itself:

स्वरः स्वयं राजते हि ।

be formed without the vowels, of which, as it has been shown, अ, इ, and उ are the primitive ones. In the same way, none of the twelve notes of the diapason could be formed without the help of the three gramas, *sa*, *ga*, and *ma*, with which the three vowels are, respectively, compared.*

THE SEVEN NOTES.

THE seven notes, according to Hindu music, are designated Sharja, Rishava, Gandhara, Madhyama, Panchama, Dhaivata, and Nishada, corresponding very nearly to the notes C, D, E, F, G, A, and B of the European scale.

Sharja means *Shat jayante yasmat* or that from which the six are derived. Sharja is the principal note and the originator of the six notes which follow.

Rishava is so called because the *Rig* Veda is said to have been chanted to its key.

Gandhara is so named because the use of the Gandhara grama is confined to the regions of the Gandharvas (celestial musicians).

Madhyama means the middle. It stands between C, D, and E on the one hand, and G, A, and B, on the other.

Panchama means the fifth. It stands the fifth in serial number beginning with C.

Dhaivata means that note which stands unaffected when any of the preceding notes is made the key-note. When C, D, E, F, and G, stand, respectively, as the key-note, the Dhaivata (A) stands A, G, F, E, and D, respectively, in relation to it, without moving from its own position.

* The principle underlying the three gramas is observed in the arrangement of the frets of the instrument setar. The diatonic scale is represented by the Sa grama, the chromatic scale is represented by the ga grama, the frets representing the notes F, G, A, B, C, and D respectively making D flat, E flat, F, G, A flat, and B flat, of that scale. The Ragini Bhairavi which is made up of these notes can thus be played upon the setar without necessitating the moving up of the frets, when ga is made the key-note. The fret B flat makes the F of the scale formed by makig ma the key note, and the fret F sharp the B of the scale which is sometimes formed by making G the key-note.

Nishada means the note with which the scale terminates, that is, the one beyond which there is no note but the first of the next tetrachord into which it glides.

THE EIGHT RASAS.

THE order in which some of the Sanskrit writers have enumerated the Rasas chimes in with the theory of evolution. Sringara (love) is, as has been already said, a feeling common to all sentient beings, and lies at the root of the law of procreation. Even such small specimens of animated nature as flies are governed by this sentiment. The next in order is Vira (heroism), which is observed in the next higher stages of created beings, such as mice and snakes which are known to fight with each other. The third in the gradation is Karuna (tenderness). This feeling is non-existent in the lower creations, such as fish, frogs, mice, snakes &c., which are known to eat up their spawns or young ones. The sentiment called Raudra (anger), which comes next, is found in the next higher grades of living beings, such as dogs, lions, tigers, &c., in whom the power of exhibiting anger is manifest. Then comes Hasya (mirth, as expressed by laughter). This is a sentiment confined to the highest creation, man. The feeling of terror (Bhayanaka), which follows, is that of man in a state of barbarism, in which any thing grand or awe-inspiring in nature or art becomes to him an object of terror. The next sentiment in gradation is Bibhatsa (disgust), which is the feeling of man when he has made strides in the path of civilization. Aborigines and and cannibals are known to exhibit no disgust in eating raw flesh or putrid matter. The sentiment of Adbhuta (surprise), which follows, is realized by man only when he has reached the summits of civilization. For instance, when a large piece of diamond will elicit no surprise from a barbarian who has no idea of its rarity and value, it will cause surprise in one who has had experience of precious stones and has the power of being impressed with the beauty and singularity of the specimen. Santi (quiescence) is, as has been already observed, the highest development of human feeling and its

exclusion from the domain of music is due, perhaps, to the fact that it is not capable of being reflected by the art.

MUSIC AND ASTRONOMY.

When the sun enters the signs of the zodiac, Vrisha (Taurus) and Mithuna (Gemini), the summer season is opened. When he enters the signs of Karkata (Cancer) and Sinha (Leo), the rainy season comes on. When he enters the Kanya (Virgo) and Tula (Libra), the autumn is introduced. When he enters the Vrischika (Scorpio) and Dhanu (Sagittarius), the dewy season is ushered in. When he enters the Makara (Capricornus) and Kumbha (Aquarius), the season goes by the name of winter; and when he enters the Mina (Pisces) and Mesha (Aries), the spring makes its advent. It will be seen that the contiguity of certain signs of the zodiac to the sun or their distance from him determines the six seasons. In the same way, the present writer ventures to think, the contiguity or distance of the fundamental note (C) of the heptachord, with reference to the other notes, has produced the six original Ragas. The key-note C might be compared with the sun, it being fixed like him, and it having the six other notes, like the planets, placed at different intervals of space with reference to its position. C keeping to its own position has taken a prominent part in the formation of the Raga Natanarayana, (*vide* page iii, Appendix). When a note has approached C at the distance represented by the position of D, it has formed the Raga Megha. In a similar way, notes approaching C at the distance represented by the positions of E, F G, and A, respectively, have respectively, produced the Ragas Sri, Panchama, Bhairava (not Bhairavi as has been misprinted on page iii, Appendix), and Vasanta. The order of succession in which the Ragas have been produced, as given above, does not tally with that given in the Sanskrit works on music, which put Sri first, Vasanta second, Bhairava third, Panchama fourth, Megha fifth, and Natanarayana sixth. This order of classification might be accounted for in the

following way. The first, Sri, which consists of one semi-tone and two quarter-tones, represents the earliest efforts of the human voice at intonation. In the infancy of the art, the human voice was not capable of taking the intervals of full notes. Hence the use of smaller intervals. The next Raga, Vasanta, does away with the use of quarter-tones and deals with two semi-tones, and by ignoring the note G shows the hexatonic scale. The third, Bhairava, consists of three semi-tones (D flat, A flat, and B flat) and also introduces an occasional use of E rendered slightly flat to differentiate the Raga from *Ramakeli* which it resembles very closely in form and construction. The fourth, Panchama, deals with only one semi-tone, namely, D flat. The fifth Megha, makes use of only one semi-tone (B flat), and is practically a specimen of the pentatonic scale, as it does away with the notes A and E, the latter being used only in the descending scale immediately following F and preceding D, and not as an independent note of any sensibly long duration. The last, Natanarayana, shows the formation of the diatonic scale, as it consists of the seven full notes of the heptachord and excludes lesser intervals.

It is worthy of note that while, according to Hindu Astronomy, or, rather, Physical Geography, the year commences with the Hemanta (dewy season), which introduces the five other seasons in succession, the Ragas, according to the musical system of the Hindus, begin with Sri, which is sung also in the dewy season, commencing with the month of Agrahayana (signifying *agra*, first, and *hayana*, year) Sri is another name for Lakshmi (Ceres—goddess of corn and tillage), and this is the harvest season. Vasanta, as its name indicates, is sung in the spring. Panchama is sung in the summer. This Raga is said to be the substitute or another name for Dipaka, which means a burning lamp, and is associated with heat. Megha (which is the Sanskrit for clouds) is sung in the rainy season. Bhairava is sung in the autumn, and Natanarayana in the winter. The former is represented as Mahadeva, who and whose consort Durga come

in for special worship in the autumn. The latter is associated with the sentiment of heroism, the Raga being described as a warrior, and the winter is generally considered the convenient season for engaging in war. There are the twelve months and the six seasons. So there are the 12 notes (7 full and 5 half notes), and the six Ragas.

MUSIC AND ASTROLOGY.

EXCLUDING Rahu and Ketu (the ascending and descending nodes), there are seven principal planets, namely, Ravi (Sun), Soma (Moon), Mangala (Mars), Budha (Mercury), Vrihaspati (Jupiter), Sukra (Venus), and Sani (Saturn), corresponding with the seven notes, Sa, ri, ga, ma, pa, dha, ni.

The following are the colours attributed to the seven planets by writers on Astronomy and according to the Tantras, as also to the seven notes by the Sanskrit anthorities on Music.

		Astronomy.	Tantras.	Musical works
(1)	Ravi	Blood red with deep blue	Blood red	Black (sa)
(2)	Soma	Yellow	White	Tawny (ri)
(3)	Mangala	Orange	Blood red	Golden (ga)
(4)	Budha	Grass green	Yellow	White (ma)
(5)	Vrihaspati	Yellow	Yellow	Yellow (pa)
(6)	Sukra	Deep blue	White	Purple (dha)
(7)	Sani	Black	Black	Green (ni)

The resemblance is striking in some cases.

COMPARATIVE TABLE OF CASTES.

(1)	Ravi	Kshatriya	Sa—Brahmana
(2)	Soma	Vaisya	Ri—Kshatriya
(3)	Mangala	Kshatriya	Ga—Vaisya
(4)	Budha	Sudra	Ma—Brahmana
(5)	Vrihaspati	Brahmana	Pa—Brahmana
(6)	Sukra	Brahmana	Dha—Kshatriya
(7)	Sani	Antyaja	Ni—Vaisya

The sinilarity in the case of No. 5 is marked, though it is not so in the other items. No (7) Sani is called Antyaja, *i. e.*, as belonging to a low caste to touch whom is pollution. This is much the same case with No. (7) Ni, which is, in many Ragas, not touched except in combination with, or with a view to introduce, the next note, C.* It has been aptly compared with Anusvara (see page 8, notes), which, as the representative of a sound, has no existence except in conjunction with a vowel or a consonant.† The note Ni is called Napunsaka, that is, of the neuter gender, perhaps (because it does not possess the power of forming or developing a Raga. It has already been stated that the note took no part in the formation of the six original Ragas.

MUSIC AND MEDICINE.

The power of music in soothing the afflicted heart and mind is acknowledged in both the East and the West. Its power of charming ferocious beasts and venomous reptiles is also referred to by writers of both ancient and modern times. Some accounts have been given, in the body of this book, of the healing powers of music so far as some of the savage nations are concerned. Ancient writers as well as medical authorities have dilated upon the power which music has of curing some of the ailments of humanity. The writer of the present work believes that a hospital was, a few years ago, established in London, with a view to cure certain diseases by means of music. It would be useful to enquire what the results have been of those interesting experiments.

The musical note has for one of its names the Sanskrit word *Dhatu*, which is the medical term for the constituents of

* From the meditations of the Nine planets it would appear that Sani is the son of Ravi. This accords with the musical idea that *Ni* is intimately connected with *Sa*. The seven notes are respectively under the control of the following deities: Agni, Brahma, Sarasvati, Mahadeva, Lakshmi, Ganesa, and Surya (Ravi).

† अनुसूर्यते संयोगं यच्छते इति अनुस्वार ।

(*Kalapa*).

The *Anusvara* glides into or is absorbed with the letter to which it is attached. This is exactly the characteristic of Nishad (Ni) which means the termination of the scale and the gliding of the note into the next following *Sa*.

the body (which, as has been mentioned on page 9, notes, of this book, are also seven in number). As without the seven *Dhatus*, the body cannot be formed, so without the seven notes, the Ragas cannot be formed.

Music is the union of *Dhatu* (note) and *Matra* (unit of measure). According to the Sanskrit medical works, the Matra may be determined by the winking of the eye or the beating of the pulse.

MUSIC AND POETRY.

Mention has been made, on page 4 of this work, of the fact that "music and poetry have been combined from time immemorial." "Pure composition," says Mr. Nathan, "unites music and poetry in indissoluble bonds; and so intimate is their connection, so equal their value, so indispensable the strictness of their union, that the rules of sense and propriety render them the echo of each other." Sentiment and metre are the groundwork of both musical and poetical compositions. The part which sentiment plays in music has already been mentioned. The object of metre is not only to diversify the time-movement but also to clothe the composition in such a garb as would best fit in with the feeling which the composition seeks to embody. A composition dealing with a solemn and serious subject cannot be put to a sprightly metre; similarly a light theme cannot be put to a sombre metre. The variety of metres used in Hindu music has given the names of the various *talas* to which the compositions are set.* The writer of the present work has attempted to add to the diversity of the time-measures of Hindu music by making use of about 40 among the *chhandahs* (metres) that are recognized in Sanskrit Prosody, such as the Totaka, Vasantatilaka, Sragdhara, Sarddula Vikririta, &c. A reference to his work, Yantra Kshetra Dipika, will show that not only a large number of metres ranging between the simplest and the most complex have been reproduced therein

* Mana and Yati, corresponding with accent and pause, are recognized in both music and poetry. The Sanskrit metre is divided into four parts. So is the measure (Tala) of Hindu music—Sama, Vishama Atita, and Anagata.

from the Sanskrit works on Prosody, but also that several of them have been utilized, by way of illustration, with a view to show how they could be made to add grace and beauty to the airs to which they might be tacked on.

MUSIC AND GRAMMAR.

The rules of counterpoint have their counterpart in Grammar. Thus, according to the *Kalapa*,

समानः सवर्णे दीर्घी भवति परश्चलोपः ।

Letters of the same class join each other, the latter being merged in the former, whose shape is elongated. For example, पद अन्त becomes पदान्त In Music, too, notes of the same denomination and caste (वर्ण) make chords. Thus C of the middle octave and C of the higher octave make chords, they being of the same denomination and caste (namely, Brahmana). In striking the chord, the sound of the higher C will appear to merge in that of the middle C.

अ वर्ण इ वर्णे ए ।

The Vowel अ unites with the vowel इ and produces ए ; *i. e.*, the first unites with the third. Similarly, C and E make a chord.

उ वर्णे ओ ।

The union of अ and उ produces ओ ; *i. e.*, the first unites with the fourth (उ being the fourth of the series of principal vowels, अ, आ, इ, उ, ए ओ * Similarly, C and F make a chord.

न व्यञ्जने स्वराः सन्धेयाः ।

There is no conjunction when a consonant follows a vowel, as देवी and इह remains देवीइह In the same way, there can be no chord between mere words (which are here compared with व्यञ्जनवर्ण) and notes (which are here compared with स्वर वर्ण).

इ वर्णो यमसवर्णे न च परोलोप्यः ।

---

* The Anusvara may be considered a vowel sound when affixed to a vowel, and a consonant sound when affixed to a consonant.

When the vowel इ is followed by a different vowel, the former is converted into य, but the latter does not merge in it. Thus रवि and आदि becomes रव्यादि Similarly, when E (corresponding with the third vowel इ) makes a chord with, say, G, (which is of a different value and caste), the sound of G does not merge its individuality in E.

The aphorism of *Kalapa* अनतिक्रमयन् विश्लेषयेत् means that, when necessary, letters joined to each other can be separated, keeping in view the rules of gender. In music, however, letters rendered long by the union of vowels, or otherwise united, can be pronounced each by itself, without reference to the rules of gender. As Bharat says

पौनरुक्तं नदेश्रीये गोते दोषोऽभिजायते ।
शीघ्रोच्चारेण वर्णानां तथाचैव प्रसारणे ॥
लिङ्गान्यत्वे विसन्धौच संयुक्ताक्षरमोचणे ।
परिवर्त्तेऽक्षराणाञ्च ह्रस्व दीर्घव्यतिक्रमे ॥

It is a recognized rule in grammar that the letter preceding a compound letter becomes one of a long sound. Thus the letter र is sounded long in the word रक्त This length is rendered preceptible by the mode of pronunciation. Similarly, in the chord made of E and G, the value of the Srutis preceding E is increased, and this increase is perceived by the ear only.

दुराह्वाने गाने रोदने च प्लुतास्ते लोकतः सिद्धाः ।

The plural measure (प्लुत) is used in calling out from a distance, in songs, and in crying. According to the view of Trilochana Das, the commentator of Kalapa, the use of the प्लुत is extensively made in Drama, &c., and Dramas come under the purview of music, having regard to the definition of the word सङ्गीत :—

सङ्गीतं द्विविधं प्रोक्तं दृश्यं श्राव्यं च सूरिभिः।

which means: the sages have divided music into two classes; ocular and auricular. Dancing and dramatic representations fall under the class of ocular music.

According to an aphorism of Kalapa, the rules governing the pronouns cease to have effect when the pronouns are preceded by the word अति (which means *excess).* Thus, the pronoun विश्व when declined in the first person of the dative case, becomes विश्वस्मै ; but when the word अति precedes, the word becomes विश्वाय; *i. e.*, the inflexion proper to a pronoun becomes inoperative. So, in rendering a Raga, the use of a note with Srutis in *excess* of those which are proper for the expression of that Raga vitiates its character. Thus, in the Raga Bhairava, D flat is used ; but if, by an excessive use of Srutis, the full note D is used, the character of that Raga is lost.

The essentials of words are धातु (roots), प्रत्यय (affixes) and विभक्ति (inflexions). The essentials of Ragas are notes (Dhatu), the affixing of other notes with reference to its position, and their declension, so to speak, with reference to time and other ingredients.

There is such a thing as निपातन (irregularity or exception) in music as there is in grammar. For instance, the Ragini Sindhu is constructed on a scale which has E flat for ore of its notes. But sometimes E natural is used and yet the character of the Ragini is not destroyed.

The following is the substance of the definitions which *Panini* gives of the three groups of the heptachord which are accepted and recognized in Hindu music :—

If the musical sounds combined with letters which are pronounced from the palate and other organs of speech are pronounced from the upper parts of such organs, such sounds are called by the name of *Udatta.* If they are pronounced from the lower parts of such organs, they are designated *Anudatta* ; and if they are pronounced in a combined manner, *i. e.*, the first half in the *Udatta* and the second half in the *Anudatta* method, they come under the class of *Svarit* or *Samahara.* In pronouncing the *Udatta* (acute) notes, the singer feels wearied in body, and the cavity of his throat becomes a

little contracted. The notes too show a degree of harshness. In pronouncing the *Anudatta* (grave) notes, the singer feels a kind of mildness and coolness about his body, and the cavity of his throat becomes a little dilated.

In the following aphorism, the Kalapa sanctions the adoption of whatever may have come down by usage :—

लोकोपचरात् ग्रहण सिद्धिः ।

This is exactly the view of the musical authorities, as the following couplet shows :—

यस्मिन् देशे यथाशिष्टैर्गीतं विज्ञस्तथाचरेत् ।

that is : whatever course the eminent adopts in singing in his country, that course the wise man should follow in that country. This sets at rest all disputes between musicians of different countries regarding the principles and practice of music.

MUSIC AND LOGIC.

In the Bhasha Parichchheda, or the introductory portion of the Nyaya Philosophy, occurs the following stanza :—

शब्दो ध्वनिश्च वर्णश्च मृदङ्गादिभव ध्वनिः ।
कण्ठसंयोगादिजन्या वर्णास्ते कादयोमताः ॥

which means that शब्द (sound) is divided into two classes, ध्वनिः and वर्ण The sound produced by the Mridanga and other musical instruments is called ध्वनिः and that produced from the throat, &c., such as क &c., is called वर्ण : The next stanza:—

सर्व्वः शब्दो नभोवृत्तिः श्रोत्रोत्पन्नस्तु गृह्यते ।
वीचितरङ्गन्यायेन तदुत्पत्तिस्तु कीर्त्तिता ॥

means that sound has its abode in नभः (ether) and reaches the cavity of the ear through it, unless and until it is obstructed. As a stone flung into the pond makes a circle in the water which widens and widens still it disappears on being

obstructed by the brink of the pond ; so, the sound on being produced makes circles in the air, till it is caught by the ear or dissolves into space.

कदम्बकोरकन्यायादुत्पत्तिः कस्यचिन्मते ।

This means : According to some, the origin of sound is comparable with the fibres that surround the Kadamba flower (Nauclea Kadamba). When the whole circumference of the flower is occupied by the fibres and no space left for more, then the Kadamba flower is formed. Similarly, when there is no more space for the sound to travel, it becomes audible.

THE SRUTIS.

In his notes on the Sisupala Badha, the well-known Sanskrit poem of Bharavi, Mallinatha, the prince of commentators, defines the *Sruti* as follows :—

श्रुतिर्नाम स्वरारम्भकावयवः शब्द विशेषः ॥

The sound which lies at the beginning of notes and forms its body, as it were, is called *Sruti*.

In the 10th stanza of the 1st canto of the above-named poem occur the following :

रणद्भिराघट्टनया नभस्वतः

पृथग्विभिन्नश्रुतिमण्डलैः स्वरैः ।

This refers to the sounding of the wires of the Mahati Vina of Narada through the action of air, and shows that the principle of the Æolian harp was known in olden India.

MUSIC AND RHETORIC.

Any piece of writing in which some Rasa or other prevails is called Kavya. Kavya is of two kinds—Prose and Poetry.* So is Music†—Anibaddha and Nibaddha.‡ Ani-

* गद्यपद्यमयं काव्यं ।

† गद्य पद्य प्रभेदेन द्विविधः कथितो बुधः ॥

‡ अनिबद्धं भवेद्गीतं वर्णादि नियमं विना ।
निबद्धञ्च भवेद्गीतं तालमान रसान्वितं ॥

baddha is that which is sung without the aid of words, but with given notes, the movement being made according to the pleasure of the singer. This form of singing goes by the name of Alapti or Alapa. Nibaddha is that which is sung with words, and with strict reference to the laws of measure. Anibaddha is thus comparable with Prose, and Nibaddha with Poetry. The latter is of 59 varieties. Both Kavya and music are divided into Sravya (audible) and Drisya (visible). Under the heading of the latter come dancing and dramatic representations. The sage Bharata is said to be the father of the Sanskrit drama, in the theory and practice of which he used to teach the celestial musicians and players. Lakshmi-Svayamvara is the name of the first drama of his which is said to have been played at the celestial Court of Indra. Bharat Samhita and Bharat Sutra are the names of two of his principal works on the drama. The subdivisions of Kavya are the same as those of music, namely, Bhashanga (pertaining to language), Kriyanga (pertaining to performances), and Bhavanga (pertaining to ideas or sentiments), these three being, respectively, represented by singing, instrumentation, and dancing.

According to Sanskrit Alankara (literally, ornament) or Rhetoric, the Padya or poetical Kavya is divided into three classes; namely, (1) Mahakavya (such as Raghuvansa, and Kumara Sambhava). (2) Khanda Kavya (such as Megha Duta and Ritu Samhara), and Kosha Kavya (such as Sringara Sataka). These have their counterparts in music, in Druvaka or Dhrupada, Lahacharika or Kheyal, and Jhumari or Tuppa. The Gadya or prose Kavya is illustrated in Kadamvari, Dasakumara Charita, &c., corresponding with the Alapa in music. There is another kind of Kavya called Champu, which is partly in poetry and partly in prose. This corresponds with the Kathakata, Panchali, Tarja, and other forms of sacred, popular, or pastoral music. In the composition of both Kavya and vocal music, the same four styles are adopted, namely Lati,

Panchali, Vaidarvi, and Gauri, these deriving their names probably from four different countries.

The Alankara in Kavya is mainly divided into three classes; namely, Savdalankara (figure o. words), Arthalankara (figure of meaning), and Savdarthalankara (combination of the above two). Musical Alankara is divided into four main classes; namely, (1) Sthayi (repetition of the same notes), (2) Arohi (ascending of the notes), (3) Avarohi (descending of the notes), and (4) Sanchari (which is the mixture of the above three).

The following are the seven subdivisions of Sthayi :—

NAMES. ILLUSTRATIONS.*

(1) *Prasannadi*—Sa, sa, sa.

(2) *Prasannanta*—Sa, sa, sa.

(3) *Prasannadyanta*—Sa, sa, sa.

(4) *Prasannamadhya*—Sa, sa, sa.

(5) *Kramarochita*—

Eka-kala *Do.*—Sa, ri, sa,

Dvi-kala *Do.*—Sa, ga, m., sa.

Tri-kala *Do.* Sa, pa, dha, ni, sa.

(6) *Prastara*—

Eka-kala *Do.*—Sa, ri, sa.

Dvi-kala *Do.*—Sa, ga, ma, sa.

Tri-kala *Do.*—Sa, pa, dha, ni, sa.

(7) *Prasad*—

Eka-kala *Do.*—Sa, ri, sa.

Dvi-kala *Do.*—Sa, ga, ma, sa.

Tri-kala *Do.*—Sa, pa, dha, ni, sa,

* The current system of notation is here given. From what is stated in Sangita Ratnakara in this connection, it would appear that a notation system was recognized at the time of its composition. It is mentioned there that the Mandra (lower) heptachord was to be indicated by a dot on the notes, and the Tara (higher) by a perpendicular line on them ; those belonging to the Madhya (middle) heptachord not being indicated by any signs.

The following are the twelve subdivisions of Arohi :—

(1) *Vistirna*—Sa (long), ri (long), &c., &c.

(2) *Nishkarsha*—Sa sa (short), ri ri (short), &c. &c.

Gatravarna—Sa sa sa (short,) ri ri ri (short), &c.
Sa sa sa sa (short), ri ri ri ri (short), &c.

(3) *Vindu*—3 sa (long) ri, 3 ga (long) ma, 3 pa (long) dha 3 ni (long).

(4) *Abhyuchchaya*—Sa, ga, pa, ni.

(5) *Hasita*—Sa ri ri ga ga ga ma ma ma ma pa pa pa pa pa dha dha dha dha dha dha ni ni ni ni ni ni.

(6) *Prenkshita*—Sa ri, ri ga, ga ma, ma pa, pa dha, dha ni.

(7) *Akshipta*—Sa ga, ga pa, pa ni.

(8) *Sandhiprachchhadana*—Sa ri ga, ga ma pa, pa dha ni.

(9) *Udgita*—Sa sa sa ri ga, ma ma ma pa dha.

(10) *Udvahita*—Sa ri ri ri ga, ma pa pa pa dha.

(11) *Trivarna*—Sa ri ga ga ga, ma pa dha dha dha.

(12) *Yoni*—Sa sa sa, ri ri ri, ga ga ga, ma ma ma, pa pa pa, dha dha dha, ni ni ni.

The Avarohi has twelve subdivisions, which are the Arohi subdivisions put in the descending scale.

The following are the twenty-five subdivision of Sanchari—

(1) *Mandradi*—Sa ga ri, dha ma ga, ga pa ma, ma dha pa, pa ni dha.

(2) *Mandra madhya*—Ga sa ri, ma ri ga, pa ga ma, dha ma pa, ni pa dha.

(3) *Mandranta*—Ga ri sa, ma ga ri, pa ma ga, dha pa ma, ni dha pa.

(4) *Prastara*—Sa ga, ri ma, ga pa, ma dha, pa ni.

(5) *Prasada*—Sa ri sa, ri ga ri, ga ma ga, ma pa ma, pa dha pa, dha ni dha.

(6) *Vyavritya*—Sa ga ri ma sa, ri ma ga pa ri, ga pa ma dha ga, ma dha pa ni ma.

(7) *Skhalita*—Sa ga ri ma ma ri ga sa, ri ma ga pa pa ga ma ri, ga pa ma dha dha ma pa ga, ma dha pa ni ni pa dha ma.

(8) *Parivartta*—Sa ga ma, ri ma pa, ga pa dha, ma dha ni.

(9) *Akshepa*—Sa ri ga, ri ga ma, ga ma pa, ma pa dha, pa dha ni.

(10) *Vindu*—Sa sa sa ri sa, ri ri ri ga ri, ga ga ga ma ga, ma ma ma pa ma, pa pa pa dha pa, dha dha dha ni dha.

(11) *Vahita*—Sa ri ga ri, ri ga ma ga, ga ma pa ma, ma pa dha pa, pa dha ni dha.

(12) *Urmmi*—Sa ma ma ma sa ma, ri pa pa pa ri pa, ga dha dha dha ga dha, ma ni ni ni ma ni.

(13) *Sama*—Sa ri ga ma ma ga ri sa, ri ga ma pa pa ma ga ri, ga ma pa dha dha pa ma ga, ma pa dha ni ni dha pa ma.

(14) *Prenksha*—Sa ri ri sa, ri ga ga ri, ga ma ma ga, ma pa pa ma, pa dha dha pa, dha ni ni dha.

(15) *Nishkujita*—Sa ri sa ga sa, ri ga ri ma ri, ga ma ga pa ga, ma pa ma dha ma, pa dha pa ni pa.

(16) *Svena*—Sa pa, ri dha, ga ni, ma sa.

(17) *Krama*—Sa ri sa ri ga sa ri ga ma, ri ga ri ga ma ri ga ma pa, ga ma ga ma pa ga ma pa dha, ma pa ma pa dha ma pa dha ni.

(18) *Udghatita*—Sa ri pa ma ga ri, ri ga dha pa ma ga, ga ma ni dha pa ma.

(19) *Ranjita*—Sa ga ri sa ga ri sa, ri ma ga ri ma ga ri, ga pa ma ga pa ma ga, ma dha pa ma dha pa ma, pa ni dha pa ni dha pa.

(20) *Sannivritta pravrittaka*—Sa pa ma ga ri, ri dha pa ma ga, ga ni dha pa ma.

(21) *Venu*—Sa sa ri ma ga, ri ri ga pa ma, ga ga ma dha pa, ma ma pa ni dha.

(22) *Lalita Svara*—Sa ri ma ri sa, ri ga pa ga ri, ga ma dha ma ga, ma pa ni pa ma.

(23) *Hunkara*—Sa ri sa, sa ri ga ri sa, sa ri ga ma ga ri sa, sa ri ga ma pa ma ga ri sa, sa ri ga ma pa dha pa ma ga ri sa, sa ri ga ma pa dha ni dha pa ma ga ri sa.

(24) *Hradamana*—Sa ga ri sa, ri ma ga ri, ga pa ma ga, ma dha pa ma, pa ni dha pa.

(25) *Avalokita*—Sa ga ma ma ri sa, ri ma pa pa ga ri, ga pa dha dha ma ga, ma dha ni ni pa ma.

The following seven additional varieties are mentioned by the musical authorities :—

(1) *Tara Mandra Prasanna*—Sa, ri, ga, ma, pa, dha, ni, sa, sa.

(2) *Mandratara Prasanna*—Sa, sa, ni, dha, pa, ma, ga, ri, sa.

(3) *Avarttaka*—Sa sa ri ri sa sa ri sa, ri ri ga ga ri ri ga ri, ga ga ma ma ga ga ma ga, ma ma pa pa ma ma pa ma, pa pa dha dha pa pa dha pa, dha dha ni ni dha dha ni dha.

(4) *Sampradana*—Sa sa ri ri sa sa, ri ri ga ga ri ri, ga ga ma ma ga ga, ma ma pa pa ma ma, pa pa dha dha pa pa, dha dha ni ni dha dha.

(5) *Bidhuta*—Sa ga sa ga, ri ma ri ma, ga pa ga pa, ma dha ma dha, pa ni pa ni.

(6) *Upalola*—Sa ri sa ri ga ri ga ri, ri ga ri ga ma ga ma ga, ga ma ga ma pa ma pa ma, ma pa ma pa dha pa dha pa, pa dha pa dha ni dha ni dha.

(7) *Ullasita*—Sa sa ga sa ga, ri ri ma ri ma, ga ga pa ga pa, ma ma dha ma dha, pa pa ni pa ni.

THE SEASONS.

THE three principal seasons are Winter, Summer, and the Rainy. These are represented by the three Ragas—Sri, Panchama, and Megha, which also represent the evening, morning, and noon-time, and are characterised by the predominance of the notes E, F, and D, respectively. The characteristic of the group of the "evening" Ragas is that they ascend from C and D or D flat to E; that of the group of the "morning" Ragas is that they ascend from C and D or D flat to F; and that of the group of the "noon-time" Ragas is that they ascend from C or D to F. These three Ragas might be said to represent the primitive forms of the three principal scales, namely, the pentatonic, the hexatonic, and the diatonic. Sri might in a manner be considered the prototype of the pentatonic scale (the primitive scale of the ancient nations), for it may be rendered without the use of F sharp and B. Panchama might also in a manner be taken as the originator of the hexatonic scale, as it introduces the use of F and can be rendered without B. Megha might also in a manner be considered as the nearest approach to the diatonic scale, introducing B flat (*i. e.*, B in an incomplete state), and being capable of being rendered with a skilful use of A and E in the descending scale. The evolution of the six Ragas of which a theory is given in the preceding pages might be considered as the result of development made in after times.